STRATEGIC MANAGEMENT:
TEXT AND CONCEPTS

Kent Series in Management

Strategic Management: Concepts and Cases
Barnett/Wilsted

Strategic Management: Text and Concepts
Barnett/Wilsted

Cases for Strategic Management
Barnett/Wilsted

The Human Relations of Organizations
Berkman/Neider

Personnel: The Management of Human Resources, Fourth Edition
Crane

Business Research for Decision Making, Second Edition
Davis/Cosenza

Supervision: A Situational Approach
Kirkpatrick

Understanding Organizational Behavior, Second Edition
Klein/Ritti

Environment of International Business, Second Edition
Kolde

Applications in Personnel/Human Resource Management: Cases, Exercises, and Skill Builders
Nkomo/Fottler/McAfee

Introduction to Management, Third Edition
Plunkett/Attner

Experiencing International Management
Punnett

Personnel/Human Resource Management: Environments and Functions
Scarpello/Ledvinka

The Changing Environment of Business, Third Edition
Starling

Managing Effective Organizations: An Introduction
Steers/Ungson/Mowday

STRATEGIC MANAGEMENT: TEXT AND CONCEPTS

John H. Barnett

University of New Hampshire

William D. Wilsted

University of Colorado

PWS-KENT PUBLISHING COMPANY
Boston

PWS–KENT
Publishing Company

Editor: Rolf Janke
Production Editor: Wanda K. Wilking
Interior Designer: Outside Design
Cover Designer: Sally Bindari, Designworks
Manufacturing Coordinator: Margaret Sullivan Higgins
Composition: Arcata Graphics/Kingsport
Cover Printer: Lehigh Press, Inc.
Text Printer and Binder: Maple/Vail Book Manufacturing Group

PWS-KENT Publishing Company is a division of Wadsworth, Inc.

Printed in the United States of America
1 2 3 4 5 6 7 8 9 — 92 91 90 89

Library of Congress Cataloging-in-Publication Data

Barnett, John Hayes.
  Text and concepts for strategic management.

  Includes bibliographies and index.
  1. Strategic planning.   I. Wilsted, William D.
II. Title.
HD30.28.B3683   1988   658.4′012   88–25504
ISBN 0-534-91726-7

for Vasilka and Karen

CONTENTS

Chapter 1   **The Evolution of Strategic Management   3**

The Working Concept   3
Working Concept 1: Stages of Corporate Development   4
Stages of Corporate Development and Strategic Management   8
   Business Policy   8 / Strategic Planning   8 / Strategic Management   8
Working Concept 2: Levels of Strategy   9
Working Concept 3: Strategic Business Units   11
Strategy Research   14
Business History   14
Executive Comments   16
Key Terms   17
Bibliography   17

Chapter 2   **Strategic Management and the Strategic Manager   19**

Working Concept 4: The Strategic Manager   19
Working Concept 5: Military and Holistic Strategic Managers   20
Working Concept 6: Mintzberg's Roles and Styles   23
Strategic Management   24
   The Entrepreneurial Manager   24 / The Adaptive Manager   24 / The Planning
   Manager   25
Working Concept 7: Brunswik Lens and Perception   25
Strategy and the Strategist: A Summary   27
Strategy Research and the Strategic Manager   27
Executive Comments   29
Key Terms   29
Bibliography   29
Appendixes: A: Accounting for Nonaccountants   31 / B: Strategic Financial
Analysis   32 / C: University of New Hampshire Bookstore Case   34 / D: Bookstore Case
Analysis   45 / E: The Case Method   47

Chapter 3   **Defining Purpose   53**

Personal Values   54
Organizational Priorities   56

Working Concept 8: Mintzberg's Organizational Power   *56*
Corporate Culture   58
Social Goals   59
Strategic Mission   61
Working Concept 9: Strategic Analysis   *61*
Levels of Strategy and Enterprise Mission   62
Research and Mission   65
Executive Comments   66
Key Terms   66
Bibliography   67
Appendix: The Nonprofit and Stages of Development   68

Chapter 4   **Determining Distinctive Competence**   **71**

Resources Defined   71
   Tangible Resources   71 / Intangible Resources   72
Strengths and Weaknesses   73
   Combining Related Symptoms   77 / Product Life Cycle and Internal Factors   80
Working Concept 10: Product Life Cycle   *78*
Defining Distinctive Competence   83
   Market Needs and Comparative Advantage   83 / Levels of Strategy   85
Significant Research   86
Executive Comments   88
Key Terms   88
Bibliography   89
Appendix: The Small Business   90

Chapter 5   **Identifying Opportunities and Threats**   **93**

External Environment Defined   93
   Markets   93 / Competition   96 / Technology   96 / Society   97 /
   Government   97 / The Changing External Environment   99
Strategic Analysis and Strategic Signals   101
   Identifying Strategic Signals   101 / Interpreting Strategic Signals   101 / Market
   Signals   101 / Competitive Signals   106 / Technology Signals   108 / Government
   Signals   109 / Social Signals   113 / Summarizing Strategic Signals — A Swiss
   Example   116
Working Concept 11: Customer Needs Analysis   *103*
Working Concept 12: Porter's Determinants of Competition   *106*
Working Concept 13: Technological Innovation   *109*
Working Concept 14: Stakeholder Analysis   *112*
Working Concept 15: The Precursor   *115*
Strategy Research and the External Environment   118
Executive Comments   122
Key Terms   122
Bibliography   122
Appendix: The International Business Environment   124

Chapter 6   **Formulating Strategy   136**

The Strategic Decision Process   136
Working Concept 16: The Strategic Decision Process   *137*
Decision Levels   139
   *Functional Decisions   139 / Business Decisions   139 / Corporate
   Decisions   139*
Working Concept 17: Levels of Strategy and the Decision Process   *140*
Strategic Management Tools   140
   Product Life Cycle   141 / Porter's Determinants of Competition   141
Working Concept 18: Product Portfolios   *142*
Working Concept 19: Product Life Cycle–Competition Matrix   *144*
Working Concept 20: Directional Policy Matrix   *144*
Working Concept 21: Industry Analysis   *148*
Working Concept 22: Strategic Issue Analysis   *150*
Examples of Strategy Formulation   151
   *Porter's Generic Strategies   151 / Situational Strategy   152 / Other
   Strategies   155*
Evaluating Strategy   160
   *Competitive Response Analysis   160 / Risk   162 / Synergy   163 /
   Consistency   164 / Workability   164*
An Overview of Strategy Formulation   164
Strategy Formulation Research   166
Executive Comments   169
Key Terms   169
Bibliography   170

Chapter 7   **Implementing Strategy   174**

No Right Answer   174
Implementation Defined   175
Implementation Illustrated   175
Structure and Systems Components   176
   *Administrative Systems   176 / Information Systems   177 / Compensation and
   Measurement Systems   179*
Selection Criteria   185
   Distinctive Competence   185 / Congruence   186
Working Concept 23: Implementation Selection Model   *186*
Difficulties in Implementing Strategy   187
Implementation and Strategic Levels   188
An Implementation Illustration   188
   Corporate Strategy   189 / Business Strategy   189 / Functional Strategy   190
Strategy Implementation Research   190
Executive Comments   193
Key Terms   194
Bibliography   194
Appendix: Personal Strategy   197

PREFACE

This preface presents the rationale, structure, and content of Barnett and Wilsted's *Strategic Management: Text and Concepts*. This text describes the art of strategic management and stresses both business examples of strategic management concepts and the findings and conclusions of strategic research. First, we cite many companies and quote numerous executives in our discussion of the art of strategy. Secondly, research and academic findings make up a part of each chapter.

In addition, models and theories of strategy comprise twenty-three working concepts. The text highlights these twenty-three working concepts, or tools of strategic management, including Porter's model of the determinants of competition, stages of development models, analytical matrices, and criteria for the selection of strategic implementation alternatives.

Each chapter concludes with a description of current research efforts in, and corporate executives' comments about, topics included in the chapter.

The Chapters   The first chapter describes the evolution of strategic management, and introduces the working concept of the stages of corporate development as a dual foundation — supporting both the topic of strategic management, which evolves from strategic planning and the role of the general manager, and the concept of levels of strategy, functional (or department), business, and corporate.

The second chapter introduces the working concept of the strategic manager and the related strategic topics of managerial roles, responsibilities, and perceptions. Appendices include financial tools for strategic analysis, a general approach to preparing cases, a sample case, and an illustrative analysis of that case.

The third chapter shows how the strategist defines purpose or mission. Personal values, organizational priorities, and social goals make up purpose, and these three components lead to a discussion of both the stages of development and levels of strategy and their relationship to purpose, organizational power, corporate culture, and social responsibility. An appendix shows how the nonprofit agency's mission differs from the for-profit enterprise, and how purpose evolves over stages of nonprofit development.

The fourth chapter addresses the problem of determining the distinctive competence of the enterprise. The text shows the relationship between this distinctive competence and (1) the firm's strengths and weaknesses, (2) the product life cycle, (3) market needs, (4) comparative advantage and competition, and (5) the levels of strategy. The appendix to Chapter 4 focuses on the small business.

The fifth chapter tells how the strategist must analyze the external environment to identify opportunities and threats in markets, competition, technology, government, and society. The text presents specific tools of analysis, including customer needs analysis, Porter's model of competition, the stages of technological innovation, stakeholders, and the precursor society. An appendix studies international business.

Chapter 6 discusses the formulation of strategy. The manager makes functional, business, and strategic corporate decisions based upon an understanding and utilization of topics such as preemptive competitive opportunities, product portfolio management and matrices analyses, generic and situational strategies including the new business, diversification, exit, and integration. Analysis of competitive response, risk, synergy, consistency, and workability help the strategist to evaluate strategy.

The seventh and final chapter presents a range of strategic implementation alternatives, such as organizational structure, information, compensation, and measurement systems. Distinctive competence and congruence help the manager select from among these alternatives, and the chapter shows how the manager implements strategy at the corporate, business, and functional levels. An appendix gives the student a chance to apply these strategic concepts to the student's personal strategy.

Acknowledgments   First in our acknowledgments must be Carol True. In addition, we are fortunate to have benefited from the comments and criticisms of many excellent reviewers:

William E. Burr
University of Oregon

Robert W. Carney
Georgia Institute of Technology

Edward S. Dyl
University of Arizona

David P. Gustafson
University of Missouri, St. Louis

Frederick C. Haas
Virginia Commonwealth University

William D. Kane, Jr.
Western Carolina University

Michael D. Lucas
Western Illinois University

Richard R. Merner
University of Delaware

Michael C. White
Louisiana State University

Finally we would like to thank the editorial staff at PWS-KENT Publishing Co., especially Rolf Janke.

John Barnett
William Wilsted

Survival in business depends upon the generalities of economics;
success in business depends upon the particularities of strategy.

CHAPTER 1

THE EVOLUTION OF STRATEGIC MANAGEMENT

Management is the new technology that is making the American economy into an entrepreneurial economy.

Peter F. Drucker, *Innovation and Entrepreneurship*

Chapter 1 traces the evolution of strategic management and presents the plan of this book. It begins with Working Concept 1, "Stages of Corporate Development," a concept from the field of strategic management. Working Concept 1 relates the three stages of corporate development to the evolution of strategic management, from (1) business policy to (2) strategic planning to (3) strategic management. The chapter then presents a schematic of the strategic decision process, relating that process both to strategic management and to the plan of this book. This chapter then presents working concepts covering levels of strategy and the strategic business unit. As in all chapters, Chapter 1 contains insights into current research in strategic management; and "Executive Comments," quotes from today's top managers, chief executives, and a broad spectrum of observers.

THE WORKING CONCEPT

This text illustrates the topic of strategic management through a series of "Working Concepts," beginning with stages of corporate development and levels of strategy, and including industry and competitive analysis, organizational structure and power, and directional policy matrix. These Working Concepts can be used in the same way that a builder uses working drawings. Working drawings present detailed parts of the overall building project — a foundation, a door, or a roof. Similarly, these Working Concepts present in detail one aspect of the overall field of strategic management. The twenty-three Working Concepts in this book model the real world of strategic management; they are your tools for practicing strategic management, just as a builder's working drawings are tools aiding in the construction of a building.

These Working Concepts may deal with specific areas of the strategic decision, such as product ("Product Life Cycle," #10; "Product Portfolios," #18), competition ("Porter's Determinants of Competition," #12), the customer ("Customer Needs Analysis," #11), technology ("Technological Innovation," #13), or combinations of these areas ("Product Life Cycle — Competition Matrix," #19). Other Working Concepts describe specific aspects of strategic management ("Strategic Business Units," #3; "The Strategic Manager," #4; "Military and Holistic Strategic Managers," #5; "Mintzberg's Roles and Styles," #6; "Brunswik Lens and Perception," #7; and "Mintzberg's Organizational Power," #8).

Some Working Concepts are analytical tools ("Stages of Corporate Development," #1; "Levels of Strategy," #2; "Strategic Analysis," #9; "Stakeholder Analysis," #14; "The Precursor," #15; "Industry Analysis," #21; and "Strategic Issue Analysis," #22). Finally, some Working Concepts are decision-making models ("Strategic Decision Process," #16; "Levels of Strategy and Strategic Decision Process," #17; "Directional Policy Matrix," #20; and "Implementation Selection Model," #23).

WORKING CONCEPT 1

STAGES OF CORPORATE DEVELOPMENT

As business analysts — most especially Chandler, author of *Strategy and Structure: Chapters in the History of the American Industrial Enterprise* (1962) — looked at the business enterprise over many years, they identified a general pattern of development. This pattern, the *stages of corporate development,* became a part of the theory of business policy and corporate strategy, as described initially in the business policy course by Harvard Professors Christensen and Scott, and as elaborated by Slater (1970).

The most frequently encountered version of the model identifies three stages of corporate development: the entrepreneurial (Stage One), the functional management (Stage Two), and the decentralized (Stage Three) corporations.

STAGE ONE

The Stage One corporation is an entrepreneurial organization. One person dominates the firm; this entrepreneurial owner-manager performs a wide range of duties and participates in all aspects of the business.

The strategic purpose of the business is identical with the personal objective of the entrepreneur. The business centers on one or more of the entrepreneur's skills and interests, which frequently are technical engineering or inventive abilities.

The Stage One corporation often takes bold, aggressive actions. The entrepreneur thrives on challenge and is not afraid of risk.

STAGE TWO

If the Stage One corporation succeeds, sheer growth and success bring new problems. The growth of a business can prove too much for one entrepreneur-manager to handle. Semiautomated production facilities and several hundred employees create a complexity that never confronted the entrepreneur operating out of a garage in the backyard. Growing markets might call for new promotion, advertising, or packaging skills. Increasing paperwork can strain the

Stages of Corporate Development (continued)

simple administrative systems of an entrepreneurial company. The possible entrance of a competitor or government regulator can further add to the managerial burden.

The corporation responds with *functional specialization*, by assigning an executive to coordinate market, a second executive to control production, and other executives to handle the other business functions. Thus, the dominant characteristic of the Stage Two corporation is the management group, a team of specialized functional experts. The organization chart of the Stage One corporation, if indeed one exists, changes (see Figure 1.1).

STAGE THREE

The Stage One company relied on one entrepreneur until growth forced it to become a Stage Two corporation. The Stage Two corporation that seeks further growth, or seeks to diversify to reduce risk, is forced to rely on more than one product or market group. As it introduces further market groups or product groups, the firm responds by first a divisional, then a decentralized divisional, management (see Figure 1.2).

By using decentralized division, the decision maker — the decentralized division executive — is closest to the problem. Decentralized division executives have strategic information close at hand so that they can respond immediately to problems.

The Stage Three corporation, then, has a corporate headquarters with several or many operating divisions, each of which looks and acts like a Stage Two company.

SIGNIFICANCE

The stages of corporate development provide a way for the strategic manager to analyze (1) managerial abilities and (2) opportunities and threats.

As the corporation moves through the stages of corporate development, its essential managerial abilities change. The high-energy, technical skills of the entrepreneur are less important than the coordinative and integrative skills required of the Stage Two manager. The Stage Three manager at corporate headquarters must have greater planning and financial skills than the Stage One or Stage Two executive.

The managerial skills change because the

FIGURE 1.1
Stage One and
Stage Two firms

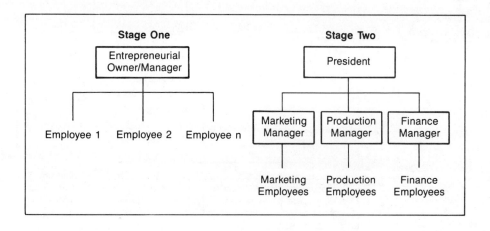

Stages of Corporate Development (continued)

opportunities and threats confronting the strategic manager change in the Stage One, Two, and Three corporations. The Stage One manager faces a series of operating crises — usually manufacturing, with occasional financial — and short-term survival problems. The entrepreneur often needs to delegate and even to decentralize decisions as the firm succeeds and grows.

The Stage Two manager, on the other hand, tries to provide organizational structures to handle longer-term problems. He or she replaces the "daily observation" measurement system of Stage One with formal reports and "responsibility" accounting systems designed to spotlight problems within each functional area.

The Stage Three strategic manager faces complex resource allocation decisions, coupled with an increasing breadth of investment opportunities. The operating and functional orientations of the Stage One and Stage Two managers, respectively, are replaced with a long-term profitability orientation, which means less reliance on personal performance and coordination and more reliance on institutional leadership, financial planning, external environment scanning, and increased research and development efforts. Outside stockholders, brought in to provide needed expansion capital, mean less managerial control. The Stage Three strategic manager must also guard against the dual internal threats of (1) an unresponsive, inflexible, risk-avoiding bureaucracy and (2) partial or less satisfying solutions within divisions, as divisional managers sacrifice long-term growth potential for short-term profits.

ILLUSTRATIONS

The experience of Peters and Waterman's "excellent" companies illustrates some of the problems incurred as a company evolves through the stages of corporate development. In their best-seller, *In Search of Excellence*, management consultants Peters and Waterman identified forty-three excellent companies. Two years later, in a cover story, *Business Week* (11/15/84) reported that at least fourteen of the forty-three companies had lost their luster. Waterman com-

FIGURE 1.2
Stage Three firm

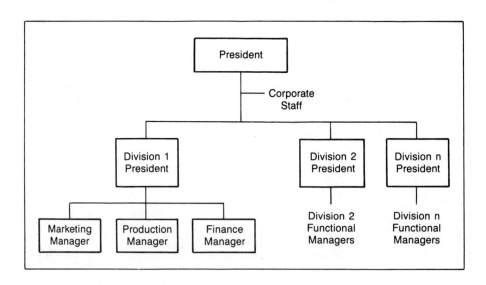

Stages of Corporate Development *(continued)*

mented, "If you're big, you've got the seeds of your own destruction in there."

The banking industry offers dramatic examples of growth and decline, success and failure. Continental Illinois National Bank and Trust Company, which collapsed in 1984, was named one of the five best-managed companies by *Dun's Business Month* in 1981.

By the end of 1985, People Express Airlines had moved well past being the entrepreneurial, Stage One firm whose organization was the champion of "management humanists." Its initial (November 1980) public offering price was $8.50 a share. The price rose to its July 1983 high of almost fifty dollars and then fell to eight dollars one year later. The nonunion, "participatory management" People Express had acquired the multiunion, bureaucratic Frontier Airlines in a pursuit of growth and geographic coverage.

People Express president Donald Burr explained the Frontier purchase as a necessary response to competition, asserting that "leadership is not pandering to what people say they need. It's defining what . . . people need" (*Business Week*, 11/25/85, pp. 80, 91). Others may view such strategic and structural changes as inevitable consequences of the stages of corporate development.

CONCLUSION

The important, long-term strategic issues confronting a company can be highlighted by the model of the stages of corporate development. Chandler's major conclusion about the management of the business enterprise was that the structure of the organization — functional, divisional, decentralized, and so on — must be determined by the firm's strategy. Not only the operating problems centering around resistance to change, but the strategic problems of changing areas of managerial focus, are identified and resolved more easily through the stages of development model.

Galbraith and Kazanjian (1986) studied firms' implementing strategies, concluding that "only under competitive conditions does a mismatch between strategy and structure lead to ineffective performance." These researchers suggested that firms may proceed from the functional (Stage Two) form along three paths:

1. *Vertical integration*: If a firm pursues economies of scale (the low cost producer strategy) it probably will integrate vertically and maintain a centralized functional structure.
2. *Related diversification*: If a firm pursues internal growth through related diversification (market or product development), it might develop a multidivisional structure.
3. *Acquisition*: If a firm pursues growth by external acquisition, it probably will adapt a holding-company structure.

BIBLIOGRAPHY

Chandler, A. D., *Strategy and Structure: Chapters in the History of the American Industrial Enterprise* (Cambridge, MA: M.I.T. Press, 1962).

Galbraith, J. R., and R. K. Kazanjian, *Strategy Implementation: Structure, Systems, and Process*, 2nd ed. (St. Paul, MN: West Publishing, 1986).

Salter, M. S., "Stages of Corporate Development," *Journal of Business Policy* 1 (Spring 1970), pp. 23–27.

Thain, D. H., "Stages of Corporate Development," *The Business Quarterly* (London, Ontario: University of Western Ontario, Winter 1969), pp. 33–45.

STAGES OF CORPORATE
DEVELOPMENT AND STRATEGIC MANAGEMENT

The model of the stages of corporate development shows the manager's task changing from an environment of (1) entrepreneurial decision making, including developing production and marketing systems; to (2) coordinating the efforts of functional managers toward a product-market objective; to (3) developing a strategic management system to allocate scarce resources among different divisions, businesses, and product markets in a way that maximizes growth and institutional objectives, such as social responsibility, while recognizing the differences in risk, competitive strengths, and opportunities that each division and business represents.

Business Policy

Just as the entrepreneur is the focal point of the successful Stage One firm, earlier writers in strategic management likewise focused their attention on the decision maker, referring to their field as *business policy*. These researchers studied the way chief executives make decisions. Cases were the dominant if not the sole method of instruction; business school teachers concentrated on the art and practice of decision making, often in an entrepreneurial role.

Strategic Planning

As researchers, tracing the stages of corporate development, moved on to the problems of coordinating functional managerial efforts and simultaneously deciding on desirable product markets, "business policy" became "strategic planning." *Strategic planning* is a process that represents part of strategic management. It is the process of analyzing the opportunities and threats in the marketplace, while building the strengths and correcting the weaknesses within the firm. Strategic planning also involves setting goals for specific product markets and for the firm.

Strategic Management

The strategist's job can be understood best from the perspective of the third stage of corporate development, that of the multidivisional, and often multinational, corporation. *Strategic management* deals with the same topics that concern the chief executive of the multinational, Stage Three corporation: creating the corporate portfolio of multiple businesses and product markets through (1) analyzing industry attractiveness, (2) analyzing each business unit's strategy, (3) formulating corporate strategy, and (4) implementing that strategy across multiple divisions and businesses.

At a very simplified level, the evolution of strategic management reads like this: business policy examined the decision maker; strategic planning studied the process the decision maker used; and what is now strategic management analyzes how to manage the entire process of planning, formulating, and allocating across time and among multiple businesses.

Just as the stages of corporate development make sense, since we would expect a successful business to evolve and grow, so also does the evolution of business policy to strategic planning to strategic management, since the strategic management field must evolve along with its subject, corporate management. The *process* underlying business policy, strategic planning, and strategic management is similarly very logical. This *strategic process* consists of reaching goals by using strengths to take advantage of the available opportunities.

Figure 1.3 summarizes the strategic process. The strategic manager (discussed further in Chapter 2) defines the mission of the enterprise — a mixture of personal values, organizational objectives, and social goals (to be discussed in Chapter 3). He or she next determines the enterprise's strengths that make up its distinctive competence (discussed in Chapter 4) and identifies opportunities — or threats — present in the markets, competition, technology, government, and society surrounding the enterprise (described in Chapter 5). The manager then formulates and evaluates a strategy (discussed in Chapter 6) which is implemented (see Chapter 7) by allocating resources; organizing; and measuring progress and performance.

This book introduces the field of strategic management in Chapter 1 and introduces the strategic manager in Chapter 2. The text then describes a step-by-step process for making strategic decisions.

Defining mission

Determining distinctive competence

Identifying opportunities and threats

Formulating and evaluating strategy

Implementing strategy

Working Concept 2 further illustrates the field of strategic management.

WORKING CONCEPT 2

LEVELS OF STRATEGY

As a firm evolves into a diversified company, strategic choices and decisions emerge that did not frequently confront — or often were not considered by — the entrepreneur. These decisions raise the following questions at the business level.

1. How are we to compete in this business?
2. What role will each function of this business perform?
3. How should each function be supported and/or developed?

At the corporate level, the president overseeing diversified divisions faces strategic decisions that include

1. What businesses should we be in?
2. What are the requirements for success in those businesses?

3. How can we provide these requirements to our organization and divisions?

The *corporate level* of strategy, then, considers multiple products, multiple industries, multiple markets, and multiple technologies. Corporate strategy determines what strategic objectives should be pursued and how individual businesses should be managed to achieve those objectives. Markets are viewed without borders, from a long-term perspective, such as two to five years. The portfolio or mix of businesses, and problems of generating and allocating resources to these businesses, are issues that confront the corporate strategist.

The *business level* of strategy considers how to use distinctive competency to compete in a specific business within a defined

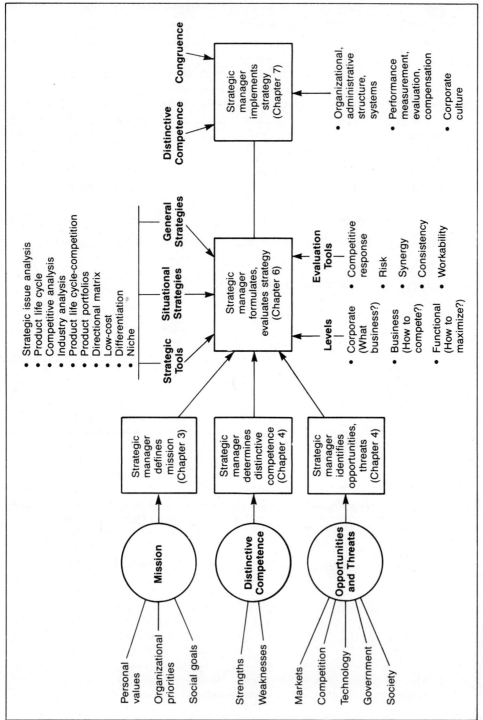

FIGURE 1.3 Strategic decision process

Levels of Strategy (continued)

product-market area. Business strategy determines where potential and profit lie within a firm's market; a typical time frame is six to twenty-four months.

The *functional level* of strategy addresses efficiency (quantity) and effectiveness (quality) decisions in maximizing the output of that functional unit, based upon inputs provided by corporate- and business-level strategic decisions about resource allocation. The time perspective ranges from less than one month up to six months. Figure 1.4 presents a spectrum of the levels of strategy. Figure 1.5 further illustrates levels of strategy by incorporating strategic levels into the Stage Three firm of Figure 1.2.

We turn to the subject of the strategic business unit and its development in the world of business (principally by General Electric) in order to provide further illustration of the levels of strategy. The strategic business unit represents General Electric's response to the increasing complexities of its strategic management.

WORKING CONCEPT 3

STRATEGIC BUSINESS UNITS

Strategic business units (SBUs) are those individual parts of a business that interact with the external environment in such a distinctive and cohesive way that they can be viewed as independent strategic units. Generally, the distinctive and cohesive way the unit deals with the environment consists of a specific product-market segment — e.g., industrial power tools — although the grouping may center around customers or geographic areas. General Electric was a pioneer in identifying strategic business units and allowing the SBU to develop its own strategic plans.

The General Electric strategist offered a broad mix of products and services to international markets. Clearly, no single strategy would have been appropriate for G.E.'s multiple products and multiple markets. Thus, the firm turned to SBUs as the organizational solution to the need for multiple strategies.

G.E. AND DECENTRALIZATION

In 1950, General Electric's new president, Ralph Cordiner, examined several barriers to the traditional corporate objectives of increasing profits and shareholder's return. G.E. was facing an increasingly competitive external environment, due in part to both a rapid business growth in response to post–World War II consumer demand and to rapid advances in technology propelled by an increase in research and development (R&D) and wartime technological advances. G.E. also was the target of frequent antitrust actions (thirteen cases between 1940 and 1950) brought about by the government. Another barrier to G.E.'s success was its extremely centralized internal environment, which produced (1) layers of bureaucracy and (2) a corporate culture of security, due in part to G.E.'s self-confidence based on its size and technology.

Cordiner formulated a strategy to bring decision making down to the levels in the organization in which market and technological changes impacted first. The company was too large, and the environment too complex, to be run as one giant corporation with a steadily growing staff. In Cordiner's view, bureaucracy was hiding, not highlighting, business environment change.

FIGURE 1.4
Levels of strategy

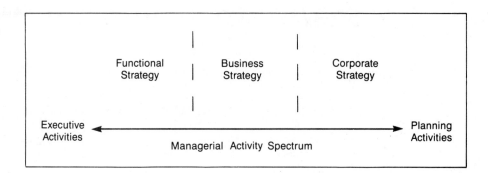

FIGURE 1.5
Stage Three firm
and levels
of strategy

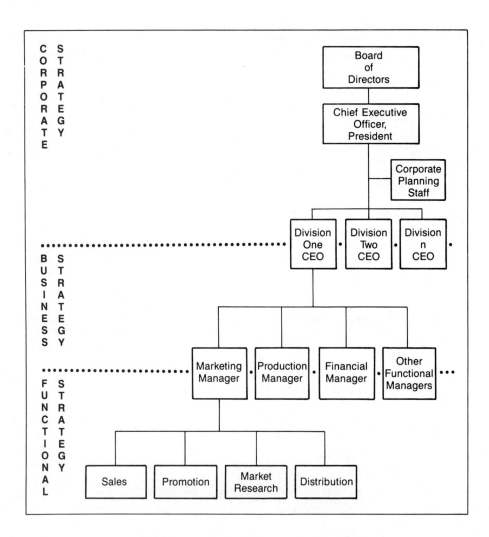

Strategic Business Units (continued)

To implement his strategy, Cordiner reorganized one highly centralized firm into twenty-seven autonomous divisions. Further, the twenty-seven divisions were made up of 110 companies; the head of each of the 110 companies was to act as the entrepreneur/boss of that business, setting budgets and approving all but major capital expenditures. This boss was to respond to competitive, technological, or antitrust problems.

DECENTRALIZATION REVERSED — THE G.E. SBU

General Electric became a decentralized company in the 1950s. During the 1960s, however, G.E. experienced profitless growth in which revenues increased but profits did not. G.E.'s 110 companies and twenty-seven divisions became 190 departments. These departments, organized into forty-six divisions and ten groups, did not generate enough profits to provide the heavy investment requirements of nuclear power, computers, and aerospace.

G.E. decided that the critical strategic objective for achieving its profitable growth purpose would be to add planning to its existing decentralized control system. During the 1970s, then, G.E. carried out the following implementation of its strategic objective.

1. Company operating units were reorganized into SBUs that had a unique business mission and unique competitors and that could plan for and implement long-term strategic plans. The 190 departments reported to and were part of forty SBUs.

2. The general manager of each SBU prepared an annual SBU strategic plan that was reviewed by sector executives. These SBU plans included environmental assessments; statement of objectives; strategy for

business and resource development; and a five-year, long-range forecast. Sectors were major business groupings determined by common markets, customers, products, or technology. Thus, the television and air-conditioning SBU managers forwarded their SBU plans to the Consumer Products and Services Sector executive vice president. Other sectors included Industrial Products and Components, Power Systems, and Technical Systems and Materials.

3. The sector executives reviewed and approved the SBU plans, then gathered them and forwarded the aggregated plan for review and approval to the Corporate Executive Office (CEO), which consisted of G.E.'s chairman and two vice chairmen. The aggregate SBU profit and investment needs were often below total planned profit and above total available investment funds. In this case, the CEO assigned higher profit targets and restricted investment amounts to the sectors for sector distribution to the SBUs.

4. The CEO also defined specific corporate planning challenges, such as productivity and general product-market targets for corporate and SBU growth. These target areas, called *arenas,* included such fields as energy, transportation and propulsion, and communication.

5. After finalizing its plans, each SBU developed an operating budget within the SBU plan guidelines. The approved budget then became the basis for monthly monitoring of current operating profit performance; profit responsibility was still decentralized down to the department level. This monthly monitoring included a series of financial statements that became less detailed at higher levels of the management hierarchy.

6. In addition to their financial goals, each G.E. manager developed a statement of nonfinancial objectives by which to be evaluated. These financial and nonfinancial

---

Strategic Business Units (continued)

objectives — in G.E. terms the *perfor-mance screen* — were reviewed with the manager's superior; together they assigned relative weights to each measure.

7. Performance evaluation sessions using the performance screen were held at least once a year. Further, the performance screens were used to rank managers for annual salary reviews, which also included substantial incentive compensation.

Thus, SBUs develop business opportunities in existing product markets; sectors develop new SBU opportunities within major industry groups; and the CEO develops new sector opportunities.

The Stage One, entrepreneurial company can be viewed as a single SBU; but the SBU is just one of many businesses within the Stage Three, divisionalized corporation. In the evolution of the corporation, the top executive moves from business policy to strategic planning and, finally, to strategic management.

STRATEGY RESEARCH

Each of the following chapters in this book will review research efforts in its subject area. In this introductory chapter, we will mention the work of Chandler, Andrews, and Ansoff, three researchers who shaped the strategic management field.

Alfred Chandler, in *Strategy and Structure* (1962), described in detail the strategic decisions made by General Motors; Sears, Roebuck; du Pont; and Standard Oil of New Jersey. Chandler not only analyzed the linkage between a firm's strategy and its environment, but he argued that a firm's structure should follow its strategy.

Kenneth Andrews was one of the main authors of the Harvard Business School text *Business Policy* (1965), and led the policy field toward suggesting what strategy should be, namely "objectives, purposes or goals and major . . . plans for achieving these goals, stated in such a way as to define what business the company is in or is to be in and the kind of company it is or is to be."

Igor Ansoff, in *Corporate Strategy* (1965), urged strategic managers to make decisions about growth and product markets based upon distinctive competence — one's competitive advantage — and synergy — the opportunity for 2 + 2 to achieve a sum greater than 4.

BUSINESS HISTORY

Research in business policy and strategy is hindered not only by the reluctance of managers to spell out decision factors and by the number and complexity of the variables involved in a strategic situation, but also by the difficulty of researching a company's strategy over time. Business histories often overcome this time restriction. The following text of a letter from C. F. Sise, the president of Bell Telephone of Canada, to F. G. Beach, the general manager of the Central Union Telephone Company of Chicago, written January 5, 1895, provides an example of the relevance of business history.

Dear Sir:

I beg to acknowledge receipt of yours of the 2nd instant, in reference to competition in the business.

It would hardly be possible, within the limits of a letter, to give you our experience in dealing with competition; but we may assume as the principal element in the matter, that there is no friendship in the business, and that if another Company can give as good service at a less rate, they will get your Subscribers. Of course you and I would naturally doubt the possibility of their giving as good service, but the Public is not so easily convinced.

I should recommend preparation for competition before it materializes, by making exclusive-franchise contracts with the Towns and Cities where you are operating, for say ten year terms. For this Franchise you can afford to give the City five per cent of your net receipts (in fact if these net receipts are to be figured by you, you could afford to give them ten per cent). We also make contracts with all Railroads, Telegraph Companies, and Electric Light Companies, whereby we interchange facilities; the Railroad for instance giving us free transportation and the exclusive right to enter their premises, in consideration of free telephone service on our part. Electric Light and Telegraph Companies are handled in practically the same manner; but they are important as they have pole rights which may be made available to your competitors.

We also take three year leases from our Subscribers (copy of one of which I enclose herewith), and of course a slight reduction is made to a Subscriber taking a three year lease. If the local rate were $50 I suppose we would take them at $45. They are very reluctant to break these leases, because if they do so before the expiration of the three years you have a claim for the full amount of the rental from the date of the lease. You will note that our rentals are payable every six months in advance.

It is far easier to stop competition in embryo than after it has got well started. Of course if the Public understands as it doubtless will, that competition means reduced rates, it will foster competition. For this reason your efforts should be devoted to opposing their franchises by securing to yourselves the exclusive rights in Cities and Towns, where possible to do so. The longer the opposition is deferred, the stronger you are getting, and the more difficult it will be to compete with you; and if the authorities can be convinced that you are giving a good service at a fair rate, they will be reluctant to allow competitors to come in for blackmailing purposes, and poling the streets of the City for that purpose. I attach great value to our relations with the Railways. Perhaps these are more important in Canada than in the United States, but in the smaller Towns in Canada no Merchant has any use for the telephone unless he can communicate with the Railway Station; and while doubtless efforts will be made through the Courts to compel the Railways to allow opposition Telephone Company's wires to be carried into their Stations, I have no doubt that such efforts can be defeated with the cooperation of the Railway Company. More than this I fear legislation compelling one Telephone Company to receive and transmit the messages of another, giving the opposition connection with your Exchange.

I shall be very glad to give you any other information, but you will of course understand that the subject is a very wide one, and efforts which are successful here may fail in your Territory. We are still constantly threatened with competition, but, with our City and Town contracts and the other alliances I have referred to, we do not give ourselves any uneasiness.

Yours truly,

C. F. Sise
President

This letter demonstrates how the history of business can provide a useful perspective for today's manager. Mr. Sise urges an entrepreneurial strategy: preparing for competition before it comes, and defending and seeking allies, such as the railroad (see Working Concept 5 in Chapter 2). How entrepreneurial is the telephone company executive today? Has today's executive the same view of "the Public" as President Sise?

EXECUTIVE COMMENTS

Finally, the comments of executives — and, occasionally, other observers of executive action — will appear at the end of each chapter to serve as real-world opinions against which to test the chapter's suggestions, prescriptions, and Working Concepts.

I know how not to make decisions. I know how to make decisions. Part of the secret of making decisions is to know which decisions not to make.
  Mario Cuomo, governor of New York, 9/30/84

The book [In Search of Excellence] has been so popular that people have taken it as a formula for success rather than what it is intended to be. We were writing about the art, not the science, of management.
  Robert M. Waterman, Jr., *Business Week*, 11/5/84

Our strategic planning process [at General Motors] is straightforward. Instructions, in the form of sets of questions, are sent out each year to each division and are divided into categories that form a series of steps: (1) business definition, including market segments, (2) key success factors, (3) situation analysis of relative competitive strengths and weaknesses, and (4) strategy development [systematically comparing] individual strengths and weaknesses against each key success factor for each of the major competitors.
  M. E. Naylor, General Motors executive

The brand of leadership we propose has a simple base of MBWA (Managing By Wandering Around). To "wander," with customers and vendors and our own people, is to be in touch with the first vibrations of the new.
  Tom Peters and Nancy Austin, *A Passion for Excellence*

"Would you tell me, please, which way I ought to go from here?"
"That depends a good deal on where you want to get to," said the Cat.
"I don't care much where . . ." said Alice.
"Then it doesn't matter which way you go," said the Cat.
". . . so long as I get somewhere," *Alice added as an explanation.*
"Oh, you're sure to do that," said the Cat, "if only you walk long enough."
        Lewis Carroll, *Alice's Adventures in Wonderland*

KEY TERMS

business policy (page 8)

business strategy (page 9)

corporate strategy (page 9)

functional strategy (page 12)

levels of strategy (page 9)

strategic business unit (SBU) (page 12)

strategic management (page 8)

strategic planning (page 8)

BIBLIOGRAPHY

Andrews, K. R., *The Concept of Corporate Strategy* (Homewood, Il: Richard D. Irwin, 1980).

Andrews, K. R., E. Learned, C. R. Christensen, and W. D. Guth, *Business Policy: Text and Cases* (Homewood, IL: Richard D. Irwin, 1965).

Ansoff, H. I., *Corporate Strategy: Business Policy for Growth and Expansion* (New York: McGraw-Hill, 1965).

Bower, J. L., "Business Policy in the 1980s," *Academy of Management Review*, 1982 (vol. 7, no. 4), pp. 630–638.

Chamberlain, N. W., *Enterprise and Environment: The Firm in Time and Place* (New York: McGraw-Hill, 1968).

Chandler, A. D., *Strategy and Structure: Chapters in the History of the American Industrial Enterprise* (Cambridge, MA: M.I.T. Press, 1962).

Cyert, R. M., and J. G. March, *A Behavioral Theory of the Firm* (Englewood Cliffs, NJ: Prentice-Hall, 1963).

Drucker, P. F., *Innovation and Entrepreneurship: Practice and Principles* (New York: Harper & Row, 1985).

Drucker, P. F., *Management: Tasks, Responsibilities, Practices* (New York: Harper & Row, 1974).

Evered, R., "So What Is Strategy," *Long Range Planning* 16 (June 1983), pp. 57–72.

Freeman, R., *Strategic Management — A Stakeholder Approach* (Boston: Pitman, 1984).

Hise, R., and S. McDaniel, "CEO's Views on Strategy," *Journal of Business Strategy* 4 (Winter 1984), pp. 79–86.

Kotter, J. P., *The General Managers* (New York: The Free Press, 1982).

Mintzberg, H., *The Nature of Managerial Work* (New York: Harper & Row, 1973).

Mintzberg, H., "Strategy-Making in Three Modes," *California Management Review* XVI (Winter 1973), pp. 44–53.

Naylor, M. E., "Regaining Your Competitive Edge," *Long Range Planning*, vol. 18, no. 1, pp. 30–35.

Peters, T. J., and R. H. Waterman, Jr., *In Search of Excellence: Lessons from America's Best-Run Companies* (New York: Harper & Row, 1982).

Schenkel, S., *Giving Away Success* (New York: McGraw-Hill, 1985).

Summer, C. E., and J. J. O'Connell, *The Managerial Mind* (Homewood, IL: Richard D. Irwin, 1971).

Sutton, C. J., *Economics and Corporate Strategy* (Cambridge, England: University of Cambridge Press, 1980).

Vancil, R. F., and P. Lorange, "Strategic Planning in Diversified Companies," *Harvard Business Review* (January–February 1975), pp. 81–90.

CHAPTER 2

STRATEGIC MANAGEMENT AND THE STRATEGIC MANAGER

If you really want to advise me, do it [during the game] on Saturday afternoon . . . [in] 25 seconds. Not on Monday. I know the right thing to do on Monday.

Alex Agase, former Purdue head coach (*Fortune,* 5/13/85)

This chapter will focus on the strategic manager, that executive who must make real-time (Saturday afternoon) decisions within the field of strategic management. We will discuss this strategic manager from both a military and a holistic perspective, and will consider the questions of managerial style — how decisions are made — and managerial perspective — how problems are perceived. Our first Working Concept examines an artificial being, the strategic manager.

WORKING CONCEPT 4

THE STRATEGIC MANAGER

No known firm has a position called "strategic manager." Nonetheless, the previous chapter's description of strategic management and the levels of strategy has shown that (1) managers at the operating, functional levels, such as research and development, or marketing; (2) divisional presidents at the product-market level; and (3) corporate executives at the multinational, multibusiness level (whether members of the board of directors, officers, or managers) all make strategic decisions that are both long term and of significance to the enterprise. Strategic decisions guide the enterprise in moving from its present position of products, markets, and technologies to its desired future position. Thus, the time perspective of the strategic manager is al- ways the long term; moving from a present position in products or technologies to a future position is a long-term movement.

Thomas Urban, chief executive of America's biggest seed-corn supplier, Pioneer Hi-Bred International, spoke about strategy and long-term perspectives:

Quarter-to-quarter doesn't cut much around Pioneer. We have a hard time thinking about year-to-year changes. I'm not in the dress business; it takes us ten years to make a new product. If you want to know how good a job I'm doing, come see me in 1990. (Fortune, 10/28/85, p. 38)

This artificial being, the strategic manager with the long-term view, is used as a Working Concept in order to highlight

---

The Strategic Manager (continued)

the strategic management duties from other managerial activities of executives (Kotter, 1982). This Working Concept may even be used to point out situations in which no one was the strategic manager. For example, commenting on Coca-Cola's introduction of New Coke and its reissue of Classic Coke four months later, Coca-Cola president Donald Keough said, ''Some critics will say Coca-Cola made a marketing mistake. Some cynics will say that we planned the whole thing. The truth is we are not that dumb and we are not that smart.''

The next Working Concept presents military and holistic versions of the strategic manager. The military version of the ''general'' stresses the authority and responsibility of the strategic manager. While researchers focus on the business enterprise, the strategic manager functions in the human arena; the holistic version of the ''executive householder'' stresses the interrelationship between the strategic manager as executive and human being. The strategic manager develops not just as a business executive, but grows in the emotional, mental, and psychological dimensions.

WORKING CONCEPT 5

MILITARY AND HOLISTIC STRATEGIC MANAGERS

THE GENERAL

Business texts often cite the military warrior origin of strategy, as evidenced also by the Random House Dictionary's definition of *strategy* as ''generalship . . . the art . . . (of formulating) a series of maneuvers . . . for obtaining a specific goal.''

Top Management Viewpoint

Three points should be made about this ''generalship'' definition. First, the viewpoint is that of the general, or, for our purposes, that of top management. Rather than being presented only with a financial problem or a limited marketing question, top management is presented with financial and marketing issues that affect the entire organization. These overall organizational issues must be considered from the point of view of the top executive, the *general (manager)*, who has authority — and responsibility — for the organization. The general manager must resolve conflicts between financial, marketing, and production goals, between the firm's perspective and functional interests.

The Art of Strategy

Second, the strategic process is an art. Accounting principles, mathematical models, and statistical formulae may provide answers for some business problems, but most often they cannot provide solutions for strategic issues. Analysis and mathematical techniques are extremely useful in determining the quantitative dimensions of problems — such as, how probable it is that competition will result in price cutting. However, these techniques can only provide measures to assist the top executive in making strategic decisions, which often must be based not only on hard facts and data, but also on judgment and intuition.

Military and Holistic Strategic Managers *(continued)*

For example, consider a military general, who has estimates of enemy troop strength, forecasts of weather conditions that might affect the battlefield, subordinates' assessments of the fighting potential of the troops, and dated descriptions and maps of the ground surfaces. With these data, which have varying degrees of reliability, the general must produce a battle strategy that will be based, at least in part, on personal judgment. In the business arena, the same principles apply; the principal organizer of General Motors, Will Durant, was "a man who would proceed on a course of action guided solely . . . by some intuitive flash of brilliance" (Sloan, 1941). Evered (1983) describes the link between military and corporate strategy. He asks "So What *Is* Strategy?" and answers in part by quoting von Clausewitz in *On War*, that "strategy forms the plan of the war, makes out the proposed course of the different campaigns which compose the war and regulates the battles to be fought in each."

In the mid-1980s, Canon, the Japanese manufacturer of office equipment, adopted a goal of direct competition with IBM in the international market of office automation products. *Business Week* (5/13/85, p. 98) quoted Canon's president, Ryuzaburo Kaku:

> *When you are climbing Mt. Fuji you can do it with wooden clogs, but when you are going to climb Mt. Everest, you have to be better prepared. [Business is becoming an age of] warring feudal lords. You look ahead for a time when there is a change in the marketplace. Then you move in.*

Students initially may feel frustrated as they try to understand and practice the art of strategy, due to the fact that in strategy, as in any other art, there is no one right answer. Strategy can provide reasonable answers; an instructor's reluctance to provide *the* answer must be seen from this perspective. Instructors are interested primarily in students developing their own strategic decision-making capabilities.

Goals and Direction

Third, and finally, the general has a specific goal. When trying to decide between various strategic alternatives, a strategist is not without guidance. Which alternative is most likely to achieve the desired result? The general has some strategic objective in mind, whether it is capturing enemy personnel, resources, and territory; or creating a diversion so that another general may achieve a strategic objective.

What is the "battlefield" of the general (manager) in business? Business organizations compete in markets and in technologies; the battlefield is the external environment of the firm. The resources of the internal environment of the firm, including managers, employees, capital, equipment, and other tangible and intangible assets, are the organization's "troops." The job of the strategic manager, and the responsibility of the general, is to define and implement a timed sequence of movements that will reach the objective — to move through the competitive market process toward success. Commenting on its competition with Procter & Gamble, Colgate's CEO Reuben Mark said, "We're just starting to take the hill. Now we've got to work on getting more ammunition out to the troops" (*Business Week*, 11/11/85, p. 138).

Harrigan (1985) analyzed Mao Tse-Tung's principles of guerrilla warfare (consolidating resources in areas of relative strength — guerrilla bases — and attacking the enemy only with slack resources on the enemy's turf — guerrilla fronts). Harrigan showed how guerrilla warfare is an

Military and Holistic Strategic Managers (continued)

appropriate tactic for the weaker firm and/ or one with low market share. These firms engage "in skirmishes where market leaders cannot respond without shooting themselves in the foot." Guerrilla bases are "market niches where competitors are unlikely or unable to enter . . . . guerrilla fronts are . . . for drawing out opponents and wasting their resources . . . [guerrilla bases] will necessarily have to be defended with a *kamikazelike* devotion."

Acquisitions, and especially hostile takeovers, are a form of competitive warfare. The year 1985 saw mergers in oil, advertising, entertainment, and consumer goods. Phillip Morris bought General Foods and Procter & Gamble bought Richardson-Vicks. But the biggest merger in history, outside of the petroleum industry, was General Electric's $6.3 billion acquisition of RCA. The concept of generalship is apparent in G.E. chairman Jack Welch's explanation of the merger:

> *Being powerful domestically is an integral part of being powerful internationally. Every day we're meeting the Toshibas of the world, the Hitachis of the world. We have to get larger and more powerful to be able to compete or just give up and let the imports take over.* (Business Week, *12/30/85, p. 48*)

Burrough's successful $4.8 billion takeover of Sperry was called a tale of a "dogged pursuer and unwary prey . . . Sperry's management misjudged the determination of [Burrough's] Blumenthal . . . [and] had to rely on crisis management" (*Business Week*, 6/9/86, p. 29).

As opposed to the unidimensional model of the general, the holistic model that follows presents the strategic manager as a stage (the successful householder) on a path that moves from student to service and retirement.

THE EXECUTIVE HOUSEHOLDER

Some holistic philosophers divide human life into four phases of growth, of which the first is the student. The student learns from the instruction and example of the teacher. The second phase is the householder, in which the householder works and raises children, thus contributing to the economic well-being of the family. The third phase of life (service) involves a gradual deemphasis of the material world. The fourth stage (contemplative) is a retirement from life, in which one continues spiritual growth (Hopkins, 1971). These phases of life mark each person's growth and development within a lifetime. Of these four phases, great emphasis is placed on the householder phase; thus, Hopkins makes the following conclusion.

> *Householdership was the keystone . . . study was important, but preservation of the entire society depended on the householder. . . . Householdership was . . . highly valued as the base for all activities, and the productive and fruitful householder was given great honor by the students, teachers, priests and ascetics whom he supported.*
>
> *The householder did more than just support others, however. Householdership in the . . . system was not an alternative to a genuine religious life but an essential stage of personal spiritual development. (p. 77)*

The path of the householder is the foundation for further growth. By fulfilling the role of the householder, one understands and then grows beyond the pursuit of wealth and sensual pleasure. This world's material and sensual attractions are to be pursued and understood, not avoided.

In summary, the general model provides a model of how to be a good householder and of how to make a living. The householder model shows how to make a life.

The next Working Concept explores what managers do by elaborating on managerial roles and styles.

MANAGERIAL ROLES

In a study of the nature of managerial work, Mintzberg (1973) described ten different managerial roles. First, among the *interpersonal* managerial roles, a manager performs (1) a leader role, exercising authority with the organization; (2) a liaison role, coordinating various functions and subordinates; and (3) a figurehead role, attending activities of a primarily ceremonial nature.

Second, within *informational* roles, a manager can be (4) a spokesperson, providing information about the organization to the outside world; (5) a disseminator, providing data within the organization; or (6) a monitor, receiving and collecting data.

Lastly, in *decision-making* managerial roles, the manager can be (7) a negotiator; (8) a disturbance handler; (9) a resource allocator, directing organizational effort toward specific activities; or (10) an innovator, introducing change.

STRATEGIST'S ROLES

Mintzberg's ten managerial roles include six roles of the strategic manager. Initially, the informational and decision-making roles are central to the activities of the strategic manager. The strategic manager is most concerned with receiving and collecting data (Role 6) about the internal strengths and external opportunities of the organization. The strategic manager then makes decisions that will become the organization's strategy. When these decisions require change, which they most frequently do, the strategic manager functions as a decision-making innovator (Role 10).

Implementing these strategic decisions encompasses four other managerial roles. As the strategic manager implements the formulated strategy, both leader (Role 1) and liaison (Role 2) roles will come into play. As details of the strategic plan are described to various organizational units, the strategic manager acts as an information disseminator (Role 5). In allocating specific resources, such as research monies for product development or capital funds for asset acquisitions, the strategic manager functions in a resource allocator, decision-making role (Role 9).

Depending on both the nature of the strategy and on the implementation tactics decided upon, the strategic manager could also serve as a disturbance handler and/or as a negotiator (Roles 7 and 8).

INTERNATIONAL ROLES

Do differences exist between strategic managers? Managers from different countries will, of course, have viewpoints shaped by their home countries' experiences. Three of the four business rules of British entrepreneur Richard Branson — (1) Keep overhead low; (2) Encourage entrepreneurship among employees; and (3) Never venture outside your core market — seem appropriate for many entrepreneurs. But Branson's fourth rule — (4) Avoid major capital investments — may make sense only in terms of the raging inflation experienced by Great Britain for two decades. Further, countries might basically differ in style (although resorting to generalizations may prove unwise). The American Management Association president, T. R. Horton, describes U.S. managers as being generally "impatient," and Japanese managers as having "enormous patience and enormous sense of detail." British managers "muddle through" and Russian managers "cover up" (*Dun's Business Month*, July 1985,

Mintzberg's Roles and Styles (continued)

pp. 69–70). Certainly there are greater differences between managers within a country, however, than between countries.

GENDER ROLES

National differences between managerial experiences and managerial style can be matched by differences in the experiences conditioning female and male strategic managers (Schenkel, 1985):

Only in the limited spheres of raising and educating children have women been allowed to control the behavior of others. We lack sufficient female role models for leadership in the larger world. As a result, when it comes to asserting authority,

many of us have a gap in our concept of authority, our self-image and our behavioral repertoire.

These environmental differences between male and female managers are decreasing, in part due to the elimination of stereotypes. We need only to note that the strategic manager includes male and female managers, as the term *strategic manager* is used in this book. The strategic manager is androgynous, requiring both the Jungian characteristics of the masculine, *animus* archetype (action, linearity) as well as those of the feminine, *anima* archetype (creativity, nurturing).

STRATEGIC MANAGEMENT

How does the strategic manager perform these strategic managerial roles? There are as many strategic management systems as there are strategic managers. The strategic decision can involve so many complex variables and can be so situationally specific that to generalize about the detailed steps of strategic management is difficult, even with the benefit of hindsight.

The strategic manager's job can be better understood by looking at how that job is performed. Mintzberg (1973) describes three modes of strategic management: entrepreneurial, adaptive, and planning modes.

The Entrepreneurial Manager

The entrepreneurial strategic manager is a strong leader who takes bold, often risky actions in an active search for new opportunities. This manager operates in an economically risky environment and aggressively pursues growth.

The Adaptive Manager

As opposed to the dramatic leaps of the entrepreneur, the adaptive strategic manager reacts to existing problems rather than aggressively searching for new opportunities. The adaptive manager proceeds in halting, uneven steps, since the organization lacks clear goals for issues such as growth. The adaptive strategic manager often can be found in bureaucratic organizations. Lindblom (1959) commented that the adaptive manager "is nevertheless a . . . problem solver who is wrestling bravely with a universe that he is wise enough to know is too big for him." While the entrepreneurial manager seeks the risky spectrum of the environment, the adaptive manager prefers an environment that is free of risk.

The Planning Manager

The planning strategic manager uses a systematic, and often formal, comprehensive analysis to foresee opportunities and anticipate problems. The planning manager is "proactive," versus the "reactive" adaptive manager; has a longer-term time frame for strategy making; and feels comfortable with or without risk.

The planning strategic manager, then, is one who systematically carries out a strategic planning process. Studies, such as those by Robinson (1982) or Karger and Malik (1975), have shown that companies that plan outperform nonplanners. Most strategic managers and business analysts believe that the planning strategic manager will make better strategic decisions than the nonplanner. Certainly that same belief underlies this text.

This chapter closes with the topic of managerial perceptions and the Working Concept of the Brunswick lens model. As a student of the strategic management process, your perspective, or "lens," will open to include more strategic data. Before describing the nature of those data, we will present this concept of perspective not only to provide deeper understanding of the strategic manager and strategic management, but also to encourage students to participate in the widening of their own lenses.

For example, appendices to this chapter review some accounting and financial tools and discuss the case method. As a student, you will need to understand the strategic concepts embedded in financial and accounting measures. Greater benefit also will be derived from in-class discussions of cases if you have come to a decision about the case before class. Experiential learning is the best — if not the only true — learning. If you learn through the class discussion about issues you did not see from your perspective, then you have learned about opening your perspective, or widening your own lens. This is only possible if you participate fully in the discussion and bring to the discussion a committed position and decision.

WORKING CONCEPT 7

BRUNSWIK LENS AND PERCEPTION

No strategist has a perfect view of the environment, and no strategist has perfect intuition. The strategic manager must (1) improve the quality of information received and (2) refine the accuracy of strategic judgments and managerial perceptions.

Figure 2.1 summarizes the process of managerial perception. This figure is derived from the framework of human judgment developed by the psychologist Egon Brunswik. Signals indicate the state of the environment (a market, technology, or competitor). These signals interact in much the same way as a competitor's advertising campaign interacts with customer demand and another firm's technology advance through an improved product. The strategic manager perceives these signals. Various strategic managers differ in (1) the accuracy of their perception and their degree of under- or overperception of the signal (i.e., the relative weight of each signal) and (2) the quality of their judgment, a combination of experience and information base, common sense, and intuition.

The perception of the general and the perception of the executive householder would clearly be different. The householder would add holistic concepts of growth, teaching, and mentoring to the general's attack/maneuver/retreat lenses. This lens model helps us stress the refinement of managerial perceptions and the improvement of information quality.

Brunswik Lens and Perception (continued)

FIGURE 2.1
Perceptions of the
strategic manager

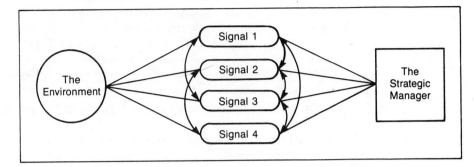

Refining managerial perceptions is part of the process of managerial development. The case methodology of the strategic management course tries to improve your strategic perceptions. As the student and strategic manager reassess their original assumptions, whether through a periodic review of conditions or through the process of class discussion, their ability to perceive strategic signals is refined.

The strategic manager improves the quality of the information received by

1. Recognizing the impossibility of perfect information.
2. Balancing the value of information and its cost.

3. Minimizing the danger of information overload by eliminating excess information through summarized feedback and exception reports, since every communication channel has a capacity limit.
4. Viewing the information system as evolutionary and flexible as opposed to formal and fixed.
5. Increasing, within cost constraints, the timeliness, format, and accuracy of reported data.

Figure 2.2 expands on the Brunswik lens model to include issues relating to improving the quality of information received and refining the accuracy of strategic judgments, decision, and managerial perceptions.

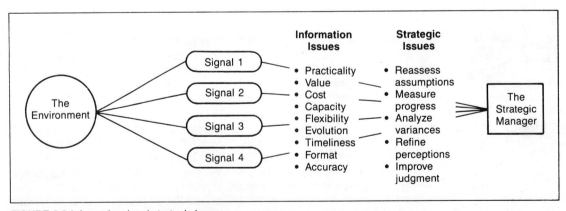

FIGURE 2.2 Informational and strategic issues

STRATEGY AND THE STRATEGIST: A SUMMARY

Before discussing research efforts, the most important messages of these first two chapters may be summarized as follows:

1. Successful firms grow in a discernible pattern.
2. Firms at different stages of growth require different managerial skills as they face changing yet predictable issues.
3. The required management skills change from entrepreneurial decision making to strategic planning to, lastly, strategic management.
4. The mature firm's specific strategic management skills include an understanding of functional strategy, business-level strategy, and corporate strategy.
5. Functional strategy addresses efficiency (quantity) and effectiveness (quality) decisions to maximize outputs, given a set of allocated resources.
6. Business-level strategy builds strengths into distinctive competence so that the firm may compete in a specific business within a defined product market.
7. Corporate strategy balances the corporate portfolio of existing business; analyzes industries, markets, and technologies for growth opportunities; and allocates resources among existing and potential new businesses to achieve overall corporate objectives.
8. Managers have many roles, but our focus is on the manager as strategic manager.
9. We may view the strategic manager either as a function — the general — or as a human being in a particular stage of personal development — the householder.
10. Strategic managers may have different styles — entrepreneurial, adaptive, or planning.
11. Strategic managers and students of management have viewpoints and capabilities limited by their lenses of perception.
12. This course of study seeks to open the lenses of perception.

STRATEGY RESEARCH
AND THE STRATEGIC MANAGER

Classical research efforts include those of Argenti, Chamberlain, Cyert and March, and Lindblom.

Argenti's *Systematic Corporate Planning* (1974) not only addressed the procedures of corporate strategy formulation, but also urged the strategic manager to ensure that the formulated strategy (1) took advantage of major opportunities and (2) defended against major threats. Further, Argenti encouraged the strategist to make contingency plans in the face of significant strategic threats.

Chamberlain's concept of ''counterpoint'' was presented in *Enterprise and Environment* (1968). While the operating supervisor tries to maintain equilibrium, the strategic manager must lead the firm through time (events) and space (markets) to

deal with strategic changes in the environment. The strategist must deal with disequilibrium in the move from point to counterpoint.

Cyert and March presented a bargaining model that underlies the formulation
of strategy in their book *A Behavioral Theory of the Firm* (1963). Organizational
slack, conflicting objectives, sequential attention to functional goals, and personal
aspirations result in adaptive, "satisficing" strategies.

Lindblom's message is similar to those of Cyert and March. Lindblom argued
in "The Science of 'Muddling Through'" (1959) that the scientific management
view of strategy formulation — the rational, comprehensive method of agreeing on
purpose and selecting from alternatives based on purpose — was often ignored or
inappropriate. Rather, he suggested that decision makers follow a successive limited
comparison method in strategy formulation. This method involves achieving a consensus on means, not ends, and occurs especially in complex situations.

Current significant research efforts in strategy formulation include studies by
the following authors.

Chaffee (1985) pointed out that definitions of strategy may be based on one or
another of the following "three models of strategy."

1. *Linear*: "integrated decisions, actions, or plans that will set and achieve viable
   organization goals."
2. *Adaptive*: environmental assessment of internal and external conditions that leads
   to the organization adjusting to a viable match between opportunities and capabilities.
3. *Interpretive*: The organization attracts individuals in a social contract or a collection
   of cooperative agreements.

Chaffee concluded that the lack of consensus on a definition of strategy is due
to its multidimensional and situational characteristics.

Ginter and Rucks studied wargame technology in 1984 and asked "Can business
learn from wargames?" They concluded that wargaming was applicable to business
as a strategic decision-making aid.

McGinnis (1984) studied strategic planning, and identified six traits that the
organization must have if the strategic manager is to function: (1) intelligence, (2)
organizational balance, (3) analysis, (4) innovation, (5) proactivity, and (6) risk
taking. Central to "strategic success" is "the ability of the firm to integrate analysis
and intuition."

Naylor studied the strategic process at General Motors (1985) and recommended
implementation and planning that included the acronym STRATEGY: **S** (Stick to
it), **T** (Think it through), **R** (Risk, responsibility, and reward), **A** (Awareness of
self and competition), **T** (Talking to each other to communicate strategy), **E** (Evaluation of each step), **G** (Growing your people), and **Y** (Yes-I-Can winning attitude).

Stopford and Wells expanded on the stages of corporate development with their 1972 model, which included international divisions, based upon a study of U.S. firms expanding abroad.

EXECUTIVE COMMENTS

One of General Motor's most important characteristics [is] its effort to achieve open-minded communication and objective consideration of facts.

  Alfred P. Sloan, Jr., *My Years with General Motors*

Cruelties should be committed all at once, as in that way each separate one is less felt, and gives less offence; benefits, on the other hand, should be conferred one at a time, for in that way they will be more appreciated.

  Niccolò Machiavelli, *The Prince*

We've seen, all too clearly, how the actions of a few can hurt an entire company and all of its employees.

  J. Welch, in a letter to General Electric employees following G.E.'s guilty plea to fraud in a Minuteman missile project, 1985

An important thing to remember is that, in terms of building an organization that is big and successful, you are going to have to pay a big price, personally. And you won't realize that until you are far enough along and have already paid that price — so you'd better be willing to live with it. . . . You have to see your professional success as part of something larger — maybe that's a way of saying you have to have a philosophy of life. Achieving success, being right — that doesn't do anything for you. Mostly what it does is bring you a lot of problems.

  Fred Smith, founder of Federal Express, in *Inc.*, October 1980

KEY TERMS

adaptive manager (page 24)

entrepreneurial manager (page 24)

managerial perceptions (page 25)

managerial roles (page 23)

planning manager (page 25)

strategic manager (page 19)

BIBLIOGRAPHY

Argenti, J., *Systematic Corporate Planning* (New York: Wiley, 1974).

Brunswik, E., *Perception and the Representative Design of Psychological Experiments* (Berkeley, CA: University of California Press, 1956).

Chaffee, E. E., "Three Models of Strategy," *Academy of Management Review* 10 (1985), pp. 89–98.

Chamberlain, N. W., *Enterprise and Environment: The Firm in Time and Space* (New York: McGraw-Hill, 1968).

Cyert, R. M., and J. G. March, *A Behavioral Theory of the Firm* (Englewood Cliffs, NJ: Prentice-Hall, 1963).

Evered, R., "So What Is Strategy?" *Long-Range Planning,* vol. 16, no. 3 (1983), pp. 57–72.

Ginter, P. M., and A. C. Rucks, "Can Business Learn from Wargames?" *Long-Range Planning* 17 (June 1984), pp. 123–128.

Hanna, R. G. C., "The Concept of Corporate Strategy in Multi-Industry Companies," D. B. A. dissertation, Harvard Business School, 1969.

Harrigan, K. R., *Strategic Flexibility: A Management Guide for Changing Times* (Lexington, MA: D. C. Heath, 1985).

Hopkins, T. J., *The Hindu Religious Tradition* (Encino, CA: Dickenson, 1971).

Jung, C. G., *Man and His Symbols* (London: Aldus Books, 1964).

Karger, D. W., and Z. A. Malik, "Long Range Planning and Organizational Performance," *Long Range Planning* (December 1975), pp. 60–64.

Kotter, J. P., *The General Managers* (New York: The Free Press, 1982).

Lindblom, C. E., "The Science of 'Muddling Through'," *Public Administration Review* (Spring 1959), pp. 79–88.

McGinnis, M. A., "The Key to Strategic Planning: Integrating Analysis and Intuition," *Sloan Management Review* (Fall 1984), pp. 45–52.

Mintzberg, H., *The Nature of Managerial Work* (New York: Harper & Row, 1973).

Mintzberg, H., "Strategy-Making in Three Modes," *California Management Review* XVI (Winter 1973), pp. 44–53.

Naylor, M. E., "Regaining Your Competitive Edge," *Long Range Planning* 18 (February 1985), pp. 30–35.

Organ, T. W., *The Hindu Quest for the Perfection of Man* (Athens, OH: Ohio University Press, 1970).

Robinson, R. B., Jr., "The Importance of Outsiders in Small Firm Strategic Planning," *Academy of Management Journal* (March 1982), pp. 80–93.

Schenkel, S., *Giving Away Success* (New York: McGraw-Hill, 1985).

Simon, H., "On the Concept of Organizational Goals," *Administrative Science Quarterly* (June 1964).

Sloan, A., Jr., *Adventures of the White Collarman* (New York: Doubleday, 1941).

Sloan, A., Jr., *My Years with General Motors* (Garden City, NY: Anchor Books, 1963).

Steiner, G., "Formal Strategic Planning in the U.S. Today," *Long Range Planning,* 16:3 (June 1983), pp. 12–18.

Stopford, J., and L. Wells, *Managing the Multinational Enterprise* (London: Longmans, 1972).

Weber, C. E., "Strategic Thinking — Dealing with Uncertainty," *Long Range Planning* 17 (October 1984), pp. 60–70.

Appendices: Appendices follow that serve as a checklist for further "refreshers" in either accounting or financial measures. The appendices also discuss case analysis, and present an example based upon the University of New Hampshire Bookstore.

APPENDIX A: ACCOUNTING FOR NONACCOUNTANTS

Jacques's Restaurant (*Chalet Le Hamberge*) at Ultra Excellence Ski Area has the following balance sheet as of the end of Year One.

Assets

Cash	$ 500
Accounts receivable	11,000
Food, wine inventory on hand	1,500
Furniture, equipment at original cost	5,000
Depreciation accumulated to date on furniture and equipment at 10-year life	(500)
	$17,500

Liabilities

Accounts payable to merchandise suppliers	$11,000

Equity

Investment by Jacques	$ 6,000
Earnings retained in the business	500
Total liabilities, equity	$17,500

Jacques's transactions during Year Two include the following checkbook totals.

Cash receipts		
Cash sales	$24,000	
Accounts receivable collected	$35,000	
Cash disbursed		
Payroll	$30,000	($20,000 to Jacques — $10,000 to part-time employees)
Rent (long-term lease)	$ 5,000	
Miscellaneous variable costs	$ 7,000	
Paid to merchandise suppliers for accounts payable	$15,000	

Note: Cash was paid for all expenses except food and wine. All food and wine for inventory was purchased on credit, and thus would be recorded as increases in inventory and accounts payable.

Additional information included a totaling of customer accounts receivable ledger cards at year end ($13,500 due to Jacques), a total of bills from food and wine supplier ($9,000 due from Jacques), and the checkbook balance of $2,500. Finally,

Jacques counted all the food and wine inventory on hand at the end of Year Two. It totaled $2,500 at invoice cost.

1. Prepare an income statement for Year Two and a balance sheet for the end of Year Two.
2. What is Jacques's
   (a) gross profit margin?
   (b) fixed costs?
   (c) break-even sales volume?
3. What do you estimate Year Three profits will be?
4. If Jacques should decide to sell, what price should he ask for the business?

APPENDIX B: STRATEGIC FINANCIAL ANALYSIS

The strategic manager must use the financial reports prepared by the organization's accountants as one source of strategic signals. Using financial reports aids both in analyzing one's own organization and in studying competitive businesses.

Two major kinds of strategic signals are contained in financial reports; namely, profitability signals and viability signals.

PROFITABILITY

Whether looking at a competitor or at our own company, we want to know how profitable the business is. The specific data and ratios that might contain strategic information include

I. Total profits (What is the general picture?)
    1. Net profits in absolute terms
    2. Net profits as a percentage of sales
II. Operating profits (How profitable are operations, disregarding financial and tax costs?)
    1. Operating profits (sales minus cost of sales and operating expenses) in absolute terms
    2. Operating profits as a percentage of sales
III. Costs (What are the critical cost elements?)
    1. Cost of goods sold as a percentage of sales
        (a) materials
        (b) labor
        (c) overhead
    2. Selling costs as a percentage of sales
    3. Administrative costs as a percentage of sales
    4. Financial, interest costs as a percentage of sales
    5. Depreciation as a percentage of sales

6. Taxes as a percentage of sales
7. Research and development as a percentage of sales

Because the strategic manager is concerned with the long term, these profitability measures provide strategic significance if they are viewed over a number of periods, preferably at least three to five years. The strategic manager really is looking for positive and negative signals contained in the *trend* of these measures. The direction in which the measures are heading is of more strategic importance than a single measure.

The strategic manager must consider not only profitability trends within the company, but also competitor-to-competitor trends. The strategic manager can put quantitative measures on the relative strength of the company versus the competition, and can begin to predict competitive strategies. For example, lower profits probably indicate a lower chance of price competition; higher research costs probably indicate a higher chance of new product innovations. Profitability measures are always a potential source for strategic signals, and often they will contain essential data for strategic judgments and decisions.

VIABILITY MEASURES

Profits indicate how well a firm is performing; viability measures depict the strengths or weaknesses of the firm's resources. The specific data and ratios that might contain strategic information include

I. Return on investment (How satisfactory are the profits?)
   1. Operating and net profit as percentages of stockholder's equity
   2. Operating and net profit as percentages of total assets
II. Value added (How important is the function performed?)
   1. Sales minus costs paid outside the firm to suppliers
III. Sources of capital (Where are resources coming from?)
   1. Funds provided by net income and depreciation
   2. Changes in net working capital (current assets minus current liabilities)
   3. Changes in net "quick" assets (current assets minus inventories and minus current liabilities)
   4. Debt as a percentage of total capital (total liabilities and equity minus current liabilities)
   5. Equity as a percentage of total capital
   6. Inventory turnover (cost of goods sold divided by average inventory)
IV. Uses of capital (Where are resources being allocated?)
   1. Dividends as a percentage of earnings
   2. Dividends as a percentage of total funds used
   3. Plant and equipment expenditures as a percentage of total funds used
V. Stock prices (How does the stock market view the firm's prospects?)
   1. Stock market prices

2. Volume of stock traded
3. Price earnings ratio

As with profitability measures, these viability measures, describing how "healthy" a firm is, should be examined from both the long term and the competitor-to-competitor viewpoints. What measures point to problems, and what measures show a firm's relative strength in comparison to its competitors'?

Specific financial ratios measure specific abilities of a firm. Liquidity ratios measure a firm's ability to pay short-term debts. A common liquidity ratio is

$$\frac{\text{Current assets}}{\text{Current liabilities}} = \text{Current ratio}$$

Many liquidity ratios suggest a ratio of about 2 to 1. Leverage ratios measure long-term debt, as follows:

$$\frac{\text{Total debt}}{\text{Total assets}} = \text{Leverage ratio}$$

A leverage ratio greater than 0.5 may indicate a debt repayment risk and/or inadequate profits and stockholder investment.

Activity ratios measure turnover of inventory (sales ÷ inventory), accounts receivable (sales ÷ accounts receivable), and asset turnover (sales ÷ fixed assets). These activity ratios may indicate that management successfully or unsuccessfully employs resources.

Finally, not all measures will be strategic signals. Viability and profitability measures must be viewed as potential sources of strategic information, not as having any intrinsic value. There is no right or wrong debt ratio, inventory turnover, or price earnings multiple. The strategic manager uses these measures as a signal of strategic problems or advantages. Financial measures thus indicate an issue that will require further strategic analysis and conclusion. The next step for the strategic manager is to analyze those factors and characteristics that resulted in a favorable or unfavorable indicator. Financial data provide input for strategic decision making; they are not ends in themselves.

∘ APPENDIX C: UNIVERSITY OF NEW HAMPSHIRE BOOKSTORE CASE

Dennis Bellucci and Dan Carr were student representatives on the University of New Hampshire special committee considering the leasing of the university-owned

Case prepared by John Barnett and Dennis Bellucci for classroom discussion purposes only. © 1985 by John Barnett.

and -operated bookstore. A conversation they had in mid-November 1983 went as follows:

> DENNIS: *Well, Dan, how do we represent the student's viewpoint now? The committee meeting is in one hour, and we think student needs can best be met through university management of the bookstore. Yet, we know the way this committee has been changed, from "Should we lease the bookstore?" to "Should we lease the bookstore to Barnes & Noble or to another private company?" And it looks like today's meeting is going to be the final one where we give in to the university administrators and forget it.*

> DAN: *It's totally frustrating. We've spent fifteen to twenty hours a week on this bookstore all fall, and for what? And who knows what is best for the university? One lesson I've learned is how you cannot accept either words or deeds at face value.*

> DENNIS: *It's not as if we have a lot of choices on the committee. We can go along, abstain, or walk out and call the newspapers and tell them how the students have been railroaded again.*

Dennis sat back in his chair in the Student Senate office, and reviewed in his mind the events leading up to the forthcoming meeting and this decision.

THE UNIVERSITY

The University of New Hampshire (U.N.H.) was founded in 1866 as the first land-grant institution in the United States. Located in Durham, a small seacoast community about midway between Boston and Portland, Maine, U.N.H. today has ten thousand students enrolled in a wide range of undergraduate and graduate programs.

The University System of New Hampshire board of trustees oversees U.N.H. and two state colleges. Of the twenty-five trustees, eleven are appointed by the governor; six are elected by alumni; one, a student, is elected by the students of U.N.H., Keene State College, and Plymouth State College in rotation; and seven are ex officio. The ex officio members are the governor; the commissioner of education; the commissioner of agriculture; the chancellor of the university system; and the presidents of U.N.H., Plymouth State College, and Keene State College. A chart of the university administration appears in Exhibit 1.

Various classifications of organizations or enterprises exist within the university or college. The bookstores fall into what are known as auxiliary enterprises. These organizations by state law cannot be subsidized with monies appropriated for the university; they are essentially "stand-alone" enterprises, and should generate a surplus. Any surplus so generated remains within that enterprise in a reserve account; monies within this account can only be reused by that same enterprise, whether it be for renovations or extraordinary expenses, or to offset losses. The university administration is prohibited from moving monies from one auxiliary enterprise to another.

Conversely, other organizations that are not auxiliary enterprises within the univer-

EXHIBIT 1
Partial U.N.H.
organization chart
(1983)

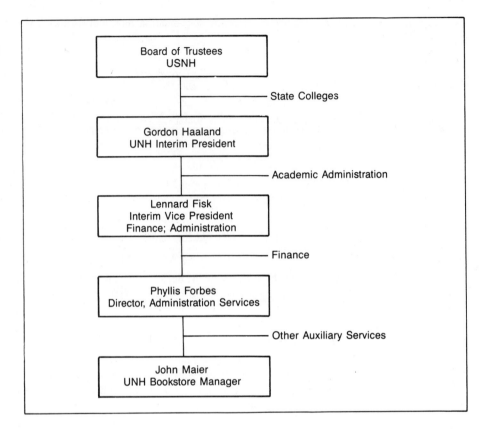

sity system — such as the library, the computer center, and athletic teams — are subsidized by appropriations. Monies generated by these activities can be moved by administration officials where needed.

Some university administrators view the auxiliary enterprises as services more than as profit centers, but feel that services such as the bookstore should not lose money. A well-stocked store, serving the needs of the students, faculty, and general public, was thought desirable.

GUBERNATORIAL REVIEW

In 1981, New Hampshire governor Hugh Gallen created a management review task force to analyze the operations of the state and find areas where the state could save money. One of the topics of the resultant report was an evaluation of the state's university system. The task force produced fourteen specific recommendations, one of which was to lease out the bookstore businesses at U.N.H. and Keene State College. The U.N.H. bookstore had shown a steady decline in income since

EXHIBIT 2
Management
Review
Commission
recommendations

Recommendations	Financial impact	Estimated amount
University System of New Hampshire		
Centralize all personnel services	Annual saving	$ 65,000
Consolidate information services	Annual saving	732,000
Terminate two positions on central Art Design and Graphics staff	Annual saving	35,000
Eliminate redundant physical plant activities	Annual saving	479,600
Identify and dispose of surplus property	One-time income	2,000,000
Eliminate the branch purchasing office at U.N.H.	Annual saving	38,400
Improve U.N.H. housekeeping services	Annual saving	455,000
Reduce inventory control staff at U.N.H. by one position	Annual saving	13,800
Raise fares for U.N.H. bus service	Annual income	253,800
Advance funding for U.N.H. steam system reconstruction by 12 months	One-time saving	1,000,000
Require adequate cost justification for U.N.H. research analyses	Annual saving	82,700
Designate all U.N.H. health services as limited auxiliary enterprises	Annual saving	290,000
Subcontract the bookstore operations at U.N.H. and Keene	Annual income	194,000
Develop housekeeping contracts for Plymouth	Annual saving	54,000

1980. Exhibit 2 presents excerpts from Governor Gallen's Review Commission Report.

THE UNIVERSITY BOOKSTORE

The University Bookstore spent most of its eighty-nine-year history as a monopoly. During the past decade, it grew at the rate of 10 percent a year and produced enough to cover its fixed expenses and allow it to at least break even or make a small profit of 1 or 2 percent. In the 1970s the bookstore built an image as a textbook and school-supply store; it stressed service and avoided competing with downtown merchants' soft lines or other products.

Problems started in 1981 when a private citizen, William Zucker, opened the Durham Book Exchange in a very advantageous downtown location. The Book Exchange broke the monopoly on textbooks held by the bookstore for years. The Book Exchange, through advertising its 5 percent discount of textbooks, succeeded in creating a desirable alternative to the high prices of the University Bookstore. The Book Exchange began to take some of the U.N.H. bookstore's business, resulting in an unanticipated decline in University Bookstore sales. From 1981 to 1984, the University Bookstore's sales declined, creating deficits. In fiscal year 1983 the bookstore suffered its greatest loss in its eighty-nine-year history, $75,000. Exhibit 3 presents a summary of the bookstore's results.

EXHIBIT 3 University Bookstore, summary of results, July–June fiscal year

	1978	1979	1980	1981	1982	1983
Revenues net of student discounts	$1,526,562	$1,723,754	$1,995,629	$2,167,325	$2,017,414	$2,054,393
Expenditures	$1,452,491	$1,662,439	$1,902,607	$2,145,039	$2,012,474	$2,158,149
Net from operations	$ 74,071	61,315	93,022	22,286	4,940	(103,756)
Inventory adjustment (see inventory investment, below*)	(46,554)	(32,498)	(161,660)	15,402	(39,140)	28,192
Building cost adjustment	—	26	—	—	—	—
Transfers to plant funds for capital additions	(75,000)	—	—	—	—	—
Net increase (decrease)	$ (47,483)	$ 28,843	$ (68,638)	$ 37,688	$ (34,200)	$ (75,564)
* Reserves invested in inventories	$ 202,727	$ 235,226	$ 396,887	$ 381,484	$ 420,624	$ 392,432

At approximately the same time the Book Exchange opened, the governor's management review task force began their analysis of the university system's financial situation. The task force recommended that the U.N.H. bookstore attain a 5.5 percent "net from operations" income by the end of fiscal year 1983. To help the bookstore achieve this goal, they also recommended that it become a "full-line" campus bookstore, incorporating the sale of books, art materials, office supplies, and other soft lines and souvenir merchandise customary to campus bookstores.

In the past an unwritten agreement had existed between the university and the Durham merchants that the University Bookstore not carry soft lines and no downtown merchant sell textbooks. After the entrance of the Durham Book Exchange, the trustees removed this restriction on the bookstore in October 1982. The University Bookstore then was given a nine-month deadline by which to increase the net income from operations from 1 to 2 percent to the 5.5 percent range. Failure to meet this goal would result in the Finance and Budget Committee's recommendation to develop specifications and solicitations for bids on the bookstore from outside companies.

MAIER'S STEPS

John Maier had worked for the University Bookstore since graduating from U.N.H. in 1972, and became its manager a few years before the 1981 management review.

Faced with financial and profit pressure, Maier, with the assistance of some U.N.H. business faculty, first undertook a study of revenue possibilities. He added higher margin soft lines, along with used books, the latter offering greater profit potential than the 20 percent margin allowed by textbook publishers. Finally, he also raised margins on nonbook items. The bookstore also turned to nonstudent markets, expanded its holdings of trade (i.e., nontextbook) publications, and dramatically increased advertising from $10,000 a year to $31,000 in an attempt to attract not only Durham, but seacoast New Hampshire customers as well.

Maier also directed his attention to cost control. He eliminated eight clerical personnel, five by attrition and three by termination. Exhibit 4 presents details of the July-to-June fiscal year's operating results. John Maier's nine-month deadline ended June 30, 1983 (the end of fiscal year 1983). The gubernatorial review had taken place in 1981 during the 1982 fiscal year (July 1 to June 30).

EXHIBIT 4 University Bookstore, selected operating data for the twelve months ending June 30

	1983		1982		1981	
	Percent	*Dollars*	*Percent*	*Dollars*	*Percent*	*Dollars*
Sales						
Textbooks	58	1,320,000	67	1,455,000	72	1,630,000
General books	15	355,000	11	240,000	7	160,000
Supplies	25	565,000	22	470,000	21	460,000
Clothing	2	55,000	–0–	–0–	–0–	–0–
Total sales	100	2,295,000	100	2,165,000	100	2,250,000
Computed gross profit						
Textbooks @ 20% (new 17%, used 33%)	43	265,000				
General books @ 30%	17	105,000				
Supplies @ 40%	36	225,000				
Clothing @ 50%	4	25,000				
	100	620,000				
Expenses						
Salaries, wages		390,000				
Student and sale discounts		170,000				
Supplies, office		55,000				
Advertising		30,000				
Accounting		10,000				
University interest, utilities, allocated costs		60,000				
		715,000				
Period profit (loss)		(75,000)		(35,000)		40,000

STUDENT INVOLVEMENT

Dennis Bellucci first became involved with the University Bookstore during the summer of 1983. Dennis, a member of the Class of 1985, had served as a representative from his dormitory to the Student Senate during his sophomore year. Representatives from the dormitories, fraternities, and commuters made up the elected senate.

Dennis was reelected to the senate for the 1983–1984 year. The student body president appointed Dennis to the seven-person executive board of the fifty-person Student Senate, as chairperson of Financial Affairs and Administration. This financial function led to his connection with the bookstore.

The Student Senate executive board routinely attended University System of New Hampshire board meetings as observers when the trustees were in Durham. The July 23, 1983, trustees meeting in Durham first made Dennis aware of the bookstore. Dennis later commented,

> *The board and President Haaland had been going along under the assumption that the bookstore would make its goal of 4.5 percent return. One of the trustees asked President Haaland if he thought the goal would be met. President Haaland said he thought so. John Maier, who was sitting with the public observers, stood up and said he didn't think the goal would be met. When asked further how the bookstore would do, John said he thought they would lose about $100,000. Jaws dropped. I felt especially embarrassed for the president.*

Later in the meeting the trustees directed that the situation be investigated further by U.N.H. administration.

Following the traditional decision-making format found at universities, Vice President Fisk put together a committee composed of Phyllis Forbes, the director of Administrative Services, John Maier, two faculty members, two administrators experienced both in purchasing and leased operations from other state colleges, and two student members, Dennis Bellucci and Dan Carr. The committee was called the Bookstore Bids and Specifications Committee. Dennis commented further:

> *Our committee met during the fall semester. Dan and I felt that the initial purpose of the committee was to see if the bookstore should be leased. We were also to prepare specifications to describe a minimum level of service an independent operator would have to provide, if a decision was made to lease.*
>
> *When I would report back to the Senate Executive Board, we would all discuss the question of the trend in student services. About three years ago the university had subcontracted out all the vending machines. Last year the student bus service was turned over to a private company that opened student buses to the public and changed student bus routes. Now there are rumors that the printing and rapid-copy service will be the next university activity to ''go private and for-profit.''*
>
> *As an example of how the university can get hurt, U.N.H. had to subsidize the private bus service with several hundred thousand dollars because the public demand expected*

by the private operator never materialized. But we were mostly concerned about the effect on the students of all this "for-profit" move.

Late in the summer Dennis and the executive board helped draft a resolution for the president. The resolution, one of the best forms of communication that the Student Senate has with the university, requires senate approval to be sent to the university president. The board decided that the resolution should be brief, and should ask for a delay in the bidding process until January 1, 1984, in order to see how the fall book rush went. *Book rush* is the time of the year when textbooks are sold at the beginning of classes; it is a peak revenue raising period for the bookstore. The resolution would represent a call to the university's attention that students were concerned with the bookstore matter.

The resolution addressed four central issues to be examined before leasing the bookstore. The first and most important issue was the bookstore's location. The present location was not near any major path running through campus and was too great a "psychological" distance from the center of campus; it was a ten-minute walk from the hub of campus activity, the Memorial Union Building. The resolution suggested that the Memorial Union Building would be a better location for the bookstore. A 1973 architectural study of U.N.H. also recommended a Memorial Union Building site for the bookstore. This proposed location would also provide a more direct position to compete with the downtown establishments.

The second resolution issue was that the views of faculty and students, as the main source of business and economic support to the university, should be considered before any action to be taken. Currently, the service was generally satisfactory to faculty; students were concerned mostly with the textbook service. Students will buy books at the location that provides texts at the lowest cost along with acceptable service levels.

Third, the Student Senate was concerned about products sold. For example, why were children's books included in the bookstore? John Maier noted that the faculty appreciated this children's book service and that they were the people most responsible for maintaining this service. Further, the bookstore's soft lines had the reputation of not being the best in the area. The senate felt that the bookstore should make a greater effort in this area, especially considering that these products had the highest margins.

Finally, the last area that the resolution examined was the Department of Administrative Services and the management of the bookstore. The Student Senate feared that the university would contract out too many vital services and would create future problems in controlling service levels and costs.

Dennis commented,

As students, it was felt that we really could accomplish something at the outset. We had the belief that deep down, we could prevent something from happening. The committee, as we viewed it, did not want to sell the bookstore and was searching for ideas to turn the slump around. The first thing that we picked up in committee was the constant reference to Barnes & Noble by the director of Administrative Services, Phyllis Forbes. It did not strike us as odd until the end of November.

The basic question among students concerned was, "Why would someone bid on an operation that was losing money? We felt that if there was money to be made, the university should make it."

CALL FOR BIDS AND REACTION

As fiscal year 1983 came to a close with a bookstore loss, and as the university trustees announced their decision to call for lease bids and proposals, bookstore employees and John Maier began talking to the press. This "media campaign" was not in full swing until the fall semester was under way in late 1983. The campaign centered on (1) "open" letters to the trustees from bookstore employees printed in the student newspaper and (2) bookstore employee interviews with a staff writer from the local daily newspaper, *Foster's Daily Democrat*. The three most active bookstore spokespeople were Roland Goodbody, Ted Whittemore, and Lauren Hill.

In November 1983 *Foster's Daily Democrat* reported:

The most recent recent letter was written by one of the bookstore's clerks. It is the second such letter from the bookstore in the past few months correcting [University trustee] Paul Holloway. . . . Holloway said he is tired of the letters from the bookstore and what is "getting to be a non-professional performance" on the part of bookstore employees. "If the management would spend more time managing and less time writing letters, they'd do a better job," he said.

Ted Whittemore, . . . one of the bookstore clerks active in the fight . . . noted that the bookstore workers are taking on the job of representing themselves to the public because they feel no one else will. (11/7/83)

Bookstore employee Lauren Hill . . . visited the trustee Finance and Budget Committee Wednesday. . . . The staff, he said, felt that the manager of the bookstore "had a personal feud with the competition, which we don't feel comfortable with." The staff felt the issue was much larger, that the atmosphere of an academic bookstore might be lost and in fact their jobs might be lost if trustees follow the route of contracting the management to a private operator.

Trustees seemed surprised that Hill made the comments directly to them, instead of pursuing the normal avenue of communication through bookstore manager John Maier.

Some praised his courage, but others said the matter shouldn't have been brought directly to them. Len Fisk, U.N.H. interim vice president of financial affairs, expressed having a "great deal of difficulty with the thought that the operating staff came directly to the trustees. It's a free country, but I sincerely hope you are on annual leave." (11/10/83)

Roland Goodbody sent a letter to all U.N.H. faculty pointing out the service objectives of the store and problems with leasing (see Exhibit 5, page 44–45).

Despite all these efforts, the committee agreed under pressure from Phyllis Forbes to solicit bids from eleven private companies, four of whom replied. The four formal bids received are summarized as follows:

1. *Barnes & Noble*: Would pay a fixed annual rent of $190,000 for the first three years and $215,000 for each of the last two years. In addition, renovations of $200,000 would be undertaken at the present bookstore location. Textbooks would be offered at a discount.

2. *Brennan College Services*: Would pay a fixed annual rent of $34,430 plus 2.48 percent of net sales. If sales were over $3 million, they would offer a 5.1 percent commission fee.

3. *Campus Services*: Would pay a fixed annual rent of $175,000 or 7.5 percent of net sales, whichever was higher. They also planned major renovations to maximize sales.

4. *College Stores*: Would pay a fixed annual rate of $50,000 plus a percentage of net sales, 3 percent on sales less than $4 million and 5 percent on sales over $4 million. They planned to discount supplies but not textbooks.

Dennis frankly admitted to himself that he was pretty tired of the bookstore issues. He eventually ignored repeated phone calls from John Maier, as Maier's direct (and indirect through the employees) press campaign became more of an annoyance than news. "If I never get another phone call from John Maier or his aides, Roland Goodbody or Ted Whittemore, I'll be happy," Dennis thought.

Maier himself had lost some credibility as the champion of the university-managed bookstore when it became known that several of the companies submitting bids for leasing the bookstore had contacted Maier about becoming their manager. Maier then resigned from the committee and was replaced by another bookstore employee.

Dennis and Don walked over to the committee meeting, talking about the change in Phyllis Forbes's questions from "Should we lease the bookstore?" to "Should we lease the bookstore to Barnes & Noble?" Despite constant rumors that the university and/or Maier would submit a bid for the university to continue running the bookstore, a bid had yet to materialize.

As Dennis reviewed his options of acquiescence, abstention, or adversarial accusation in the press, he was startled to see Vice President Fisk come to the meeting with Phyllis Forbes. "Looks like even a delay is going to be impossible," Dennis thought.

"The discussions of this committee today are to remain strictly confidential," Fisk began. "We are not here to decide if the bookstore is to be leased. President Haaland and I will decide on that and make recommendations to the trustees. What this committee should deal with, and the only thing it should deal with, is: If the bookstore is leased out, to whom should it be leased?"

EXHIBIT 5
Letter from
bookstore staff

24 October 1983

TO: All Department Chairpersons

FROM: UNH Bookstore Staff

RE: Impact on Faculty of Leasing of UNH Bookstore

We feel that the following information is of particular importance to you as faculty. We urge you to share it with others in your department and to support us in our effort to oppose the leasing of the bookstore.

A year ago, acting on GMR #153 (subcontracting the system bookstores), the Board of Trustees mandated that the UNH bookstore show a 5.5% profit margin, failing which bid specifications were to be prepared for possible contracting of operations in Fiscal 1984. In June the bookstore reported an operating deficit and so bid specifications were drawn up and sent out to prospective subcontractors earlier this month.

The bookstore leasing issue is therefore already at an advanced stage. Bidding will close on November 10, at which time a team of University administrators will review the bids and make appropriate recommendations. But this does not *mean that the issue is closed. On November 9 the Trustee Finance and Budget Committee will meet to review the current financial status of the bookstore. If, as is expected, the figures indicate an upward trend toward achieving the mandated 5.5% profit margin, there is a chance that the Committee will recommend reconsidering the leasing question.*

We believe, however, that the decision whether or not to lease the UNH bookstore should not rest on a simple comparison of profit margins, but should be based on an examination of all aspects of the issue. The Student Senate and some members of the faculty have already independently expressed their support for a more comprehensive approach. We urge you to examine the following information and voice your opinion on this issue.

1. *Service and Academic Resource.* The present UNH bookstore functions as a crucial educational resource for the institution and provides a high level of service. There is much evidence to suggest that many, and perhaps all, of these services will be drastically reduced or eliminated altogether under leased operations.

2. *Criteria Used.* The significance of this comparison lies in the fact that both the Governor's Management Review team and the Trustees specifically used the Plymouth store as the standard against which the UNH store was measured. According to one GMR member, the team simply abstracted Plymouth's financial arrangement and applied it to the UNH bookstore, having no reason to believe that such an application was inappropriate. This is where the 5.5% profit margin originated.

3. *Financial Viability.* For the five years prior to 1983 the UNH bookstore recorded a profit. This financial year has seen increased sales of 12% over last year and 33% more traffic in the store. Operating costs have also been cut by not moving Bookrush out of the store and by hiring work-study students in place of hourly staff. What this all indicates is that the bookstore is a financially viable operation which, given proper time for the recent changes to take effect, would demonstrate its capabilities.

4. *Other Options.* Rather than leasing the UNH bookstore to a private operator, it would be more fruitful for the institution to consider alternative profit-increasing options for the store. The possibility of relocating the store more centrally could be explored. Other considerations could include a student and staff operated co-op store, such as those at Dartmouth and the University of Connecticut, or a system-wide bookstore operation.

Please address your response to the Trustee Finance and Budget Committee, c/o Edward F. Smith, Dunlap Center, Lee, no later than October 31. *We apologize for the short notice, but hope that you will find time to respond to this.*

For the Bookstore Staff

Roland Goodbody

Roland Goodbody
Bookstore Clerk

APPENDIX D: BOOKSTORE CASE ANALYSIS

CASE OVERVIEW

Dennis Bellucci, student representative, is trying to decide what action he should take regarding the leasing of the U.N.H. bookstore to a private operator.

The bookstore has operated as a monopoly for almost a century. Now local competition has hit hard, and the former service strategy of the bookstore seems inappropriate to the store's critics, including some U.N.H. trustees and the recommendations of a gubernatorial "management review."

The bookstore has been given a deadline; instead of producing a profit, it has handed in a significant loss.

One of the issues that must be resolved is that of perspective. Should the case be analyzed from the point of view of Dennis Bellucci, the student representative? John Maier, the bookstore manager? A university administrator? Three levels of strategy present themselves. Dennis Bellucci might be thought of as representing the functional level: he is to express the student viewpoint. John Maier should have the business strategy perspective. How can he achieve success in his product market? The university administrators, President Haaland and Vice President Fisk, can represent the corporate strategy viewpoint. They seek to determine and implement a long-term direction for the university, of which the bookstore is only a small part.

This case, then, illustrates the Brunswik lens effect, for perception varies according to the role taken. This point is covered in the following section.

IDENTIFYING AND EVALUATING OPTIONS

In identifying his options, Dennis has three choices: (1) to give in to the university administration's wishes, (2) to abstain, or (3) to continue the fight to keep the bookstore within the university system.

Perspective is critical in evaluating the various options in the bookstore issue. Through John Maier's lens, the university has an ethical responsibility to its employees. A nine-month test does not seem adequate.

From the university's perspective, Barnes & Noble or other private operators are a source of "hard" dollars. The state's enterprise system sees to it that the university never gets any funds out of the owned bookstore; but lease payments would be available to the university administration if a private operator were installed.

From the students' perspective, the past has shown that the intangible feature of service is not as important as price. If Dennis Bellucci takes the long-term perspective of the strategic manager, under which option — lease or not lease — is the overall price level likely to remain the lowest? Will a Barnes & Noble lease lead to increased competition in the long run? Certainly in the short run, competition might increase; the Durham Book Exchange might not have the resources to compete effectively against a Barnes & Noble.

MAKING RECOMMENDATIONS
AND IMPLEMENTING STRATEGY

It is presumably too late to save the University Bookstore, but one wonders if, in any event, the present management is capable of effective competition and profitable operation. Nonetheless, Dennis as strategic manager might try to establish a price-level monitoring system for student protection in the long term. Perhaps a price monitoring service for popular texts might be established with Boston universities and other nearby universities.

AFTERWORD

Over the Christmas recess, the university announced the decision to lease the bookstore to Barnes & Noble. John Maier then mailed a letter to all faculty announcing he would become the Barnes & Noble manager in May, and pledging the continuance of high levels of service. Barnes & Noble indicated they would review all employees

July 1. John Maier then left Barnes & Noble in July to become manager of the Phillips-Exeter Academy Bookstore in Exeter, New Hampshire.

APPENDIX E: THE CASE METHOD

The primary teaching method used in strategic management is the case method. Cases allow you to apply the art of the strategic process in real-life situations.

Two basic principles apply to case work. First, the cases are not designed to prepare you for a specific incident you may meet in your business career; they are simply vehicles that force you to practice systematic analysis and decision making. Second, there are no school solutions to the cases. Your job is to analyze the situation, define the major problem(s), decide on appropriate courses of action, and logically and rationally present and defend your recommendation. Recommendations to the cases may differ considerably, and many recommendations might be creditable alternatives. Your work will be evaluated in terms of how clearly, precisely, and logically you think the problems through and defend your recommendations.

The following outline provides a very broad, general checklist. In any specific case used in this course, only parts of this outlined analysis will be appropriate. Make sure you use this checklist only as a general reminder, not as a "cookbook" appropriate to every situation.

GENERAL APPROACH

Case analysis generally proceeds through the following seven stages or steps.

1. Sizing up the situation
2. Evaluating the present strategy
3. Identifying issues and options
4. Evaluating options
5. Making recommendations
6. Implementing strategy
7. Monitoring results

Sizing up the Situation

What is the enterprise doing at present? In what circumstances? With what results? As you answer these questions, you are getting a feel for the situation. You are obtaining the facts in a meaningful order and placing dimensions upon them.

1. Analyze the economics of the situation.
    1.1 Attributes of products and of the demand for them (the demand curve)
    1.2 Attributes of the technology, including the productive and distributive processes

      1.3 The input mix, the cost mix, the unit (average) cost curve

      1.4 The competitive situation both in the market for the inputs and in the market for the finished products

      1.5 The price-cost-volume-profit relationships resulting from 1.1 through 1.4

2. Analyze opportunities and constraints, and strengths and weaknesses relative to them.

3. Identify the strategy of the enterprise, which refers to established company policy concerning

      3.1 Mission, objectives, and goals

      3.2 Strategy being employed

         3.2(1) to improve opportunities

         3.2(2) to overcome constraints

         3.2(3) to meet competition

         3.2(4) to gain access to markets, both as buyer and as seller, on favorable terms

      3.3 Basic decisions concerning

         3.3(1) products and markets

         3.3(2) technology

         3.3(3) make-or-buy

         3.3(4) resource procurement

         3.3(5) location

         3.3(6) scale

         3.3(7) standards

From the outline you should derive insight into what the enterprise is trying to do — its "game plan" — and the circumstances in which this effort is being made. You will assemble and order the available facts, analyze them objectively, and withhold a decision until the size-up has been completed.

As you attempt to identify the strategy of an organization, you may study (1) its pronouncements as to its purpose, (2) its resource allocation, (3) its products and markets, and (4) its method of competition.

Pronouncements. Often you will come across a statement of strategy, such as "We want to be the General Motors of XYZ industry"; "We want constantly rising earnings"; or "We want to be on the cutting edge of technology." You should look for statements about what a company wants to be or what it wants to do.

Resource Allocation. Strategic pronouncements might be too general to be of help, or they might be contradictory or misleading. Assuming that the company has a logical procedure for allocating monies for capital expenditures, you may be able to deduce what the company's strategy is by where it spends its money. Unfortunately, a company might not have a logical procedure for capital budgeting. Certainly political and bureaucratic processes might outweigh strategic considerations, especially in a huge bureaucracy like the General Electric of 1950.

Products and Markets. What is the company selling and to whom? Reduce the product to its essential nature, if possible, in order to understand where the company's skills lie: Does a cruise line transport people or entertain them? Does a technical school train people or place them in jobs? The answer often varies, and you need analytical and judgmental tools to answer questions about the product.

The market may be described geographically, or as a customer or consumer group, or as one or more segments within customer groups. Again, use a very broad definition of markets; neat and tidy definitions may not work for many companies. What is Sears, Roebuck's market? Catalog and store customers? Financial consumers? Real estate purchasers and sellers?

Competitive Focus. The nature of a company's competitive thrust reveals a lot about a company's strategy. Does the company compete on the basis of price, quality, technology, and/or marketing skills? Is it a leader or a follower in product research? How important is service? A firm often competes on the basis of what it believes is the most significant resource in its internal environment.

Summary. To begin analyzing a company's strategy, identify critical aspects of the strategy by asking

What does the company say its strategy is?

How does the company spend its resources?

What does the company sell and to whom?

How does the company compete?

Analyzing the individual answers and the relationship of each answer to the sum of all four answers should move you beyond the identification of strategy to the more demanding evaluation of strategy.

Evaluating the Present Strategy

A company's game plan may or may not make sense or work well. Evaluate a game plan in terms of the following criteria.

1. Are the separate elements that make up the strategy consistent with each other and mutually supportive?
2. Is the strategy appropriate considering the surrounding circumstances (externalities) and the internal situation (resources, purpose)?
3. Are these policies and strategies likely to enable the enterprise to meet not only short-term goals but long-term objectives as well?
4. Have considerations of ethical and social responsibility been properly taken into account?
5. How satisfactory are the results?
6. Is the strategy practical and workable?
7. Does the strategy adequately consider risk?

Identifying Issues and Options

Against the background of the size-up and evaluation that you have made, what policy/strategy issues are most important? What are the alternatives to these issues — the realistic options open to the enterprise?

Try to distinguish between primary and secondary issues, the latter being either derived from and dependent upon the first, or of lesser importance. Concentrate on *one*, or, at most, *a few* primary issues. You will analyze more effectively by narrowing your field and sharpening your focus. Carefully and thoroughly considering a small number of important issues is far preferable to an extensive and, therefore, more superficial coverage. Cases often contain an "action" question which is only symptomatic of the real problem(s).

Evaluating Options

Develop the arguments for and against each option, including the option of making no change from the present course of action. Remember to consider *costs* and implications for *organization* and *personnel*. At a minimum, consider the following criteria for each option.

1. *Appropriateness*: Will the option allow us to achieve our objectives?
2. *Feasibility*: Do we have the resources — tangible and intangible — to achieve our objectives?
3. *Reality*: Do we want to go with this option? Will or does top management buy into it?
4. *Workability*: Can we gain corporate-wide organizational committment?

Making Recommen- dations

What would you recommend for change in the present strategy? And how should these recommendations be accomplished? Useful policy/strategy recommendations are specific, making explicit the *rate* of change and any scheduling or phasing being recommended; the additional resources, if any, to be procured; and any organizational and personnel changes involved.

Implementing Strategy

A proposed strategy is useless unless the organization commits to its adoption. When implementing a recommendation you must consider (at a minimum): *Who* will be in charge of its implementation? What *time* frame is involved in its implementation? Does the organization need to restructure, or is the present structure appropriate? Why? How will people be affected by its implementation? Will a new motivation or compensation system be necessary? How will you know if the plan is not working?

Monitoring Results

Timely and accurate information assists the strategic manager in determining if the proposed recommendations are working. The ongoing nature of the strategy process entails a constant monitoring and appraisal of results. Any variances must be quickly identified and corrected, so that operating remedies may be identified, evaluated, and implemented.

By following these seven steps to analyzing a case study, you will more quickly develop a logical approach to strategic problems. Nonetheless, since each case is unique, some aspects of some or even all of these steps may not be appropriate, given the nature of the case issues and alternatives.

INDUSTRY ANALYSIS

Since a company's success depends in part on the economics of its industry, you should look for information about the industry in general. Ideally, you would like to be able to answer the following four questions about the industry.

1. How does the general economy affect the industry?
2. How does the industry affect the economy?
3. What is the general trend of industry sales?
4. What are the characteristics of the industry?
   — number of companies
   — percentage share of industry sales
   — barriers to entry
   — capital versus labor intensity
   — value added
   — level of competition
   — method(s) of competition
   — rate of technological change
   — research and development expenditures
   — international factors
   — regulatory factors

Industry trends and industry characteristics will have important strategic implications. The strategic manager in a declining industry may be very reluctant to make major capital investments. The manager in an increasingly competitive industry may revise marketing promotion and pricing policies.

In addition, the performance of a specific company versus the performance of the industry as a whole can tell you a great deal about the success of a company's strategy and its strength relative to that of the industry.

CLASS PARTICIPATION

The primary role of the instructor is to facilitate discussion. Generally, the instructor will try to direct the discussion only when critical issues are being ignored or the discussion is not progressing. Occasionally the instructor may intervene in order to make sure your analysis is complete or to give you practice in defending your recommendations. These occasional interventions should be viewed as ultimately helpful, even if they may prove somewhat stressful. Since there is not one correct answer, the instructor will serve as a listener for reasonable suggestions and logical analyses.

Exhibit 1 includes some general guidelines for effective versus ineffective class participation.

EXHIBIT 1
Class participation factors

Positive Factors/Effective Participation

1. A complete analysis of one or more important case issues and problems
2. A well-reasoned conclusion following logically from a complete analysis
3. A reasonable recommendation for action while recognizing the consequences of that action
4. Constructive criticism of another student's comments
5. The integration of concepts and theories from other courses and/or from other cases
6. Effective communication

Negative Factors/Ineffective Participation

1. Repetition of case facts without analysis or conclusion
2. Irrelevant comments
3. Lack of participation
4. Poor communicative ability

CHAPTER 3

DEFINING PURPOSE

A man in Boston has dedicated
  himself
to telling about injustice.
For three-thousand dollars he will
come to your town and tell you
  about it.

William Stafford, "Things I Learned Last Week"

This chapter describes the three components of enterprise purpose: (1) personal values of managers, (2) organizational priorities, and (3) societal goals. The strategic manager analyzes these components and defines the enterprise purpose, or mission. The relative importance of each component depends upon the strategic manager's perspective.

In the long term, selling a product or service to a customer is the essence of mission. During some crises in the history of an enterprise, its mission can be stated very simply — *survival*. Corporations such as Lockheed, Chrysler, Continental Illinois National Bank and Trust, Braniff, American Motors, and Penn Central reached periods in their history during which their only motivation was to survive.

U.S. Steel chairman David Roderick issued survival orders based upon the concept that nothing is sacred. As *Business Week* reported (2/25/85, p. 50), Roderick

Closed 150 manufacturing sites.

Reduced capacity by 30 percent.

Eliminated 54 percent of administrative positions.

Dismissed one hundred thousand workers.

Sold $3 billion in assets.

Lee Iacocca commented on Chrysler's mission of survival in *Iacocca: An Autobiography*:

Everyone talks about "strategy," but all we knew was survival. Survival was simple. Close the plants that are hurting us most. . . . Fire the people who aren't absolutely necessary . . . two moves alone cut out $500 million in annual costs, but the firings were just tragic, and there's no way to pretend otherwise.

A popular assumption is that firms pursue growth. The pursuit of corporate growth was especially in evidence in the automobile industry in 1985. Both U.S. and West German automobile giants pursued high-tech growth by turning to the aerospace industry for major acquisitions. General Motors acquired Hughes Aircraft Company in a dramatic sealed-bid purchase, and Daimler-Benz purchased Germany's second-largest aerospace manufacturer, Dornier.

Leslie Wexner, founder and chairman of The Limited, the chain of women's clothing stores, talked about growth:

My vision of the business is always to have a large one. When I had two stores, ten stores seemed like a lot. [Now with 2,500 stores] . . . I'd like to believe that trees can grow to the sky. None have yet, but that doesn't mean it's impossible. (Fortune, 8/19/85, p. 154)

Although the pursuit of growth is necessary for survival in the face of increasing competition, the strategic manager must develop a perspective broader than the simplistic purposes of survival and growth. Figure 3.1 shows that the strategic manager views the enterprise purpose through a tri-focal lens. Defining purpose means identifying (1) personal values of managers, (2) organizational priorities, and (3) relevant social goals.

PERSONAL VALUES

Key managers have values that are personal, and thus are determined independently of the organization. The manager's personal values, held regardless of the organization, are the values of interest to the strategic manager. The personal values of top management may be the dominant, single driving force behind the entire enterprise. Edwin Land dominated Polaroid; Harold Geneen was the single force driving ITT;

FIGURE 3.1
Strategic managerial perspective

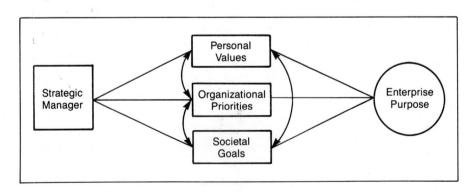

and Thomas Watson shaped IBM. Although one executive rarely dominates a large corporation (the preceding three being exceptions), little difference exists between the objectives of the small business and the personal values of its founder or leader.

In his autobiography, Lee Iacocca elaborated on personal values. At this stage in his life, money and "the good life" were important personal values:

I often ask myself why I didn't quit [Ford] at the end of 1975. Why did I accept the fate Henry [Ford] was dishing out? How could I let a guy take my destiny and pummel it?
First, like anybody in a bad situation, I hoped things would get better. . . .
I was also greedy. I enjoyed being president. . . . I was getting soft, seduced by the good life. And I found it almost impossible to walk away from an annual income of $970,000.

Examples of personal values of key managers include (1) personal development and psychological/spiritual growth, (2) active parenting, (3) the acquisition of personal wealth, (4) prestige and recognition, (5) altruism, and (6) increase in the quality of life.

T. Roland Berner, the second of three chief executives at Western Union in four months, commented on personal values (in his case, active family and personal life) and work: "It was a tough job. The biggest Christmas present my family wanted was for me to become human again" (*Business Week*, 1/14/85, p. 36). The Limited's Leslie Wexner expressed another dimension (the drive to succeed) of personal values: "My biggest frustration is that I never feel I can work hard enough. I read *The Agony and the Ecstasy* three times and empathized with Michelangelo" (*Business Week*, 2/25/85, p. 78). And Sony's Morita forced the development of the Walkman cassette over strong opposition within Sony because he wanted music while he played golf!

W. L. Gore & Associates, Inc. in Delaware shows the influence that managers' personal values have on organizational priorities. Chairman Bill Gore, his wife and the company's secretary-treasurer, Genevieve, and other family members control the company stock with others who work at Gore. Gore's personal values, specifically his distaste for boss-employee relationships, has led to this worker-ownership of Gore. At Gore, workers are called *associates*, work units are led by group and area leaders, and plants are kept to the small size of two hundred workers. Although Gore has over thirty plants, employee productivity and morale are high.

The activities of corporate raiders put the spotlight on managers' personal values during the mid-1980s. Many speculate about a future stage of corporate development — Will professional managers be turning large, institutional (Stage Three) corporations over to institutional investors?

Raider Saul Steinberg made $32 million (plus $28 million in expenses) when Walt Disney bought his stock at a premium. Carl Icahn has made more than $100 million on takeover bids, while the "greenmail" (stock price premiums) profits of T. Boone Pickens and his partners have exceeded $800 million. British raider James Goldsmith asserted that raiders operate "for the public good, but that's not why I do it. I do it to make money" (*Business Week*, 3/4/85, p. 80).

Business Week's survey of executive salaries (5/6/85, p. 79) showed that arch-raider T. Boone Pickens received total compensation of $22,823,000 in 1984 from Mesa Petroleum; shareholders received only $14 million in dividends. Pickens's pay was equal to the total received by the chairs of Chrysler, Wang, Ford, IBM, Exxon, and Dun & Bradstreet combined. Pickens's primary target, oil companies, included some that responded to corporate raid threats and growth problems by getting rid of shareholders. Those that bought back their own stock included Phillips Petroleum (53 percent, after raids by Pickens and others), Atlantic Richfield (25 percent), Pennzoil (16 percent), Sun (13 percent), Exxon (12 percent), and Amoco (10 percent).

Among the questions raiders raise about mission and managers' personal values are:

1. If managers try to maximize shareholder returns, why do they pay "greenmail"?
2. Do raiders force managers to focus on short-term profits to keep stock prices up?
3. Do raiders assist in the efficient distribution of resources, correcting the mismanaged assets of the complacent, arrogant corporate giant?

ORGANIZATIONAL PRIORITIES

What are organizational priorities? How are they determined? How are they perpetuated?

While exceptional cases exist in which organizational priorities can be expressed simplistically as survival, growth, or profit maximization, the priorities of the organization reflect its economic, political, and social components. Thus there are economic priorities, such as a minimum level of profitability and return on investment, or the development of production and distribution systems. There are also political priorities, such as the development of a managerial budget negotiation system. And social priorities might include the provision of employment during times of high unemployment, and equal opportunity.

How do companies determine these priorities? Working Concept 8 on organizational power describes the mechanism for priority determination.

WORKING CONCEPT 8

MINTZBERG'S ORGANIZATIONAL POWER

EXTERNAL SOURCES

Mintzberg's theory of organizational power and goals (1979) addresses organizational priorities from the perspective of power. Mintzberg first looks at those external sources of power—such as owners, unions, and the public—who directly influence the organization's priorities, through membership on the board of directors, employee labor contracts, social norms, or government regulation. These external power groups may be focused and gathered together by a dominant power; they may be divided; or they may be passive.

INTERNAL SOURCES

Mintzberg then looks at sources of internal power, including top management, middle line managers, operators, technical analysts, and support staff. He identifies four systems of influence through which organizational priorities are determined. The first is the personal control system dominated by the CEO and top management. Mintzberg's second system is the bureaucratic control system that replaces the top manager's power with a system of rules, policies, and procedures. The third is a political system which — because of ambiguities in formal goals, inclination to pursue one's personal values, group pressures, and political skills of people throughout the organization — consists of political power games. The games are played through (1) the decision-making process, (2) the provision of information and advice, and (3) the interpretation and implementation of policies. The fourth system is the ideology control system, in which dominant ideas — such as a religious doctrine or a social need — focus the organization.

Mintzberg concludes that internal power can then lead to (1) autocratic coalitions, (2) bureaucratic coalitions, (3) politicized coalitions, (4) ideologic coalitions, or (5) meritocratic coalitions. A meritocratic coalition is one in which a complex technology or professional service becomes the "best" or most meritorious coalition, and can then dominate priorities.

POWER CONFIGURATIONS

Mintzberg completes his model by grouping these external and internal power sources into six commonly encountered power configurations: (1) continuous chain, (2) closed system, (3) commander, (4) missionary, (5) professional, and (6) conflictive. One of these six power configurations determines the organization's priorities.

The continuous-chain power configuration couples a dominant external control force with clearly understood goals. The organization with this power configuration has "simple, mass-output systems" so that common goals can exist and power flows from the external controllers throughout the organization. Some examples of continuous-chain organizations are the stock exchange or, in the public sector, the post office.

One step removed from the continuous-chain organization is the closed-system power configuration typical of many widely held, divisionalized corporations. The closed system differs in that it has only a passive external power group, such as stockholders. It is more politicized and less autocratic or bureaucratic than its continuous-chain counterpart since it is not dominated by external power and does not have clear goals.

The commander, the third power configuration, is based upon an autocratic leadership. Commander power emerges in firms confronting extreme crisis, so that external and internal power groups surrender control to the leader for survival. Entrepreneurial firms also employ commander power configurations to determine priorities.

The fourth and fifth power configurations are the missionary and the professional, representative of the ideology and meritocracy groups respectively. Volunteer agencies and legal firms illustrate the missionary and the professional configurations.

Sixth and last is Mintzberg's conflictive power configuration, which may occur when any of the first five power configurations are under attack or experiencing internal dissension, such as separate but conflicting missions or a harsh conflict between two leaders. In these situations the organization's priorities are determined in a purely political way. Conflictive power organizations are usually short-term anomalies, since most organizations cannot survive continuous, prolonged conflict.

To review, priorities are determined by one of the following six power configurations:

A *continuous chain* dominated by an external control force determining priorities

A *closed system* determining priorities through internal political and social means

A *commander*, in which a leader determines priorities

A *missionary*, in which the ideology defines the priorities

A *professional*, in which professional aims determine priorities

A *conflictive*, in which politics alone determine priorities

Once these priorities are determined, however, they must then be reinforced and perpetuated. Because organizational priorities are embodied in the corporate culture, their existence is ensured.

Mintzberg's power configurations also influence the personal values of key managers. Clearly, the manager's personal values interact with the priorities of the organization; the degree of the interaction and influence will depend on the degree to which the manager internalizes the organizational priorities. Internalizing and strengthening individual values and beliefs are subjective and dependent upon each specific circumstance. Nevertheless, it is recognized that, while the degree of interaction is an individual matter, it is a real phenomenon.

CORPORATE CULTURE

The shared values, beliefs, and traditions of an organization make up its corporate culture. The corporate culture is determined by the organization's priorities as defined by the commander, the external power control group, or another of Mintzberg's power configurations. Thus, organizational power determines organizational priorities, which then form the corporate culture, as Figure 3.2 depicts. The corporate

FIGURE 3.2
Power, priorities, and culture

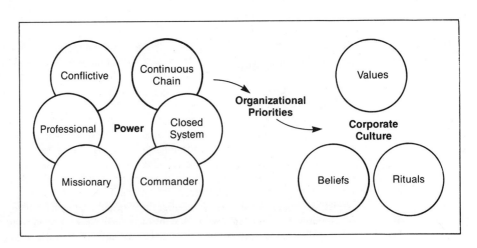

cultures applied to Mintzberg's six power configurations might include (1) accountability in the continuous-chain system, (2) productivity in the closed system, (3) loyalty in the commander system, (4) zeal in the missionary system, (5) objectivity in the professional system, and (6) competition in the conflictive system.

EXAMPLE: *Corporate Culture*

The effects of corporate culture can be seen in these observations about Heinz, Polaroid, Fluor, and St. Joe in 1985. Heinz's 1985 strategy (*Fortune*, 6/24/85, pp. 44–54) of becoming a low-cost producer resulted in a corporate culture of cost reduction. The result was referred to by the manufacturing vice president as a "culture [that] has been chip, chip, chip." Management and hourly employees formed cost-reduction suggestion teams, package size was reduced, and production was shifted offshore to Puerto Rico and Samoa.

Polaroid, whose Personnel Policy 251 guaranteed lifetime employment to those employees with ten years' experience, had to end the policy in 1985 in the face of a "civil service mentality," that is, a corporate culture requiring only the bare minimum from its employees. Polaroid needed to enter new industries, but lacked the talented, entrepreneurial executives necessary to accomplish the task.

"Incompatible corporate cultures" was one of the main reasons cited by *Business Week* in its analysis (6/3/85, pp. 92–93) of the failure of the merger of Fluor, an engineering and construction firm, with St. Joe, a mining company. St. Joe's managers, reflecting the company's corporate culture, were used to taking big risks. They had a streamlined overhead budget and freely exercised management initiative. Fluor, however, had a corporate culture that reflected its large, bureaucratic managerial structure. Their large overhead budget was evidenced in their fleet of helicopters and planes, and managers could expect a long wait in the decision-making process. The merger also failed because the deal was made in one week's time, while St. Joe was trying to escape from a Seagram takeover attempt. St. Joe's chairman described it as a time "so brief it was embarrassing."

An expert on corporate culture, Management Analysis Center's Howard Schwartz commented on the difficulty of "instant" changes in corporate culture: "You can't change culture by working on it directly. You must have some strategic ground to stand on, then build a vision of what a company wants to be before rubbing their noses in what they are" (*Fortune*, 10/17/83, p. 69). Schwartz and Davis (1981) stressed the importance of matching corporate culture and business strategy.

SOCIAL GOALS

The enterprise exists in a social environment that has goals. In a pluralistic society, such as in North America, different groups within society may have different goals. Some may consider personal liberty to be the ultimate social goal. For these libertarians, no social programs, including police procedures, must ever interfere with one's personal civil liberties. Others may feel that equality in all senses — especially economic equality — is the ultimate social goal. Egalitarians sacrifice elements of personal liberty in areas such as employment in order to achieve equality. Other alternative social goals are technological progress versus environmental integrity.

The enterprise in a pluralistic society thus finds itself with a spectrum of competing goals. Society also has a set of generally supported social goals (i.e., education; adequate, affordable health care; minority rights; religious freedom; and a strong military defense) which different individuals may be expected to prioritize in different ways.

Social goals, then, are ends that society views as important in themselves. Individual perceptions of the relative importance of these social ends differ significantly.

Social goals have greater impact as the enterprise becomes a more important member of society. An enterprise could grow more important because of its size, its goods and services, or a variety of other factors. As the enterprise increases its connections to society — and thus its social importance — through increasing product lines, growth in employment, or geographic expansion, it becomes more aware of its social responsibility.

Social responsibility may be defined as the obligation of the enterprise to act in accordance with social goals. Unfortunately, definition of social responsibility is deceptively simple, since it still raises some questions. First, how can an enterprise act in accordance with social goals if a pluralistic society does not agree on the priority of social goals? An enterprise may argue that a plant closing furthers the social goal of technological progress because an inefficient plant is no longer competitive. But what about the employees' loss of income, or the resulting increased welfare cost? It is relatively easy to agree on some acts of social *irresponsibility* (such as pollution), but it is not always easy to define social *responsibility*. To whom in society is the enterprise to be responsible? Shareholders? Unions? Communities? These groups have different priorities and different needs.

Second, even if it were possible to agree on the definition of socially responsible acts, measuring the specific impact of social responsibility on the decision process still would be difficult. One could always argue that a firm undertook a certain social program not for altruistic reasons but for sound business reasons, such as public relations and general advertising.

An individual's perspective on social responsibility depends on his or her view of the relationship between business and society. Does a business have the "right" to do business based upon property rights, or is a business "allowed" to do business and to make profits because society wants it to? The latter opinion seemed to be behind the aggressive stance that the Connecticut state banking commissioner took against E. F. Hutton. After the large investment banking firm was convicted in May 1985 of mail and wire fraud, which primarily centered on overdrawing accounts and transfering funds to take advantage of banking processing delays, or *float*, the banking commissioner, Brian Woolf, commented: "Integrity is at the core of this. To do business in Connecticut, Hutton has been given a license. That's a privilege and a trust, and they should be held to the highest standards'' (*Business Week*, 7/15/85, p. 33).

STRATEGIC MISSION

The strategic manager, understanding the three components of strategic mission — (1) personal values of key managers; (2) organizational priorities, embodied in the corporate culture; and (3) societal goals — now turns to the definition of *mission*, the first of three steps in the process of strategic analysis.

WORKING CONCEPT 9

STRATEGIC ANALYSIS

Defining strategic mission is the first of three analytical steps the strategic manager must complete in preparation for the formulation of strategy. The three preparation steps, as shown in Figure 3.3, consist of (1) defining mission; (2) analyzing the firm's strengths and weaknesses in order to determine its distinctive competence; and (3) identifying opportunities and threats in the external environment of the firm by means of product market, competition, and industry analysis.

FIGURE 3.3
Strategic analysis

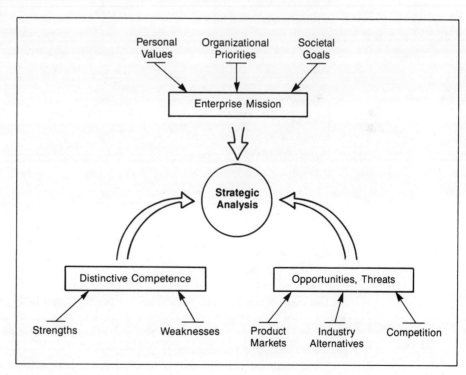

LEVELS OF STRATEGY
AND ENTERPRISE MISSION

Each enterprise naturally has organizational priorities that are specifically its own, although profitability is a common priority among all enterprises. The strategic manager prepares an explicit statement of these organizational priorities. Specific priorities depend upon the specific enterprise, but statements of organizational priorities encompass the following topics.

Earnings
   absolute amounts
   percentage increases
   minimum levels required for research, capital expenditures, dividends, etc.
Distinctive competency and competitive advantage
   present
   planned
Product and markets
   target markets
   innovation levels
   service levels
Growth
   sales
   assets
   earnings
   markets
   products
Responsibilities and obligations
   human resources
   political
   social
   ethical
   environmental
Legitimacy
   markets served
   social functions

The consistency between organizational priorities and both personal values and social goals must now to be considered. Experience has shown that inconsistencies may occur, as Table 3.1 suggests. You can expand this table to include your own personal values and social goals.

These inconsistencies in enterprise mission are more easily understood from the point of view of the levels of strategy. Working Concept 2 in Chapter 1 described the three levels of strategy. In the corporate level of strategy, the strategist seeks

TABLE 3.1
Possible
inconsistencies in
enterprise mission

Organizational priorities	versus	Personal values
Cost, including executive salary, minimization		Wealth accumulation
Hierarchical structure of formal organizations		Prestige
Dedicated, hardworking management		Parenting
Specialized functions		Personal development
Increase in public shareholders' wealth and fiduciary responsibilities		Top management's "taking private" a public company

Organizational priorities	versus	Social values
Minimizing labor costs		High employment
		Increasing living standards
Minimizing production costs		Job safety
		Environmental protection
Minimizing changeover costs		New products
Salary incentives		Economic equality

to achieve long-term objectives through managing the portfolio of new and existing product markets, technologies, industries, and opportunities. In the business level of strategy, the strategic manager seeks to compete in a defined business with a given product-market scope. In the functional level of strategy, the functional manager seeks to maximize output of a functional department. To define enterprise mission, the strategic manager must use the perspectives of both the three levels of strategy and the stages of corporate development, as depicted in Figure 3.4. The relative

FIGURE 3.4
Defining mission

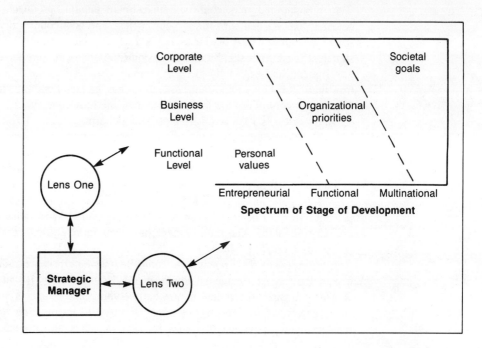

importance assigned to each component of mission — personal values of key managers, organizational priorities, and societal goals — will depend on the lens, or viewpoint, of the manager.

Long-term opportunities and long-term priorities are matched and managed at the corporate level of strategy. Thus the strategic manager carefully considers social responsibility and societal goals in both the analysis of opportunities — what social goals and trends will create what opportunities — and in the mixing and balancing of such long-term priorities as investment in human resources, capital appreciation, and asset growth.

Societal goals become somewhat less important, although always significant, at the business, and especially at the functional, levels. The functional-level manager, with a short-term perspective and a concern for maximizing outputs, must emphasize intradepartmental and functional cooperation, and thus give significant weight to the personal values of associates.

Similarly, the entrepreneurial manager attaches a great deal of importance to personal values of challenge and risk. In both the small business and the entrepreneurial enterprise, the personal values of the entrepreneur and the small-business owner will be reflected in the organization's priorities.

At the multinational, Stage Three level of development, however, societal goals are of increasing importance. Consider, for example, the attention the multinational manager must pay to a foreign host country's cultural values and goals, and especially to the host government. The relative strength and influence of the government and the multinational depend on the relative importance of each party's contributions. The multinational may contribute investment capital, products, technology, and potential exports that earn foreign currencies. The host country may be a source of scarce resources, new markets, and a low-cost labor supply. The multinational strategist must understand the relative contributions of the corporation and the host government, and especially the host country's societal goals. The strategist for the firm that contributes important technology has greater flexibility than the manager who desperately needs the low-cost labor of the host country.

Merck & Co.'s 1983 acquisition of Banyu Pharmaceutical of Tokyo led to difficulties when Merck misjudged its strength relative to that of the Japanese government. The increased cost of health care, given Japan's aging population, has been one of its government's major concerns. Accordingly, the government announced reductions on controlled drug prices. Merck-Banyu's drug prices were reduced by 12 percent overall, but the price of Banyu's best-seller, an oral antibiotic, was cut by 32 percent. Merck's head of Japanese operations said, ''Well, what are we going to do? Cry about it? The environment has been more difficult than we expected'' (*Fortune*, 3/18/85, p. 48).

Elf Aquitaine, the French state-controlled oil enterprise, acquired Texasgulf in one of the largest foreign takeovers in the United States. Because of the franc's weakness against the dollar in the early 1980s, and France's societal goal of a stable currency, the French government refused to let the over $1 billion debt be reduced by the payment of francs for dollars. Thus the original $1.3 billion Elf

Aquitaine debt cost the company the equivalent of over $3 billion a year as the franc fell almost one-third against the dollar in the mid-1980s.

The appendix to Chapter 5 discusses the international business perspective further. The relationship between societal and organizational goals and the evolution of strategic mission is illustrated by a nonprofit agency in an appendix to this chapter.

RESEARCH AND MISSION

Classic research studies of mission include those by Galbraith and Wood.

Galbraith, in *The New Industrial State* (1971), theorizes that managers (technocrats) have personal motives (e.g., wealth, status, and self-preservation) that are inconsistent with shareholder priorities. He believes that organizational priorities (the reduction of risk and uncertainty) become so important that they are translated into social goals (economic growth, elimination of downturns of the business cycle, high defense spending, and consumer expectations of constantly increasing standards of living). This transformation is achieved by the power of the corporation and big business.

Wood analyzed organizational priorities in *A Theory of Profits* (1975). Wood concluded that firms have priorities of sales — not profit — growth, since sales are generally something the manager can both influence and understand easily. This sales growth priority is also coupled with a minimum acceptable level of profits in absolute terms. Once this level seems reasonably assured — often through an annual budgeting process — the manager concentrates on sales. The minimum level of profits, furthermore, is determined by the level of investment needed to support dividends and sales growth.

Current research on mission, managerial values, and social responsibility include works of the following researchers.

Carroll and Hoy (1984), concluded that social policy and social responsibility had been a "residual factor" for too long. They urged the "need for incorporating social policy into strategic management process," and suggested steps to "integrate corporate social policy into strategic management."

Kirton (1984) evaluated managers by studying their missions. Kirton evaluated managers as the firm's internal resource (especially managerial capabilities with new initiatives) using an Adaption-Innovation Inventory; he concluded that "the change agent can be either an adaptor or an innovator."

Shrivastava and Grant (1985), in an empirical study of strategic processes, described four strategic decision making models that reflected varying degrees of importance of organizational priorities, personal values, and social goals. These strategic process models were (1) the managerial autocracy model, (2) the systemic bureaucracy model, (3) the adaptive planning model, and (4) the political expediency model.

EXECUTIVE COMMENTS

Go back ten years. Polaroid and Xerox could have been on everyone's list of the ten best-managed companies. How did they lose their way when they became multibillion-dollar corporations? When you start growing like that, you start adding middle management like crazy. . . . People in the middle have no understanding of the business. . . . To them, it's just a job. The corporation ends up with mediocre people that form a layer of concrete. We're trying to keep Apple as flat as possible.

    Steven P. Jobs, founder of Apple Computer, in *Business Week* (11/26/84)

I firmly believe that [IBM or] any organization, in order to survive and achieve success, must have a sound set of beliefs on which it premises all its policies and actions. Next, I believe that the most important single factor in corporate success is faithful adherence to those beliefs.

    T. J. Watson, Jr., IBM CEO, 1963

I don't know how you can run a company with a board of directors.

    Richard Branson, British entrepreneur

We would never forsake those who kept this [United] airline going during the work stoppage. That is the word of this corporation, and it is worth something.

    R. J. Ferris, United Airlines CEO, 1985

You've got to be stubborn. You've got to believe you're right. Most organizations are the shadow of one man. I've got about two hundred more patents to get out of my system before I kick the bucket.

    Paul Taylor, American entrepreneur, 1985

A lot of people thought working at Polaroid was like having a government job. That just couldn't keep going on.

    R. W. Young, Polaroid CEO, 1985

In Washington they sometimes *hit a man when he's down. In New York, they* always *hit a man when he's down.*

    Harry S. Truman

If the arts, with all their power to accentuate and clarify, to explore and criticize, to teach and persuade, to stimulate and enhance, were left entirely reliant on government, not only would the pluralism of the arts be imperiled, but that of our social structure itself.

    W. H. Krome George, Alcoa (Aluminum Company of America) CEO

KEY TERMS

corporate culture (page 58)

Mintzberg's theory (page 56)

organizational priorities (page 56)

personal values (page 54)

purpose, or mission (page 53)

social responsibility (page 60)

societal goals (page 59)

BIBLIOGRAPHY

Andrews, K. R., *The Concept of Corporate Strategy* (Homewood, IL: Richard D. Irwin, 1980), *cf* Chapters 4, 5.

Barnett, J. H., "Nonprofits and the Life Cycle," *Program Evaluation and Planning* (1987, in press).

Bell, D., *The Cultural Contradictions of Capitalism* (New York: Basic Books, 1976).

Capon, N., J. Farley, and J. Hulbert, "International Diffusion of Corporate and Strategic Planning Processes." *Columbia Journal of World Business* (Fall 1980), pp. 5–13.

Carper, W. B., and R. J. Litschert, "Strategic Power Relationships in Contemporary Profit and Nonprofit Hospitals," *Academy of Management Journal* 26 (June 1983), pp. 311–320.

Carroll, A. B., and F. Hoy, "Integrating Corporate Social Policy into Strategic Management," *Journal of Business Strategy* 4 (Winter 1984), pp. 48–57.

"Corporate Culture," *Business Week* (October 27, 1980), pp, 148–160.

Doz, Y. L., and C. K. Prahalad, "Headquarters Influence and Strategic Control in MNCs," *Sloan Management Review* 23 (Fall 1981), pp. 15–29.

Firstenberg, P. B., "Profit-Minded Management in the Nonprofit World," *Management Review* (July 1979), pp. 8–13.

Fitzpatrick, M., "The Definition and Assessment of Political Risk in International Business: A Review of the Literature," *Academy of Management Review* 8 (April 1983), pp. 249–254.

Galbraith, J. K., *The New Industrial State* (New York: New American Library, 1971).

Gupta, A., "Contingency Linkages Between Strategy and General Manager Characteristics: A Conceptual Examination," *Academy of Management Review* 9 (July 1984).

Hatten, M. L., "Strategic Management in Not-for-Profit Organizations," *Strategic Management Journal* (April-June 1982).

Hout, T., M. Porter, and E. Rudden, "How Global Companies Win Out," *Harvard Business Review* 60 (September-October 1982), pp. 98–108.

Iacocca, L., with W. Novak, *Iacocca: An Autobiography* (New York: Bantam Books, 1984).

Kimberly, J. R., "Initiation, Innovation, and Institutionalization in the Creation Process," in *The Organizational Life Cycle: Issues in the Creation, Transformation and Decline of Organizations,* J. R. Kimberly, R. H. Miles, and Associates, eds. (San Francisco: Jossey-Bass, 1980).

Kirton, M. J., "Adaptors and Innovators — Why New Initiatives Get Blocked," *Long Range Planning* 17 (April 1984), pp. 137–143.

Leibenstein, H., *Beyond Economic Man* (Cambridge, MA: Harvard University Press, 1980).

McKie, J. W., ed., *Social Responsibility and the Business Predicament* (Washington, DC: The Brookings Institution, 1974).

Mintzberg, H., "Organizational Power and Goals," in *Strategic Management,* D. E. Schendel and C. W. Hofer, eds. (Boston: Little, Brown, 1979), pp. 64–80.

Mitroff, I., and R. Mason, "Business Policy and Metaphysics: Some Philosophical Considerations," *Academy of Management Review* vol. 7, no. 3 (1982), pp. 361–371.

Newman, W. H., and H. W. Wallender, III, "Managing Not-for-Profit Enterprises," *Academy of Management Review* (January 1978), pp. 24–31.

Nutt, P. C., "A Strategic Planning Network for Non-Profit Organizations," *Strategic Management Journal* (January-March 1984).

Ouchi, W. G., "A Framework for Understanding Organizational Failure," in *The Organizational Life Cycle, op. cit.*

Ronstadt, R., and R. Kramer, "Getting the Most out of Innovation Abroad," *Harvard Business Review* 60 (March-April 1982), pp. 94–99.

Schwartz, H., and S. H. David, "Matching Corporate Culture and Business Strategy," *Organizational Dynamics* (Summer 1981), pp. 30–48.

Shanks, D. C., "Strategic Planning for Global Competition," *Journal of Business Strategy* 5 (Winter 1985), pp. 80–89.

Shrivastava, P., and J. H. Grant, "Empirically Derived Models of Strategic Decision-Making Processes," *Strategic Management Journal* 6 (April-June 1985), pp. 97–113.

Simon, H., "On the Concept of Organizational Goals," *Administrative Science Quarterly* (June 1964).

Stevens, J. M., and R. P. McGowan, "Managerial Strategies in Municipal Government Organizations," *Academy of Management Journal* 26 (September 1983), pp. 527–534.

Unterman, I., and R. M. Davis, "The Strategy Gap in Not-for-Profits," *Harvard Business Review* (May-June 1982), pp. 30–40.

Wood, A., *A Theory of Profits* (Cambridge, England: Cambridge University Press, 1975).

APPENDIX: THE NONPROFIT AND STAGES OF DEVELOPMENT

Barnett's analysis (1987) of 119 nonprofit agencies led to the identification of three stages of nonprofit development: (1) start-up, (2) professionalization, and (3) institutionalization.

START-UP

In the start-up stage, a small group of individuals perceives a need. Based upon this perceived need — or, in the case of the arts, a perceived area of artistic interest — a group experiments with alternative ways to service the need. Group members generally participate on a part-time basis; the group's board of directors is a working board, active in all areas of the agency. Service technology, or the method of providing service to clients, undergoes experimental changes during start-up as the technology is improved upon. Since the service technology is in the process of being developed, the group has informal, flexible operating procedures. Finally, the group's funding during start-up is limited, often based on one initial infusion of capital.

PROFESSIONALIZATION

The two principal characteristics of stage two in the nonprofit, professionalization, are the resolution of service experimentation and the creation of a professional service staff. The group, or agency, has agreed upon a way to service the perceived need that caused its start-up. A professional staff is now working full time to provide this service. With the service technology in place and the agency seeking funds, the board becomes less a working board and more a financial board. Though the agency is accumulating funds, it is doing so at an unreliable rate, with significant fluctuations.

INSTITUTIONALIZATION

Once the nonprofit agency reaches the third stage of development, institutionalization, it has a reliable, steady flow of revenues that provides at least an adequate base. The service technology is fully supported throughout the agency. The agency has standard operating procedures, an administration executive, and a formal organization structure. This administration executive, usually called the executive director, is often not a member of the professional staff. The administration executive performs or oversees grant writing and financing, so that the board's role evolves further from a financial role to an advisory and/or social one. By the institutionalization stage, an agency has developed an administrative group that is often separate from the group delivering the agency's service. Delegation, specialization, and the fine-tuning of administrative structure and systems have reduced the organizational stress and executive burnout that led to the turnovers in management of developing agencies. The institutionalization agency now builds its constituency and looks for additional revenue-generating activities based on its current capabilities, rather than responding to perceived areas of need.

Exhibit 1 summarizes this life-cycle model for nonprofit organizations. During start-up, the strategic manager's objective is experimentation, as the agency explores different ways to service a perceived need. During professionalization, the manager focuses all efforts on supporting the professional service resource. During institutionalization, after the professional service system is in place, the manager concentrates on the strategic objective of increasing agency legitimacy through expanding the agency's constituency.

The model suggests that the critical determining factor in the move to the institutionalization stage is legitimacy with the agency's constituency, or the degree of congruence between agency goals and the objectives of the society that is affected by the agency. An agency at this time must avoid the temptation to deviate from the norms of the society it serves. The agency whose goals are the same as society's goals will receive support, but "failure will occur . . . when the society deems the basic objective of the organization to be unworthy of continued support" (Ouchi, 1980). Exhibit 2 depicts the importance of legitimacy and goal congruence.

EXHIBIT 1 Nonprofit development stages

Factor	Start-up	Professionalization	Institutionalization
Strategic objective	Serve (altruistically) a perceived need	Strengthen and support the service vehicle	Increase legitimacy
Strategic time frame	Present	Medium term based upon service vehicle	Longer term based upon constituency
Service vehicle	Experimental	Focused	Formalized base for new revenue
Structure	Informal "zealots"	Functional hierarchy supporting professiona	Formal, joint professional service and administration
Critical issue to resolve for next stage	Select service vehicle	Align organizational and social goals	N/A
Board role	Working	Financial	Advisory/social
Staff makeup	Part-time volunteers	Full-time, paid professionals; new manager supplements founder	Separate administrative group and new executive director
Funding	One-shot "angels"	Variable amounts, increasing sources	Reliable "public" base
Causes of failure	Early burnout of founders	Staff fails to support chosen service vehicle, resists formal structure; organizational drift away from objective; staff burnout	Lack of legitimacy
Causes of success	The founders	Service provider commitment	Society-agency congruence

EXHIBIT 2
Toward institutional-
ization

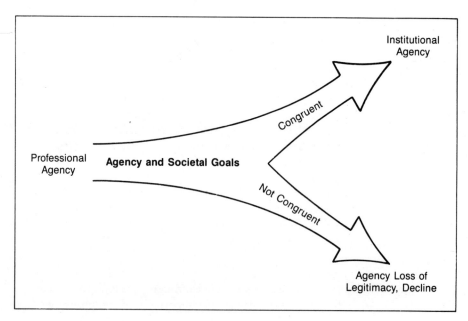

CHAPTER 4

DETERMINING DISTINCTIVE COMPETENCE

Opportunity without the organizational competence to capture it is an illusion.
A. A. Thompson, Jr. and A. J. Strickland, III, *Strategy Formulation and Implementation*

This chapter describes the second step in strategic analysis: how a firm's distinctive competence is determined. The strategic manager analyzes the firm's strengths and weaknesses, characteristics of the firm's resources, to determine distinctive competence. The importance of various competencies change depending on the stage of the product life cycle.

RESOURCES DEFINED

The resources of an organization are the tangible and intangible means by which it carries out its activities. The tangible resources of the organization include (1) people; (2) physical facilities and equipment; (3) product markets, including those bought from suppliers and those sold to customers; (4) distribution and communication systems to reach these supplier and customer product markets; and (5) financial assets. An organization's intangible assets might include (1) managerial processes and skills; (2) special relationships, such as marketplace reputation or banking connections; (3) other special skills and synergies, such as research capabilities; and (4) legal relationships, such as patents, licenses, or long-term contracts.

Tangible Resources

People Resources. The people who carry out the organization's goals include the management, administrative, and functional employees. People who serve as less obvious people resources are the shareholders and bankers and other creditors. The organization's part-time people resources include consultants in such areas as design, systems, and public relations, who are hired by the organization for a specific project or period of time.

Physical Facilities and Equipment. Production lines, assembly plants, research and development laboratories, computers, machine tools, warehouses, and transportation equipment are just a few examples of the many different kinds of facilities and equipment an organization can use. These can be catalogued by location (North American, European), by function (manufacturing equipment, office equipment), or by more subjective terms (fully utilized, inefficient). Finally, the organization can have different levels of investment in a facility or piece of equipment. Physical assets can be leased or owned, and fully owned equipment and facilities can be partially or fully depreciated.

Product Markets. Product groups include suppliers' products and products for customers. Suppliers' products are those goods and/or services purchased by the organization that will be resold directly after being produced, or that will be used in other functions (such as office supplies). Customers' products include all goods and/or services sold by the organization. Both suppliers' and customers' products are part of the organization's inventory at any one time.

Distribution and Communication Systems. An organization has one or more methods of distributing its products to its customers. A distribution system might be through wholly owned retail outlets and catalog locations at one end of the spectrum, or, at the other, more limited end, might only involve delivering items out the back door of the manufacturing facility to an independent trucking service.

The communication system for a product market also can range from the simple to the complex. The organization might communicate with its customers and suppliers using the regular mail service. Or, the organization might communicate through leased or owned computer terminals, transmission and telecommunication lines, and a host computer within the organization.

Financial Assets. The organization's financial resources include cash, and other resources that can be turned into cash. In the short term, government and other marketable securities represent resources that can be turned into cash to finance the organization's activities. Accounts receivable that can be factored and inventory that can be pledged represent other intermediate sources of cash. Land and buildings that can be mortgaged represent longer-term cash sources.

Intangible Resources

Managerial Processes and Skills. As well as being composed of resources that are tangible and can be described definitively, an organization also includes intangible resources, such as managerial procedures, processes, and skills. Nissan possesses special managerial skills for increasing employee productivity; Procter & Gamble is especially well known for its brand-management abilities; General Electric has a worldwide reputation for its managerial budgeting procedures. Whether these skills or processes encompass such diverse management functions as capital budgeting, employee development, or human resource management, they are as much a part of the internal working environment of the firm as distribution systems and assembly lines. The organization and its leaders specifically created these intangible resources.

Special Relationships. Caterpillar Tractor Company has been praised for its special relationship with its worldwide dealers; Dartmouth College has a very active alumni association; Joseph A. Seagram, Ltd., has developed a professional relationship with provincial liquor control boards across Canada. These are examples of special relationships that have been cultivated by top management. These relationships provide the specific means by which management operates, and thus they are resources — intangible, but real — of the organization.

Special Skills and Synergies. *Synergy* is an interaction between parts that increases the effectiveness of each part; in synergy, the whole is greater than the sum of the parts. (In other words, two plus two equals five.) An organization may have special skills such as synergy between research and customer service. Problems studied by a customer service manager, who reviews returned products or studies a major customer's special needs, might trigger solutions within a research technician's mind, who has been researching theoretical aspects related to the same product problem or to the same customer need. Similarly, two managers who previously had been working independently to develop new products might each individually improve the new product through the synergistic effect that information exchange, and the cross-pollinization of ideas, can produce.

Legal Relationships. An organization also might possess an intangible resource in the form of a process or product patent, or in some other long-term contractual relationship. For example, the world's major copper-mining firms often enter into long-term price and quantity (tonnage) contracts with major copper fabricators in order to produce a guaranteed satisfactory return for their mining efforts, even when world copper prices are depressed. These copper contracts often contain clauses for perpetual renewal, called "evergreen" clauses. These legal relationships are an integral part of the way the organization does business, and thus are an important part of the internal environment.

STRENGTHS AND WEAKNESSES

The strategic manager studies the resources of the organization to identify its strengths and weaknesses. The strategic manager asks, "Where are we strong, and where are we weak?" This is not an easy task. As Andrews (1980) points out, "Subjectivity, lack of confidence, and unwillingness to face reality may make it hard for organizations as well as for individuals to know themselves." The strategic manager's list of an organization's strengths and weaknesses cannot be prepared from a checklist of all possible strengths and weaknesses; in other words, strategy does not apply a "cookbook" approach. The definition of a "strength" or a "weakness" is partly a question of fact and partly a matter of judgment. You will develop your sense of strategic judgment as you analyze the cases in this course.

For example, having only enough cash in the bank to pay one or two days of daily operating expenses may mean one thing in a profitable, relatively debt-free, well-known company, and quite another in companies such as Continental Illinois National Bank in May 1984, or Public Service of New Hampshire during major construction problems at its Seabrook nuclear power plant. Henry (1980) examined other firms and how to evaluate a company's strengths and weaknesses; small-business strengths and weaknesses are discussed in the appendix to this chapter.

The job of the strategic manager is to use business judgment by objectively and professionally studying each component of the organization's internal, working environment. This text cannot provide a ''cookbook'' approach to identify the organization's strengths and weaknesses because each situation in the business world (and each case in this course) is unique. One purpose of this course is to help you develop your skills in applying strategic judgments to the analysis of an organization's internal environment. Thus, the following list presents only some — not all — examples of strengths and weaknesses.

1. *How strong (or weak) are managers?*
   knowledge of the firm's business
   knowledge of the industry and competition
   grasp of current problems
   anticipation of future problems
   development of solutions to current and future problems
   implementation of problem solutions
   cohesion
   executive development system
   age, experience of key managers
   quality of staff support groups
   relative difficulty of management task
   continuity/turnover
2. *How strong (or weak) are employees?*
   past, current, and future productivity
   morale and motivation
   extent of employee participation in decision making
   role and attitude of unions
   absenteeism and turnover
   employee training and development
   wage and salary systems
   relative contribution of employees/skill levels
3. *How strong are connections to shareholders? debt sources? consultants? others?*
   current and future needs
   number of alternative sources
   congruence of objectives
   role of board of directors
4. *How efficient is the equipment?*
   cost versus benefit
   cost-volume relationship

flexibility
machine alternatives
obsolescence factors
rate of technological advance
reject/rework/downtime experience
expansion capability
maintenance
degree of integration (continuous process versus job shop, batch systems)
5. *How effective are the facilities?*
cost versus benefit
cost-volume relationship
location and its effect on cost and service
capital intensity
flexibility and resale potential
expansion capability
6. *Other asset considerations*
industrial engineering skills
quality of production scheduling system
financing arrangements
tax consequences
7. *How strong (or weak) are customer ties?*
nature of customer buying decision
nature of customer needs
market share
stage of product life cycle
breadth of product line
basis of product appeal (price, service, multiple-purpose, reputation, financing, brand loyalty, technology, quality)
market-research skills
advertising skills
packaging skills
promotion skills
sales force
purchase follow-up
product research and development abilities
availability of substitutes
number, concentration of customers
8. *How strong (or weak) are suppliers?*
nature of buying decision
nature of needs
relative importance of suppliers
availability of substitutes
cost
quality

service

reliability of inventory control system

number, concentration of suppliers

9. *How strong (or weak) are distribution and communication systems?*

coverage (local, regional, national, international)

cost

speed

reliability

capacity

impact on receiver

relative importance to receiver

flexibility

breadth

degree of firm's control

10. *How strong (or weak) are financial resources?*

financial requirements and needs

predictability of needs and requirements

seasonality

availability of financial resources

cost of financial resources

flexibility of financial arrangements

number of financial alternatives

tax consequences

relationship with financial community

exposure/risk (inflation, business cycle)

reliability of financial (cash management, capital budgeting) systems

percentage of requirements provided internally

present distribution/commitment of financial resources

11. *How strong (or weak) are managerial skills, processes, systems, and procedures?*

costs

response time

nature of skills

cost of improvements, managerial development

relationship between authority and responsibility

relative gap — what is versus what ought to be

availability of managerial alternatives

degree of integration of managerial systems

relative degree of bureaucracy, red tape

12. *How strong are special skills and relationships?*

nature of special skills, relationships

availability of alternatives

research and development

13. *What special legal resources does the firm possess?*

cost of legal relationships

duration

enforcement costs

flexibility

regulatory/governmental relationships

Combining Related Symptoms

In reviewing an organization's strengths and weaknesses, the strategic manager finds that each factor is really a manifestation or symptom of a larger or more common problem. Recognizing the core problem is important so that the strategic manager can deal with the real strength or weakness, not its manifestation. In other words, diagnosing the underlying illness is important so that the illness, not the symptoms, can be understood (and later, treated).

For example, you are the new owner of a manufacturing firm that produces precision electronic components that are modified frequently as customers' needs change. Your operating managers have put together the following partial list of weaknesses.

1. High level of customer complaints
2. High level of absenteeism in fabricating and assembly areas
3. Excessive level of rework in fabricating
4. Excessive overtime and high turnover in product and process engineering
5. High level of product returns

In reviewing these weaknesses, you see a common problem: Customer complaints are high, and product returns are high. You can deduce fairly safely that product quality is poor.

Next, you note that production is characterized by morale problems and poor quality (excessive fabricating rework). These morale and quality problems *in conjunction with* high overtime and turnover in the engineering department produce a further hypothesis. It seems likely that both the engineers studying the product, and those coming up with ways to fabricate the product — the process engineers — are overworked and are not performing at an acceptable level. You thus combine these five related symptoms into one strategic weakness, or "illness": The organization has insufficient engineering resources, which are manifested in poor manufacturing performance and unacceptable product quality.

Finding the opposite of the above five weaknesses — i.e., low instead of high levels of complaints and returns, rework, engineering overtime, and engineering employee turnover — would lead to the opposite conclusion: The organization has a strong engineering resource, as indicated by excellent manufacturing performance and outstanding product quality. In other words, you reach conclusions by combining related strengths and weaknesses.

Reviewing strengths and weaknesses is an exercise in fact finding. Combining strengths and weaknesses is an exercise in reaching conclusions. The skillful strategic manager, relying on a combination of experience and intuition, makes a strategic diagnosis based on the facts of the firm's resources. As you analyze cases, you will move from shuffling and regrouping strengths and weaknesses to understanding the significance of these strengths and weaknesses. You will move from the world of the business student to the world of the strategic manager.

Working Concept 10 shows how the product life cycle guides the strategic manager to those resources that are especially significant to the firm.

<table>
<tr>
<td>

WORKING CONCEPT 10

PRODUCT LIFE CYCLE

</td>
<td>

Business and marketing research has shown that products go through a distinctive cycle and that different strengths are needed at different product life cycle stages. Although there are problems of definition (product brand versus company product versus industry product versus product group) and of interpretation (such as the number of phases of the cycle), Figure 4.1 presents one model of the life cycle. This figure is a simplified version of a typical life cycle of a successful product.

Some researchers conclude that the product life cycle is an important concept (Wasson, 1974; Levitt, 1965). Other researchers have found that the product life cycle is very difficult to apply with any precision (Dhalla and Yuspeh, 1976; Polli and Cook, 1969). Nonetheless, there is general agreement that the product life cycle is a model,

</td>
<td>

albeit an imperfect one, that has significant implications for the strategic manager. These include:

1. Product importance
2. Functional consequences
3. Profit and cash-flow expectations
4. Performance standard
5. Strategic emphasis

PRODUCT IMPORTANCE

An organization carries out its business by bringing products and services to the market; it succeeds or fails based upon how well and how profitably it provides those services. All strategic plans and contributions of researchers, engineers, marketers, producers, and financiers reach their ultimate expression in the product. Failure,

</td>
</tr>
</table>

FIGURE 4.1
Product life cycle

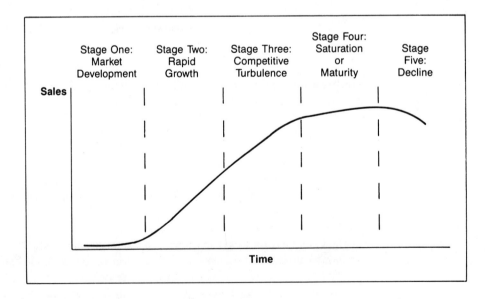

Product Life Cycle (continued)

survival, prosperity, and growth are all determined by the product's performance in the marketplace. Thus, the product life cycle is an appropriate lens for focusing management's attention on the product.

FUNCTIONAL CONSEQUENCES

The strategic manager, who has a high organizational level of authority and responsibility, must plan for and control the changing functional resources that are required as a product moves through the life cycle. During the market development stage, the developmental resources — managerial, tangible, and intangible — of product development, market research, and customer education are especially critical. The rapid growth stage of the life cycle requires increasing productive capacity and market skills to increase market share. As the company's rapid increase in sales, and then profits, attracts more competitors, the company will need the following resources: (1) advertising, customer service, selling, and promotional skills as it seeks to build market share and searches for volume; (2) industrial engineering skills to discover ways to lower costs in the production system; and (3) efficient distribution and communication systems, particularly the latter to provide feedback on competitive moves. During this stage of competitive turbulence the company changes its marketing emphasis from "Try our product" to "Prefer our brand."

Once in the saturation stage, the company emphasizes production efficiency. As margins decline throughout the industry, the company seeks a low-cost — if not lowest cost — position, possibly in combination with seeking a market niche through product differentiation. The company also tightens financial and accounting controls during the saturation stage.

The company further tightens its account-

ing and financial control systems during the decline stage. The company tries to prune any and all unnecessary costs connected with the declining product, as the strategic manager takes resources from the declining product and allocates them to other uses.

PROFIT EXPECTATIONS

The strategic manager is, among other things, a resource allocator. The product life cycle is a tool to plan for the source and use of resources, since a product typically will (1) have its lowest (or nonexistent) profits during market development; (2) show profit levels that lag behind, but follow the growth patterns of, sales during the rapid growth and competitive turbulence stages; and (3) show profits that peak and decrease faster than sales during the maturity and decline stages of the cycle, as the marginal cost of each new sale becomes greater just as lower prices are enforced. Although sales changes are generally expected, the strategic manager must also plan for unit profit changes.

PERFORMANCE STANDARD

The simplified product life cycle pattern presented here is a stereotype that never will be followed by any one product. Nonetheless, any plan is better than none, and the predicted, stereotypical life cycle pattern is a standard against which actual performance can be analyzed. The strategic manager thus can use the product life cycle as a tool for evaluation. Further, the life cycle of the industry's group of products shows changes in the total market demand, while the life cycle of the company's product helps the strategic manager to evaluate the company's competitive strength.

STRATEGIC EMPHASIS

During the life cycle phases the strategic manager is concerned with different re-

Product Life Cycle (*continued*)

sources and emphasizes different steps in the strategic analysis process. The manager concentrates on purpose, goals, and values during the first stage of the product's life. At the second life cycle stage, internal resources — especially both the productive capacity to service rapid growth and the marketing skills to reach the first-time customer — are critical. These internal re-

sources become the foundation of the firm's distinctive competence. During the competitive-turbulence stage, the strategic manager concentrates on the external environment, especially the moves of competitors and their effect on market share. This changing strategic emphasis is summarized in Figure 4.2.

FIGURE 4.2 Life cycle and strategic emphasis

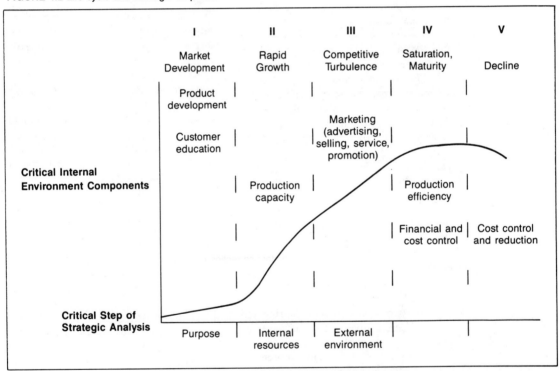

Product Life Cycle and Internal Factors

The product life cycle concept is a powerful tool for distinguishing between the important strengths and weaknesses of the internal environment and those that are less significant. Hofer (1975) concluded that "the most fundamental variable in determining an appropriate business strategy is the stage of the product life cycle."

Wasson (1974) has developed strategic objectives for the five phases of the product life cycle. These strategic objectives, and subsequent research in this important area of strategy, suggest that a number of factors are important at the five stages in the product life cycle, as shown in Table 4.1.

EXAMPLE: *Product Life Cycle Stages*

California Coolers, Schering-Plough, and AMF illustrate stages of the product life cycle. California Coolers grew at a fast rate typical of the growth stage of the cycle. Its owners, who began by making a bathtub mix of fruit punch and white wine, sold the company for $55 million in cash. Schering-Plough and AMF, however, faced problems of declining products. Schering-Plough's antibiotic Garamycin grew at a 17 percent rate for ten years, representing 25 percent of sales and 50 percent of profits (*Fortune*, 8/19/85, p. 50). Garamycin patents ran out in 1980, and Schering's profits from that year of $239 million dropped to $179 million in 1981. When AMF bet on an oil boom in 1981, its energy service business earned a high $63 million on operations for that year. By the 1983 oil bust, AMF's energy services had lost $24 million (*Business Week*, 8/12/85, p. 50).

EXAMPLE: *More on Product Life Cycles*

As MCI moved from growth to competitive turbulence with the long-distance telephone business, the strategic variable of cost became all-important. Earnings and stock prices dropped sharply from 1983 to 1984, as MCI paid higher connection charges to local telephone companies. Competitors keep pressure on revenues. *Busi-*

TABLE 4.1 Strategic life cycle factors	**Product life cycle stage**	**Significant strengths or weaknesses**

	1. Market development	1. Product introduction skills
		    a. ability to educate customer
		    b. ability to gain early use
		2. Product quality
		    a. fast correction of defects
		3. Customer education

	2. Rapid growth	1. Brand management skills 2. Distribution system 3. Productive capacity 4. Cash and human resources

	3. Competitive turbulence	1. Market development
		    a. dealer relationships
		    b. customer's perceptions/loyalties

	4. Saturation or maturity	1. Brand defense
		    a. communication and promotion system
		    b. distribution system
		2. Product improvement skills
		3. Cost advantages
		    a. production facilities, process

	5. Decline	1. Brand management in decline a. "harvest" strategy of cost minimization

ness Week (11/5/84, p. 40) reported the comment of Amy Newark, an industry analyst: "The unanswered question is who is the lowest-cost producer. Nobody knows for sure, except maybe AT&T, and they're not telling." Levi Strauss failed to see the consequences of competitive turbulence. Riding an annual growth of 15 percent in jeans sales, they spent little on local store promotions, had inflexible return policies, and refused to offer volume discounts. As blue jean wearers acquired more taste for fashions, retailers were fast to drop the Levi's line, since the company had "lost touch with its customers" (*Business Week*, 11/5/84, p. 79).

EXAMPLE: *Life Cycle Durations*

One fascinating variable within the product life cycle model is duration. How long does the product life cycle last? Selchow & Righter, the U.S. board game producer, presents an interesting example of the problem of the duration of a product life cycle. During 1984 the company sold over twenty million units of Trivial Pursuit, an amazing sales record when one considers that the company's Scrabble game has sold an annual average of three million units over its thirty-year life. (A rival game, Monopoly, sold by Parker Brothers, has sold an annual average of less than 1.5 million units over its fifty-year life.) As reported by *Business Week* (11/26/84, pp. 118, 122), Selchow & Righter are betting that the product life cycle of their game is of substantially longer duration than that of the hula hoops, pet rocks, and skateboards of other years. The company is ignoring new products and customers alike as it pushes itself to the breaking point to satisfy demand.

Capri Beachwear's filing for Chapter 11 bankruptcy in 1984 illustrates the danger of wrong product life cycle estimates. Although it had manufactured Colony beachwear almost since its founding in 1943, Capri diverted "most of its resources" (*Women's Wear Daily*, 8/9/84) in 1984 from the Colony label to Jane Fonda Workout Bodywear. Capri paid Fonda $162,500 in advance, and committed to annual payments of $650,000 in royalties to Fonda and $400,000 in Jane Fonda Workout Bodywear promotion and ads. Department store returns of $1 million out of $7 million worth of purchases, and Capri's overcutting of $1.5 million for expected orders, were direct symptoms of bankruptcy troubles stemming from the underlying illness of misjudged product life cycles. The company's $10.8 million in assets were mostly in inventory. Liabilities of $12.6 million included Century Factors ($8.3 million) and Jane Fonda herself ($157,800).

Compaq Computer's success is attributed to their completely IBM-PC–compatible line and to the professional business strategy and maturity of Compaq's executives. Compaq's chief executive, Rod Canion, spoke about the product life cycle and the resulting managerial skills:

I admire Steve Jobs and Steve Wozniak [founders of Apple Computer] . . . I don't think it takes anything away from them to then say that as markets begin maturing, those skills aren't what's important to compete. It's more business-oriented skills. (Christian Science Monitor, *5/27/86, p. 25*)

DEFINING DISTINCTIVE COMPETENCE

The strategic manager (1) identifies strengths and weaknesses of the firm's resources, (2) analyzes these strengths and weaknesses by related groups, and (3) determines the relative importance of these strengths and weaknesses based upon the stage of the product life cycle. The strategic manager then defines that important strength that (1) meets a market need and (2) gives the firm a comparative advantage over competition. That strength is the firm's *distinctive competence*. IBM's success in business computing is attributable to its strength in providing total service to businesses — services that included equipment, software, and maintenance. Subaru's success in automobiles is based on satisfying the American market's desire for quality (low maintenance) and reasonable prices. What is required for success in a marketplace? What strength is present in a firm's strategic resources that will satisfy this market requirement?

Secondly, what ability exists in a firm's strategic resources that gives it a comparative advantage? Distinctive competence comprises both market needs and competition. The strategist studies competitors' abilities and those of the firm. In what areas is a firm better than its competitor?

Sears has a comparative advantage over Montgomery Ward and J. C. Penney in its number of modern stores. The New York Yankees have a competitive advantage in higher salary scale, which allows the organization to attract skilled players. Mercedes-Benz and Cross pens have a competitive advantage in their perceived quality.

Market Needs and Comparative Advantage

Stevenson (1976) examined how firms define strengths and weaknesses, and found that executives (1) used past experience to find strengths but not weaknesses (90 percent versus 10 percent), (2) used judgment to find weaknesses but not strengths (80 percent versus 20 percent), and (3) used market and customer comparisons about twice as much to find strengths (67 percent) as to identify weaknesses (33 percent). He further elaborated:

> *The process of defining strengths and weaknesses should ideally require the manager to test his assumptions and to analyze the status quo in relationship to the requirements for future success given the competition and the changing environment. The analysis performed by managers is rarely so dispassionate. There is a great tendency toward inertia.*

The analysis of strengths and weaknesses *must* be coupled with market and competitive analyses to define distinctive competence. This chapter has presented the individual parts of the overall process of defining distinctive competence — identifying strengths and weaknesses, determining strategic importance, analyzing market needs, and studying comparative advantage versus competition — as discrete steps. In real-life situations, of course, these parts are not separate. Each time the strategist looks at a strength or a weakness, he or she also must consider the market and competition. South (1981) argued that competitive advantage is "the cornerstone of strategic thinking."

EXAMPLE: *Competitive Advantage*

Purolator Courier entered the air delivery business against the aggressive competition of Federal Express and the specialized competition of Emery, DHL Worldwide, and Airborne Express. Subsequently, Purolator's market share decreased by one-third, three chief Purolator executives moved in and out, and their stock fell from seventy dollars (1983) to twenty-two dollars (1985) per share. A competitor commented: "They made a tactical error by going into the air business. They had a marvelous ground operation in place" (*Business Week*, 8/12/85, p. 52).

Toys "R" Us, the toy discounter, pursued growth and profits in the mid-1980s by building on its distinctive competence — discount retailing — and its market base. Toys "R" Us, as *Fortune* reported (11/26/84, p. 135), opened children's clothing stores with a strategy based upon the discount prices, inventory control procedures, and volume purchasing strategy that had led to over $1 billion in toy sales.

Mayflower, predicting that high interest rates and business slowdowns would reduce household moving, turned to other segments of the transportation business — hauling computer equipment, delivering appliances, and operating school buses. They determined that transportation was their distinctive competence. Chief executive John Smith commented: "We'll look at any business that has to do with transportation. But I don't plan to take a fine company and wreck it by going into the fast-food business or running motels" (*Fortune*, 3/4/85, p. 60).

In Peters' and Waterman's study *In Search of Excellence*, two top executives commented on the importance of using your strengths and distinctive competence. Robert W. Johnson, Chairman of Johnson & Johnson, said, "Never acquire a business you don't know how to run." Edward G. Harness, C.E.O. of Procter & Gamble, commented: "This company has never left its base. We seek to be anything but a conglomerate."

EXAMPLE: *Distinctive Competence*

Few companies undergo such a dramatic change in their internal environment as did Arrow Electronics, a firm that specialized in distributing electronic components to industrial customers. The firm's strategy was to be an efficient distributor to all but the few major industrial users who were served directly by component manufacturers. During the 1970s Arrow grew from tenth to second in the electronics distribution industry, with sales exceeding $300 million.

In December 1980 Arrow held its annual budgeting sessions at a suburban conference center outside New York City. At midmorning on December 4, a fire at the conference center killed thirteen Arrow executives, including the forty-four-year-old chairman, one of the two executive vice presidents (aged forty-one), several department chiefs, the principal financial officers, and five sales executives.

The surviving executive vice president, John Waddell (then forty-three), who had skipped the meeting to wait at headquarters for announcements connected with a stock split, watched as the market price of the stock fell within thirty days to two-thirds of the price the day before the fire. Rumors of takeovers and competitors' moves, along with speculations about the fire's origins, flew through the organization. By the time the stock bottomed out, shares were trading below ten dollars from a high of twenty-six dollars per share, making the company even more vulnerable.

In what hindsight has proven was an excellent decision, Waddell, after viewing the decimated managerial resources; the concern of the financial markets; and the world of competitors, suppliers, and customers, concluded that the relationship with suppliers was Arrow's critical strategic resource. Waddell mounted an all-out campaign to reassure suppliers, such as Texas Instruments and the Silicon Valley manufacturers, that Arrow Electronics was not only here to stay but would continue its aggressive and successful growth. It took over six months to reassure suppliers; but four years after the fire earnings per share had advanced to twice the pre-fire level and sales grew to over $750 million. Waddell commented to *Fortune* (4/30/84, p. 98) that Arrow Electronics "represents the one truly creative opportunity in life that has come my way."

Levels of Strategy

During the early history of an entrepreneurial venture, the strategic concept of distinctive competence is relatively easy to understand and apply. The creator of a new product idea must have as a distinctive competence the ability to translate that invention or idea into a salable product. If the entrepreneur can subcontract production or license the product idea to an existing manufacturer, he or she may not need manufacturing skills. The entrepreneur may not need marketing skills if the product has great inherent market attractiveness. Financial resources could be managed by a venture capitalist who is willing to share profits with the entrepreneur. Nonetheless, the entrepreneur must possess the critical distinctive competence of managerial ability to overcome the barriers between the product and the marketplace. To the extent that these problems are primarily technical production problems (as they often are), the entrepreneur's distinctive competence must lie in the area of product engineering skills.

Similarly, distinctive competence is relatively easy to define at the functional level of strategy. As an organization evolves through the stages of corporate development and becomes more complex, the strategic concept of distinctive competence, while still easy to understand, becomes more and more difficult to apply.

The mature organization, because of its greater resources, has many more strategic opportunities than the young, entrepreneurial venture. The older organization, with its extensive line of products, services, and markets, faces many more threats than the entrepreneurial venture. National and international competitors, rapidly developing technologies and substitutes, and increasing governmental restraints may threaten the broad-based, diversified company; but these factors might be of little or no consequence to the small-product inventor. Multiple product life cycles are probable

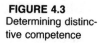
FIGURE 4.3
Determining distinc-
tive competence

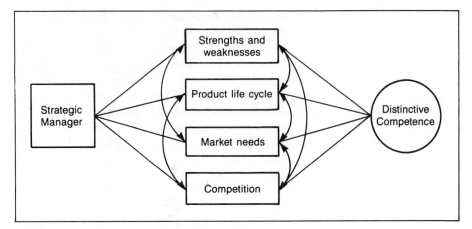

within each business division of the multiple division, multinational, Stage Three firm. Thus, at the corporate level of strategy, the strategic manager oversees scores, hundreds, or even thousands of distinctive competencies.

To summarize, distinctive competence consists of satisfying a market need while having a comparative advantage with competitors. Distinctive competence builds upon the firm's strengths — strengths that are of strategic significance based upon the stage of the product life cycle. Figure 4.3 summarizes this process. Determining distinctive competence is the second step — following defining purpose and preceding identifying strategic opportunities and threats — of the strategic analysis the manager must complete in order to formulate strategy.

SIGNIFICANT RESEARCH

Classic research studies in internal resources and competence include those of Ansoff, Schoeffler et al., and Stevenson.

Ansoff, in *Corporate Strategy* (1965), argues that the "common thread"— the common factor uniting a firm's products and markets — must be based on its competence profile. This competence profile is a list of the major skills and competences of the firm, and is used both for internal appraisal and for understanding the pattern of skills required in industries under review as possible diversification opportunities.

Schoeffler (1974) reported on the Profit Impact of Market Strategies (PIMS) study of over six hundred businesses. Those factors underlying distinctive competence and explaining profitability included (1) market share, (2) marketing expenditures, (3) research and development expenditures, (4) product quality, (5) investment levels, and (6) degree of diversification. Significantly profitable performance was linked primarily to high market share and high product quality. Thirty-six variables explained 77 percent of profitability variance.

Stevenson (1976) interviewed fifty executives in six companies to determine how they assess strengths and weaknesses. The organizational level and the area of responsibility of the responding executive significantly affected the category (financial, marketing, etc.) of strengths and weaknesses described. Further, past performance was most important in determining strengths; management theory and practice was most important in identifying weaknesses. Overall, Stevenson concluded that the process of defining strengths and weaknesses not only would improve the firm's strategy but also would serve as an instrument for managerial development.

Current studies include those by the following researchers.

Aaker and Mascarenhas (1974), describing "the need for strategic flexibility," pointed out that flexibility can come not only from diversification but also from internal resources, either through (1) "investment is underused resources" or (2) "reducing commitment of resources to a specialized use."

Hambrick and Lei (1985), to answer the question "How significant is the stage of the product life cycle?" studied ten variables, including product life cycle, as factors explaining strategy and performance. They found that the type of business (consumer or industrial) and the lack of frequency of customer purchase (once a year or less) were more important than product life cycle stage. They also studied other variables, such as technological change, degree of product differentiation, import levels, industry concentration, and instability of both demand and market share.

Lorange and Murphy (1983), researching the "concepts and practice" of "strategy and human resources," stressed the importance of human resources and strategic management.

Lucas and Turner (1982) studied the firm's information systems resource and degree of integration of the information processing function with the strategic process. They found that most firms have information systems that are concentrated on operational efficiency and are thus independent of strategy, with only a few systems supporting the strategy by producing data for standard, daily decisions. Nonetheless, the firm of the future will merge the information system into strategy formulation, especially by successfully answering the question "How can our information system provide us with technological and other trends to help us open new product markets?"

Rothschild (1984), a manager at General Electric, described the interplay between "surprise and the competitive advantage" and suggested that an "ideal" preemptive move should include (1) the possibility of rapidly occupying prime positions, (2) the difficulty of adversaries following your move, (3) the reduction of competitor's response rate, and (4) the ease of reversing the preemptive move if necessary.

Tyebjee, Bruno, and McIntyre (1983) studied the internal structure and marketing resources of rapidly growing high-tech companies. They concluded that these fast-growth companies passed through four stages of marketing for which a company must plan in advance: (1) entrepreneurial marketing (finding a market niche), (2) opportunistic marketing (penetrating the market), (3) responsive marketing (developing product markets), and (4) diversified marketing (developing new business).

Wheelwright and Hayes (1985) sought to answer the question "How does one carry out a policy of low-cost producer and other competitive strategies based upon production?" They provided some suggestions on "competing through manufacturing." They identified four stages of manufacturing strategy: (1) minimizing the negative potential of manufacturing by keeping it flexible and reactive; (2) achieving parity with competition primarily through capital investment; (3) providing support for the business strategy by systematically addressing long-term manufacturing developments and trends; and (4) providing a manufacturing base that is a competitive advantage with achieved capabilities in advance of needs. Wheelwright and Hayes cited examples at General Electric and IBM.

Williams (1984), constructed a generic matrix for "competitive strategy valuation," placing "relative competitive advantage" on one axis and "economic life in the market" on the other axis. He showed how profitability and cash flow per unit, capital investment, and managerial commitment varied within this matrix.

EXECUTIVE COMMENTS

[AMF] is an operating company, not a holding company. It's a different language. A financial man sees problems expressed in numbers and ratios, but the operations man is out there dealing with people.

J. W. Wolcott, former AMF executive, in *Business Week* (8/12/85) p. 50

[We at] Firestone would have had to invest another $150 [million] to $200 million to stay competitive in the plastics business, and if we had done that, we would have had to starve our other businesses. We are a company with extraordinary skills and strengths, but I don't think plastics was a well-advised battlefield for using those skills and strengths.

J. J. Nevin, Firestone CEO, in the *Wall Street Journal* (11/19/80), p. 37

If all you have is a hammer, everything looks like a nail.

Bernard Baruch, Wall Street investor and financier

[Our strategic] plan calls for Kaiser to identify its most promising businesses and to focus its resources on long-term development and profitability. Increased resources will be allocated to business lines where the company believes it has existing strengths, such as superior technology, low costs, or strong market positions.

C. Maier, Kaiser Chairman

KEY TERMS

comparative advantage (page 83)
competitive turbulence stage (page 78)

decline stage (page 78)

distinctive competence (page 83)

market development stage (page 78)

market needs (page 83)

maturity stage (page 78)

product life cycle (page 78)

strengths and weaknesses (page 73)

synergy (page 73)

BIBLIOGRAPHY

Aaker, D. A., and B. Mascarenhas, "The Need for Strategic Flexibility," *Journal of Business Strategy* 5 (Fall 1984), pp. 74–82.

Anderson, C., and C. Zeithaml, "Stage of the Product Life Cycle, Business Strategy, and Business Performance," *Academy of Management Journal* 27 (March 1984).

Andrews, K. R., *The Concept of Corporate Strategy* (Homewood, IL: Richard D. Irwin, 1980).

Ansoff, H. I., *Corporate Strategy: Business Policy for Growth and Expansion* (New York: McGraw-Hill, 1965).

Buchele, R. B., "How to Evaluate a Firm," *California Management Review* (Fall 1962), pp. 5–16.

Dhalla, N. K., and S. Yuspeh, "Forget the Product Life Cycle Concept," *Harvard Business Review* 54 (January-February 1976), pp. 102–112.

Drucker, P. F., *Management: Tasks, Responsibilities, Practices* (New York: Harper & Row, 1974).

Hambrick, D., "High Profit Strategies in Mature Capital Goods Industries: A Contingency Approach," *Academy of Management Journal* 26 (December 1983).

Hambrick, D., and D. Lei, "Toward an Empirical Prioritization of Contingency Variables for Business Strategy," *Academy of Management Journal* 28 (1985), pp. 763–788.

Hambrick, D., and S. Schecter, "Turnaround Strategies for Mature Industrial-Product Business Units," *Academy of Management Journal* 26 (June 1983), pp. 231–248.

Henry, H. W., "Appraising a Company's Strengths and Weaknesses," *Management Policy* (July-August 1980), pp. 31–36.

Hofer, C. W., "Toward a Contingency Theory of Business Strategy," *Academy of Management Journal* (December 1975), pp. 784–810.

Hussey, D. E., "The Corporate Appraisal: Assessing Company Strengths and Weaknesses," *Long Range Planning* (December 1968), pp. 19–25.

Levitt, T., "Exploit the Product Life Cycle," *Harvard Business Review* 43 (November-December 1965), pp. 81–94.

Lorange, P., and D. C. Murphy, "Strategy and Human Resources," *Human Resources Management* 22 (Spring-Summer 1983), pp. 111–135.

Lucas, H. C., Jr., and J. A. Turner, "A Corporate Strategy for the Control of Information Processing, *Sloan Management Review* 23 (Spring 1982), pp. 25–36.

Peters, T. J., and R. H. Waterman, Jr., *In Search of Excellence: Lessons from America's Best-Run Companies* (New York: Harper & Row, 1982).

Polli, R., and V. J. Cook, "Validity of the Product Life Cycle," *The Journal of Business* 42 (October 1969), pp. 385–400.

Rothschild, W. E., "Surprise and the Competitive Advantage," *Journal of Business Strategy* 4 (Winter 1984), pp. 10–18.

Schoeffler, S., R. D. Buzzell, and D. F. Heany, "Impact of Strategic Planning on Profit Performance," *Harvard Business Review* 54 (March-April 1974), pp. 137–145.

Salter, M. S., "Stages of Corporate Development," *Journal of Business Policy* 1 (Spring 1970), pp. 23–27.

South, S. E., "Competitive Advantage: The Cornerstone of Strategic Thinking," *Journal of Business Strategy* 1 (Spring 1981), pp. 15–25.

Stevenson, R. H., "Defining Corporate Strengths and Weaknesses," *Sloan Management Review* (Spring 1976), pp. 51–68.

Thompson, A. A., Jr., and A. J. Strickland, III, *Strategy Formulation and Implementation* (Dallas: Business Publications, 1980).

Tyebjee, T. T., A. V. Bruno, and S. M. McIntyre, "Growing Ventures Can Anticipate Marketing Stages," *Harvard Business Review* 61 (January-February 1983), pp. 62–66.

Wasson, C. R., *Dynamic Competitive Strategy and Product Life Cycle* (St. Charles, IL: Challenge Books, 1974).

Wheelwright, S. C., and R. H. Hayes, "Competing Through Manufacturing," *Harvard Business Review* 63 (January-February 1985), pp. 99–109.

Williams, J. R., "Competitive Strategy Valuation," *Journal of Business Strategy* 4 (Spring 1984), pp. 36–46.

APPENDIX: THE SMALL BUSINESS

SMALL BUSINESS CATEGORIES

We arbitrarily define a small business as any firm with less than twenty employees. Although they are insignificant in terms of assets, employment, investment, or profit when compared to U.S. multinational firms, small businesses represent over 90 percent of the businesses in the United States, according to the *Statistical Abstract of the United States*.

Two ways of categorizing these vast numbers of small businesses were suggested by both Susbauer and by Vesper in commentaries within Schendel and Hofer (1979).

Success Categories   Susbauer categorized small businesses into four groups in terms of increasing success. Least successful, but by far the most numerous, are the "survival firms," typically the "undercapitalized, undermanaged, limited-potential mom and pop stores." Next are the "attractive growth potential firms," which are small businesses on their way to success; in other words, intermediate-step firms such as high-tech companies on the verge of success.

Susbauer's third category is the "underachieving firm," the company that consciously or unconsciously does not achieve its potential. The final category is the "high success growth firm."

**Economic
Categories**

Vesper, on the other hand, groups small businesses, based upon "the economic functions they perform," into nine categories:

1. Solo, self-employed entrepreneurs
2. Work-force builders (typically service companies)
3. Product innovators
4. Unutilized resource exploiters
5. Economy of scale exploiters
6. Pattern multipliers (franchise entrepreneurs such as Colonel Sanders)
7. Takeover artists
8. Capital aggregators (such as founders of small banks)
9. Speculators

SMALL BUSINESS ENVIRONMENT

The internal environment of the small business distinguishes it from other organizations. By definition, the small business has limited resources. Although limited financial resources are cited as the most important reason for the failure of small business, the small business strategic manager may also face limited (1) managerial talents, (2) productive capacity, (3) marketing options, and (4) information.

The small business strategist, then, has a narrowly defined distinctive competence, since the small firm usually does not possess many significant strengths. This limited distinctive competence means that the small business strategist confronts a higher risk than a strategist for a larger company. Higher risk may mean that the small business tries to avoid products at the competitive turbulence or mature stages of the product life cycle.

EXAMPLE: *Small Businesses*

EMF is a privately held service company that provides repair service for personal computers and minicomputers. Its sales goal for 1984 was $1 million. In the fall of 1984, EMF had an option to pursue the maintenance-agreement end of the repair market through retail distributors. In this field, EMF faced such competitors as TRW, RCA, Honeywell, and Arrow Electronics. If EMF decided to concentrate on start-up and foreign computer manufactuers, it would face such competitors as Sinclair and Acorn, who could not afford a national service organization. The latter group of manufacturers were clearly the preferable alternative; EMF did not possess a significant distinctive competence to use in competing against such mature, resourceful corporations as TRW and RCA.

Commenting on the move into biotechnology industry by du Pont and Monsanto, a manager at one of the two hundred small, start-up biotechnology businesses said, "It's becoming the waltz of the elephants, and the fleas are going to get squashed" (*Business Week*, 11/5/84, p. 137).

Although smaller businesses have significant advantages in the commitment of top executives, time flexibility, and lower fixed costs, Drucker (1974) concluded that the "typical small business has no strategy . . . it lives from problem to problem." While focusing on the present, the small business strategic manager also must anticipate the future investment and managerial needs caused by growth.

BIBLIOGRAPHY

Drucker, P. F., *Management* (New York: Harper & Row, 1974).

Susbauer, J. C., "Commentary," in *Strategic Management*, D. E. Schendel and C. W. Hofer, eds. (Boston: Little, Brown, 1979), pp. 327–332.

Vesper, K. H., in *Strategic Management*, op. cit., pp. 332–338.

CHAPTER 5

IDENTIFYING OPPORTUNITIES AND THREATS

Every enterprise must watch what is new in the environment, for this might eventually destroy it. . . . It is discouraging that most phonograph companies did not enter the radio field, wagon manufacturers did not enter the automobile business, and steam locomotive companies did not enter the diesel locomotive business.

P. Kotler, *Marketing Management: Analysis, Planning and Control*

This chapter will identify the components of the organization's external environment, describe a method for analyzing these external components, and show how this analytical method can be used by the strategic manager. An appendix to this chapter describes the special complexities of the international business environment.

EXTERNAL ENVIRONMENT DEFINED

The external environment of the firm consists of all outside factors that affect the firm. The impact may be direct, as in the short-term acts of a competitor, or indirect, as in long-term changes in social attitudes toward business. These factors may be grouped into five segments: (1) markets, (2) competition, (3) technology, (4) society, and (5) government. Each segment includes factors that have a direct and indirect effect on the organization.

Markets

The organization succeeds or fails based upon what happens in its markets. The markets in which the organization offers its products and services include customers and competitors.

As a company grows from a small, single-product firm to a complex, diversified multinational corporation, its markets grow in complexity. As complexity grows, the strategic manager's job of analyzing the marketplace becomes more difficult

How does a firm define its market? The answer to this question depends on the type of business. For example, a small family business may think of its market in terms of its product or service, such as being in the auto parts business or the television repair business. One company might see itself in a customer needs market, such as data processing, or in a technology market, such as aerospace. A large, diversified company might be active in many markets, or even in markets without definition or delineation — borderless markets with broad ranges of products and services. In Derek Abell's view (1980), a company can define its business by (1) who it sells to (customer group), (2) what it sells (customer needs), and (3) how the product or service is produced (technologies).

EXAMPLE: *TWA's Market*

Consider the example of Transworld Corporation. Trans World Airlines (TWA), formerly the major component of the Transworld Corporation, could define its market in definite terms. The market included the transportation of passengers and the provision of supporting services (i.e., baggage, freight, and in-flight items, including food and beverages). These transportation services operated between set cities and geographic regions, and were offered at prices easily defined by a few systems of fare regulation.

By early 1984, Transworld had sold its controlling interest in TWA stock; its markets included: (1) food service, ranging from over four hundred fast food outlets, including Hardee's, to a mammoth institutional service, Canteen Corporation; (2) real estate, via a national franchise of Century 21 real estate firms; (3) hotels, through its operation of approximately one hundred Hilton Hotels; and (4) personnel services, including Dunhill Personnel System. Transworld can now clearly define its markets as encompassing anyone who works, travels, eats, or sleeps. By the third quarter of 1984, Transworld had reported operating profits of $120 million on sales of $1.5 billion, with fast food outlets and Hilton Hotels contributing two-thirds of earnings.

The marketplace may be so complex as to seem limitless or without borders. Nonetheless, market may be defined within the following categories.

Customers
   industrial, consumer
   government, not-for-profit
Locations
   regional, national, international
Types of product
   goods or services
   stage of product life cycle
Nature of product
   household, technical
Nature of buying decision
   impulse, formalized analysis

Purchase decision factors
    price
    packaging
    service/maintenance
    availability
    convenience
    credit financing
    reputation
    others
Market structure
    competitive/commodity to regulated oligopoly/monopoly

The following list shows how the Transworld Corporation might define its current markets.

Customers
    Industrial/institutional customers sold to by Transworld's Canteen Corporation, Dunhill Personnel (employer)
    Consumer customers sold to by Transworld's Hardee's, Century 21, Hilton, Dunhill Personnel (employee)

Locations
    Regional (Hardee's [Southeast])
    National (Century 21, Dunhill Personnel)
    International (Hilton)

Product Type
    Goods (Hardee's, Canteen Corporation)
    Services (Century 21, Hilton, Dunhill Personnel)

Product Nature
    Household (Hardee's, Hilton, Canteen Corporation)
    Technical (Century 21, Dunhill Personnel)

Buying Decision
    Impulse (Hardee's)
    Formalized Analysis (Century 21)

Purchase Factors
    Price (Canteen Corporation)
    Service (Century 21)
    Others (Hilton)

Market Structure
    Competitive/commodity (Hardee's)
    Regulated oligopoly/monopoly TWA [former holding]

A definition of the external environment's market, then, can be presented as follows: The *market* is the present and potential *customers* in their range of *locations*, organized into economic *market structures*, who may decide to buy the firm's *product* — a buying *decision* that varies as to nature of the product and as to decision factors.

Competition

The firm's success or failure in the marketplace depends in part upon the strategic decisions of its competitors. *Competition*, then, consists of the present and potential alternative sources of a firm's goods and services. The breadth and variety of a firm's competitors depends on the extent of the firm's product offerings and market location. A strategic manager may face aggressive international competition or a few local competitors.

Competition may be direct, such as the computer offerings that AT&T presented to Digital Equipment Corporation's customers and others following the breakup of the Bell system. Competition can also be indirect, through product substitution. The North American beverage industry has made a clear shift away from distilled spirits (especially blends) toward table wines.

Technology

Scientific and engineering principles underlie all the product design and production knowledge found within an industry. Advances in production processes and product designs represent technological progress that will affect the organization to some degree. *Technology*, then, consists of the current scientific and engineering principles embodied in an organization's processes and products, and the expected advances in these production and design systems.

Communication and computers illustrate the force and potential of technological advance. With the technological breakthrough of fiberoptics, message capacities increased and operating costs decreased. Market and industry boundaries fell before the force of fiberoptic technology. The *Wall Street Journal* and *USA Today* transmitted their daily editions to Europe via satellite. Larger corporations (such as Kodak) that acquired their own communications systems in order to control costs found themselves with excess communication capacity, and so began to compete with AT&T by offering telephone services to others.

In the mid-1980s an estimated 9,000 robots worked in the United States, 12,500 in Europe, and 140,000 in Japan. Hitachi builds videocassette recorder chassis in one plant in Japan. After they installed eleven robots and fifty-two automatic assembly machines, their assembly time per chassis fell from twenty-four to three minutes; their number of workers dropped from 170 to 33.

The rate of technological change is determined primarily within a given business by economics, and within a given society by social values. An organization facing little competition in a structured market will have little incentive to make heavy investments in technological research and development. The manufacturer of microcomputers in the 1980s cannot expect economic survival without staying in the forefront of computer technology. Similarly, few advances in manufacturing technology can be expected of societies that value rural life most highly and stress the family agricultural unit as the foundation of society. Societies that value health and longevity, however, can be expected to pursue advances in medical technology.

Society

If markets seem difficult to define, society proves to be an even more elusive concept. *Society* can best be defined as the cultural values and expectations that surround the organization. These values and expectations are embodied in the population; they affect the organization directly through the attitudes of customers, employees, and others who deal with the organization. While many fast food operators began to despair at McDonald's industry dominance (40 percent of worldwide fast food hamburger sales and a history of constantly increasing quarterly earnings), others decided to follow the social trend of increasing attention to nutrition and personal health. Several national food retailers are hatching new outlets serving unbreaded chicken broiled without oil — a dish endorsed by medical groups.

One element of U.S. society, the labor union, today faces an unfavorable trend that has resulted from changing social values. A 1983 Gallup poll ranked labor officials second from the bottom in ethical behavior, only slightly more ethical than used car salespeople. A 1985 AFL-CIO report showed that 65 percent of nonunion workers thought union leaders forced members into certain contracts and actions. Union members are the lowest (19 percent) proportion of the work force in decades. The president of the Communication Workers of America, G. E. Watts, said, "What we're now saying to ourselves is that we should, we must adjust to a changing workplace. We've got to change some every day to keep up" (2/24/85).

Columbia University sociologist David Halle (1985) provides further insights into the worker in society. Halle's findings, which were based on a study of blue collar workers in northern New Jersey from 1974 to 1981, include:

Most workers get no deep satisfaction from religion or ethnicity.

Most workers believe they are wasting their lives in dull, repetitive jobs.

Most male workers get most enjoyment from drinking with male friends, fishing, hunting, and sports events.

Forty percent of workers are unhappily married.

Eight-three percent of workers believe big business runs the country.

Ninety-two percent of workers believe all politicians are corrupt.

As social values and expectations change and evolve, they create opportunities and threats for the strategic manager.

Government

Government is an administrative system for organizing human effort. The procedures of this administrative system are political. The government's scope of activities includes defense, the judiciary, the economic infrastructure (taxes, tariffs, and incentive programs), and regulation. The government is also the major domestic purchaser of goods and services, and the instrument of the critical fiscal and monetary policies that influence economic trends.

Government regulation of business changes and evolves as it reacts to perceived problems or abuses. Early regulation of business reacted to monopolies; the first regulation effort, the 1887 Interstate Commerce Commission, was established to control the monopolistic position of railroads. This industry-by-industry approach to regulation, built upon the principle of controlling or limiting monopolistic profits, changed with the administration of Franklin Roosevelt. Regulation changed further with the legislative acts regulating social problems in the mid-1960s and mid-1970s. These social problems or issues included equal employment opportunities, occupational safety, consumer protection, and environment.

Professor Manley Irwin of the University of New Hampshire warns of a new change in regulation as we enter the age of cold war technology: regulation by the Pentagon. Professor Irwin cites the following incidents as evidence of this Department of Defense regulation of business during the fall of 1984.

Harvard University report cites campus fear of federal control of research (December 1984).

Ericsson, Sweden's largest electronics company, cancels Eastern bloc sales under U.S. pressure (August 1984).

United States gets tough with Austria over high-tech leaks (November 1984).

United States investigates computer sales to Czechs by ASEA of Sweden (December 1984).

Austria toughens export controls in bid to preserve its access to U.S. technology (November 1984).

Digital Equipment Corporation to pay $1.1 million to settle U.S. export violations (September 1984).

ITT's German subsidiary cancels telephone exchange sale to Hungary (October 1984).

Belgium abandons nuclear plant contract in Libya (October 1984).

In summary, the strategic manager seeks answers to questions encompassing the market, competition, technology, government, and society, questions including:

Market
What present economic conditions influence my ability to profitably sell my goods and services in the marketplace?
What economic trends over the next one-, two-, and five-year periods do I anticipate?
What is the anticipated impact of these trends on my ability to sell my goods and services in the future?

Competition
What present competitive conditions influence my ability to profitably sell my goods and services in the marketplace?
What competitive trends in the one-, two-, and five-year time horizons do I anticipate?

What is the anticipated impact of these trends on my ability to sell my goods and services in the future?

Technology

What present technological conditions influence my ability to profitably sell my goods and services in the marketplace?

What technological trends in the one-, two-, and five-year time horizons do I anticipate?

What is the anticipated impact of these trends on my ability to sell my goods and services in the future?

Government/Society

What present regulatory/political/social conditions influence my ability to profitably sell my goods and services in the marketplace?

What regulatory/political/social trends in the one-, two-, and five-year horizons do I anticipate?

What is the anticipated impact of these trends on my ability to sell my goods and services in the future?

The Changing External Environment

The preceding list of questions focuses on change. To underscore the dynamic nature of the external environment, some basic social and cultural values will be examined from a historical viewpoint. What are the constant values of any society? Some of the fundamental concepts might be property rights, the role of the market and individual expectations, and the nature of the Deity. This brief review of these fundamental cultural concepts will provide a means for understanding change in the external environment.

Property Rights. What is the basis of the right to property? From the viewpoint of the historian and anthropologist, property rights have been built upon a changing foundation. Initially, as nomadic hunter-gatherers roamed the earth, rights to property were based upon the foundation of first occupancy. Further, these rights usually were collective or communal rights that were based upon tribal, not individual, ownership. Subsequent foundations for property rights included (1) superiority, such as the moral superiority supporting the divine right of monarchies; (2) labor, wherein an individual's labor on or toward something, such as agricultural land, determined ownership; (3) political liberty, wherein the ultimate goal of liberty required economic freedom, which in turn required the right to own property; and (4) utility, wherein the system of private property rights was enforced because it was the most effective system.

The Market and Individual Expectations. Some anthropological economists have hypothesized that the basic economic structure has changed from (1) reciprocal societies, in which individuals exchanged surplus, to (2) administered societies, in which a centralized, administrative (often either religious or military, or both) class redistributed surpluses for everyone, to (3) market societies, in which the flow of goods and services are determined by the market's demand and supply. Other social scientists have hypothesized that societal expectations have changed from simple survival to equality, liberty, education, and most recently (in developed societies) to increasing standards of living and individual development.

The Deity. Even such a basic concept as the nature of the Deity has changed. Early pantheistic views of the Deity in nature and all things moved to a period of goddess religions in which all the head deities were female, to a period of male principal deities. One might even argue that many persons currently view the Deity as a scientific principle, a "cosmic computer."

Business and Society. "Constants" in business change, just as cultures change, as witnessed by Coca-Cola's reformulating their 99-year-old Coke formula and Procter & Gamble's abandoning a 135-year-old trademark (thirteen stars and a "man" moon). *The Christian Science Monitor* (5/6/85, p. 31) reported on the Starch Advertisement Readership Service's study of basic interest in the United States; it included the following changes. (1) Religion, which ranked first among women and fifth among men as a basic interest in 1953, had disappeared entirely from the top ten list by 1983. (2) Women's first basic interest in 1983 in fashion and clothes, replacing religion; the first basic interest for men was business, replacing sports. (3) Health entered the top ten interests in 1983 (third for women and seventh for men) while gardening disappeared. (4) Travel became a new interest for women, while homemaking dropped from third in 1953 to eighth in 1983.

Change and Opportunity. The strategic manager identifies and seeks to direct the forces of change as a source of opportunity. Cultural changes thus can be seen as major opportunities.

Health Maintenance Organizations (HMOs) are an example of a mass market opportunity that resulted from significant cultural change. North Americans' increasing health consciousness represents a cultural change; the HMO responded by addressing concerns about rising hospitalization costs. HMOs charge monthly premiums just as do the traditional health insurers; however, their monthly fees are often lower, and small physician and medication fees are significantly lower. Blue Cross-Blue Shield of Massachusetts saw an increase in its HMO subscribers from 31,000 in 1981 to 200,000 in 1985. The director of the federal government's HMO office estimated that the more than fifteen million HMO members should double by 1989 (2/4/84).

Following in this same health trend, Riunite offered jogging gear with its faddish wines. Seagram, perhaps more logically, introduced a no-alcohol wine, St. Regis, in the mid-1980s.

EXAMPLE: *Change*

Strategic managers have found themselves in great difficulty when they have refused to recognize change. Howard Head clung steadfastly to a single product, the black metal ski, in the face of fiberglass technology and trends toward more fashionable, colorful skis. Fiberglass skis ended Howard Head's industry dominance. Sewall Avery of Montgomery Ward stood firmly committed to cost cutting, store consolidation, and cash-liquidity, expecting a post–World War II recession; Sears, Roebuck aggressively expanded after World War II to take advantage of pent-up demand and the move to suburbia. The effective strategic manager recognizes change as a fact of life. Montgomery Ward saved a lot of money, but Sears gained all the business.

STRATEGIC ANALYSIS AND STRATEGIC SIGNALS

The method used by the strategic manager to analyze the external environment consists of two steps: (1) identifying strategic signals and (2) interpreting strategic signals.

Identifying Strategic Signals

The job of the strategic manager is to identify those strategic signals which show that the environment is shifting in ways that will provide opportunities or will present threats to the firm. *Strategic signals* are early warning signs generated by the external environment that reveal both the nature and direction of external environmental change. As consumer tastes evolve, markets change. As societal values shift, social programs change. As competitors take actions in the marketplace, competitive pressures change. As one governmental leader succeeds another, governmental regulations change.

Interpreting Strategic Signals

After identifying early warning signals in the external environment, the strategic manager determines whether these signals are positive or negative. Positive signals (i.e., significant increases in the percentage of customers who are repeat customers after an initial trial purchase of a product) indicate opportunities for the firm in the external environment. Negative signals (i.e., continued decreases in a competitor's manufacturing costs) represent threats in the external environment.

Market Signals

The variety and number of strategic signals seem infinite. Nonetheless, the strategist must detect *and* interpret the signals. Business experience has shown the strategic manager can expect positive and negative signals of external environmental opportunities and threats relating to present products. Table 5.1 presents selected market signals. When the strategist turns away from existing products to look for new market opportunities, new signals become important. Of primary interest is the change in consumer tastes.

EXAMPLE: *Strategic Market Signals*

Experience in the steel container (tin can) packaging industry since World War II provides an illustration of some of these strategic market signals. Positive signals in the industry included (1) increase in total number of customers; (2) increase in

TABLE 5.1
Selected market
strategic signals for
existing products

Category	Positive	Negative
Customers		
total number	Increases	Decreases
per customer volume	Increases	Decreases
Location		
firm's geographic coverage	Increases	Decreases
industry geographic coverage	Expands	Contracts
Product type		
firm's product mix	Expands	Contracts
industry product mix	Expands	Contracts
Product, buying decision nature, factors		
firm's percentage contribution	Increases	Decreases
industry margins	Increase	Decrease
purchase frequency	Increases	Decreases
product substitutes	Decrease	Increase
Market structure		
price competition	Decreases	Increases
industry advertising	Decreases	Increases
barriers to entry	Increase	Decrease

per-customer volume; (3) geographic expansion; and (4) product mix expansion, including the introduction of aerosol cans. Nonetheless, the negative signals warned of what was really happening. Alcoa, Reynolds, and the other aluminum manufacturers were successfully introducing aluminum cans. Du Pont and others were developing plastic substitutes. Libby and other major customers were producing their own cans. The industry increased price competition as a result of these other negative factors. Thus, negative signals included (1) decrease in contribution and margins as the industry cut price to keep volume, (2) decrease in product mix, (3) increase in product substitutes, (4) increase in price competition, and (5) decrease in purchase frequency.

EXAMPLE: *Retailers and the Market*

Recognizing the market opportunity represented by the increasing numbers of professional women in the work force, Chicago retailer Carson Pirie Scott & Co. created a 40,000-square-foot "corporate level" that offered designer fashions, shoes, cosmetics, and accessories for the woman executive, along with a fashion consultant, shoe repair shop, restaurant, dry cleaners, and photocopy center.

Market signals or suggestions may appear from many sources. *Business Week* (4/22/85, p. 65) reported on entrepreneur Roy Raymond, who had established Victoria's Secret lingerie shops. At age thirty-seven, after the birth of his two children, Raymond formed My Child's Destiny, a chain of children's boutiques selling natural fiber clothes and nonviolent toys. The restrooms even provided free diapers! Working Concept 11 provides a tool for understanding markets; Figure 5.1 summarizes customer needs analysis.

WORKING CONCEPT 11

CUSTOMER NEEDS ANALYSIS

The strategic manager tries to determine what factors influence the customers' choice of one company's service or product over another's. These factors influencing customer choice make up the needs that the customer seeks to satisfy; they might include price, service, credit availability, durability and other measures of ''quality,'' and location. Frequently, market research interviews will provide a number of these factors.

Through market research and market studies, the manager next determines the relative importance of these factors. These findings may range from imprecise ''guesstimates'' to numerical weights, depending on the data available. Clearly, some measure of importance is necessary; a 33-inch yardstick is better than no yardstick at all. The degree of precision will be determined by the specifics of the situation. By rating the firm's performance against competitors on each of these customer need factors, the manager can gain competitive insight.

The strategist then makes assumptions about the future likelihood of change, both as to customer need factors and as to their relative importance. The manager needs to determine how the purchase of tomorrow will differ from today's purchase. Manage-

ment analyst Peter Drucker (1974) concluded,

It is the customer who determines what a business is. It is the customer alone whose willingness to pay for a good or for a service converts economic resources into wealth, things into goods. . . . What the customer thinks he is buying, what he considers value, is decisive — it determines what a business is, what it produces, and whether it will prosper. (p. 61)

The critical functional marketing questions — What market segments should we pursue? and How should we position our products? — can best, and perhaps only, be answered after customer needs are analyzed and understood. Differing needs create different market segments. The strategic manager can meet those needs through product positioning.

The president of Pepsi, Roger Enrico, commented on customer needs and product positioning as he compared Pepsi and Coke: ''Coke . . . slapped their name on more and more kinds of products. Pepsi stands for something. . . . When people pick up Pepsi they know what they are getting. I don't think you can say that with the other product'' (*Boston Globe*, 12/1/85, p. A-1).

FIGURE 5.1
Customer needs analysis

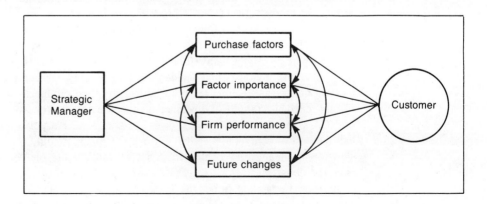

EXAMPLES: *Customer Needs*

Howard Head correctly attributed the success of his revolutionary metal ski to its responsiveness and turning ability that made skiing easier; he also stressed the importance of product longevity. Being an engineer, Head thought that people would want skis that would last a long time. However, he discounted fashion as a critical factor in the purchase decision, ignoring the striking cosmetics of the new fiberglass skis being introduced by Kneisl and other European manufacturers. Head also over-looked price as a measure of perceived quality. Inevitably, Head's market share dropped as other manufacturers positioned their skis at price points above Head skis.

The banking industry provides examples of the importance of understanding the customer. From 1980 to 1985 the Barnett Bank group climbed from number 3 to number 1 among the almost five hundred banks in Florida. The Barnett group's success in capturing the largest share of retired people's savings in this deposit-rich environment was attributed to its excellent customer services, based in turn on its knowledge of the factors that influence customer decisions. A Boston bank, on the other hand, was fined $500,000 for failing to report international cash transac-tions to the Internal Revenue Service between 1980 and 1984. Large cash transactions by alleged bosses of the New England crime syndicate were at the center of the unreported transactions. The bank asserted that it didn't know the "boss" family should be scrutinized, and didn't think to report the exchange of over $2.2 million in cash exchanged for certified checks by the "boss" family companies.

The Decision to Buy. Assessing market signals, then, is a process of (1) understanding the critical factors underlying the customer's buying decision and (2) identifying signals that will indicate strategic changes in a firm's relative position regarding these purchase factors.

EXAMPLES: *Purchase Decision*

The strategic importance of identifying the essence of the purchase decision can be seen in Beech-Nut's mid-1980s gain in the Gerber-dominated (70 percent) U.S. baby food market. Beech-Nut's biggest gain has been in its Stages baby foods, which are color-coded to four stages of infant development. Although Stages cost 10 to 30 percent more than their competition, *Fortune* reported that Stages had over 50 percent of the baby food business in some markets in 1984 (12/24/84, p. 56). Parents obviously had decided that Stages set Beech-Nut products apart from those of Gerber and Heinz, the other U.S. baby food producers. In the same issue, *Fortune* cited an example of misunderstanding the purchase decision when it reported on RCA's abandonment of video discs. Although RCA's video disc player sold at half the cost of competitors' video cassette machines, it could not record programs. This missing feature lay behind RCA's $500 million loss on "one of the decade's mangiest dogs."

In 1985 Coca-Cola turned its back on the secret Coke formula developed by John Pemberton in 1886. Coca-Cola was reacting to Pepsi's increasing market share;

FIGURE 5.2
Importance of price in the purchase decision

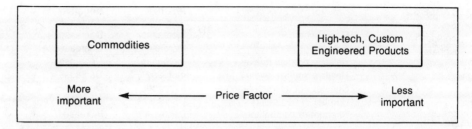

the New Coke formula was sweeter, smoother, and closer to Pepsi's taste. Loyal Coke drinkers, however, didn't want a "better" Pepsi. The Coke "loyalist" purchasers raised such a ruckus — threatening class action lawsuits, moaning about Coke's "fixin' something that ain't broke," and flooding the company with protests — that the original Coke — now called Coca-Cola Classic — was brought back to life.

Price and the Decision to Buy. Figure 5.2 illustrates price as one aspect of the basic customer purchase decision. The simple illustration of price versus all other factors leads to the following questions.

1. As your products move toward the right, don't the following become more important distinctive competencies: (a) technical knowledge, (b) flexible production, and (c) customer relations?
2. As your products move toward the left, where price is more of a factor, don't the following become more important distinctive competencies: (a) production efficiencies, (b) administrative systems, and (c) economies of scale?

The simplicity of Figure 5.2 should not obscure the difficulty of determining the qualitative and psychological purchase factors, such as the emotional brand loyalty entirely unanticipated by those who withdrew the original Coke in April 1985, only to bring it back in July.

Quality and the Decision to Buy. Product quality is a second aspect of the customer purchase decision. Quality, of course, interacts with price; price is, to some, a measure of quality. The strategic manager must recognize the perception aspects of customer needs. If a customer needs quality, creating the perception of quality is a valid strategy. Don Burr, chairman of People Express, spoke about the opposite effect, the perception of a lack of quality: "Coffee stains on the flip-down trays mean [to the passengers] that we do our engine maintenance wrong" (*Fortune*, 5/13/85, p. 23).

EXAMPLES: *Customer Needs*

A firm's misunderstanding of customer needs and customers' interest in quality can lead to trouble in the marketplace. Procter & Gamble, *Business Week* reported (2/24/86, p. 36), "virtually created" the market for the disposable diaper by recognizing the customer need. A competitor, Kimberly-Clark, introduced a better, contoured

TABLE 5.2
Selected
competitive strategic
signals

Category	Positive	Negative
Market share	Increases	Decreases
Relative profitability	Increases	Decreases
Relative product quality	Increases	Decreases
Relative service levels	Increase	Decrease
Number of market segments	Increases	Decreases
Number of competitors	Decreases	Increases
Strength of competitors	Decreases	Increases

disposable diaper; Procter & Gamble "didn't realize that consumers would pay more for a better diaper." Their 75 percent market share declined rapidly, and Kimberly's Huggies became number 1 over P&G's Pampers.

Knowledge of the whole spectrum of her high fashion customer needs is central to Donna Karan's success. Chief designer for Anne Klein at age twenty-five, and now the head of a company that expects first year sales of $12 million, Karan's designs combine sophistication, sensuality, and convenience: "A working woman has no time to shop. I want quality. I want sophistication, and I want ease. Zip on, and get on with your life" (*Business Week*, 12/23/85, p. 56).

**Competitive
Signals**

Although market research and analysis can help identify competitive strategic signals presented in Table 5.2, how can the manager analyze the strength of the competition? At the center of this dilemma is access to the competition's information. The strategic manager looks for signals of change in the relative strength between the organization and the competition. Possible measures of strength include price levels, store location, sales force, advertising budgets, R&D expenditures, inventory levels, financial resources, and management training programs. Several possible data sources contain information about these measures, such as salespeople, customers, market research, business periodicals, trade associations, and economic statistics. Porter's model of competitive activity, presented in Working Concept 12, helps the manager understand competition and its strategic signals.

WORKING **12**
CONCEPT

PORTER'S
DETERMINANTS
OF
COMPETITION

Professor Michael Porter (1980) of the Harvard Business School has identified those factors that determine the level of competitive activity within an industry. These include (1) current level of competition, (2) relative power of suppliers and customers, (3) threat of entry from potential competitors, and (4) threat of substitute products. If customers are powerful, they may force price cutting within an industry. If substitute products or companies eager to enter an industry present strong threats, profits and prices within that industry will lower and competition will grow more intense.

Porter noted further that barriers to entry include (1) economies of scale; (2) product differentiation; (3) capital requirements; (4) cost disadvantages independent of size, such as a lack of experience; (5) access to distribution channels; and (6) government policy. These conditions change and they can be changed by the actions of those in the industry. Figure 5.3 summarizes Porter's concept. The strategic manager searches for signals about the likely future state of these five determinants of competition.

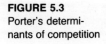

FIGURE 5.3
Porter's determinants of competition

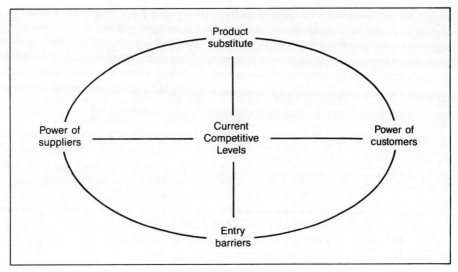

After understanding these factors that determine the level of competition, the strategist (1) positions the company in the best defensive posture, (2) influences competitive balance by strengthening the company, and (3) anticipates changes in the competitive balance and exploits these changes before competitors do. These three action plans all stem from identifying the company's crucial strengths and weaknesses.

EXAMPLES: *Competition*

Porter cited Dr. Pepper as an example of a company that strengthened its position by product differentiation, rather than by chasing after Pepsi and Coke. Polaroid, on the other hand, was vulnerable to attack (by Kodak) once its barrier to entry — its patents covering instant photography — expired.

Porter concluded that "the key to growth — even survival — is to stake out a position that is less vulnerable to attack [by competitors] . . . and less vulnerable to erosion from the direction of buyers, suppliers, and substitute goods."

In *Fortune* (4/29/85, pp. 153–166), Porter described how to attack the industry leader. Attacking the market leader requires (1) a competitive advantage in cost or in differentiation of the product, (2) an ability to counterbalance the leader's advantages, and (3) a barrier to retaliation that will keep the leader from a full-scale counterattack. Other competitive considerations include the stage of the economic cycle and the stage of maturity in the industry. More established industries, and industries within expansionary economic cycles, tend to be less competitive than younger industries and industries facing economic recessions. The greater the potential returns from economies of scale, the greater the competitive pressure.

Competition levels can also be affected by a change in top management. Jack Welch became chairman of General Electric in 1981; by 1985 he had purchased fifty businesses for G.E., including RCA. A saying circulated within G.E. that "if you put Jack in charge of a gas station at a corner with four gas stations, he wouldn't sleep until the other three guys had plywood over their windows'' (*Business Week*, 12/30/85, p. 49).

Technology Signals

Additional technology strategic signals that frequently are more significant than those in Table 5.3 are (1) the rate of technological innovation within the industry and (2) the relative degree of risk.

The smaller organization with a smaller research budget usually views an increase in the pace of technology as a negative sign. Similarly, a firm's exposure to the risk of technological innovation increases directly as its technology and product line become more narrow. The body of scientific knowledge and technology is said to be doubling every decade. Further, the time lag between laboratory development and product introduction has been reduced dramatically. How can the strategic manager forecast trends in technology given its exponential growth?

The strategic manager may be able to find objective measures of the amount of research being conducted in specific areas from industry or government sources. More subjective measures and opinions are becoming more available as interest in futurism — reflected in popular literature such as studies of ''megatrends'' — accelerates.

Those studying specific technological trends must include an analysis of Japan's research efforts. The Japanese Ministry of International Trade and Industry (MITI) has organized and funded groups of researchers from different Japanese companies to work on R&D projects in target industries such as microelectronics, biotechnology, satellites, and artificial intelligence. After groups of leading engineers and scientists perfect technology, the individual companies convert the pilot technology, or laboratory efforts, to commercial operation and full-blown production.

The strategic manager can identify ''precursor'' research projects — such as solar energy, oil shale, and space shuttles — that provide leading indicators of the direction of technological change. Especially important are robotics and other automatic control systems within the manufacturing process. The strategic manager can also call on experts on technological trends who consult with organizations and industries. One such expert is Paolo Soleri of the Arcosanti project in Arizona. Soleri identifies technological trends of increasing (1) complexity, (2) miniaturization, and (3) duration. These technological trends will accelerate the pace of high technology, which Soleri sees as a necessity for the benefit of this limited planet.

TABLE 5.3
Selected technology strategic signals

Category	Positive	Negative
Level of research	Increases	Decreases
Share of industry research	Increases	Decreases
Research of suppliers	Increases	Decreases
Research of substitute suppliers	Decreases	Increases
Public/government research	Increases	Decreases

WORKING CONCEPT **13**

TECHNO-LOGICAL INNOVATION

Technological innovation passes through three general phases: (1) research, (2) prototype testing, and (3) full-scale production.

RESEARCH

Research may consist of basic research, applied research, or a combination of both. Basic research concerns itself with general design concepts and scientific theories; but in applied research, these general design concepts and scientific theories are verified in a laboratory or some other controlled environment. In practice, it may be difficult to identify that point in technological innovation at which basic research becomes applied research.

PROTOTYPE TESTING

Prototype testing follows that phase of applied research that has verified the design or theory. It applies the design or theory in a full-scale trial, which may include commercial introduction. In other words, prototype testing takes place exclusively in the real world with real users and real customers, as opposed to applied research, which occurs in a controlled environment.

FULL-SCALE PRODUCTION

Full-scale production picks up where testing ends. The prototype tests have produced feedback on problems that need correcting or, in rare cases, on immediate acceptance in the marketplace. The project now goes into full production and is widely distributed to appropriate markets.

The strategic manager uses this model of technological innovation to track the progress of technological projects from the time they are possibilities — the research stage — to the time they become probable competitive threats. Harvey Brooks (1981) analyzed some of the forces that contribute to technological developments. His attempts to diagnose the trend of these forces follow:

1. *Economies of scale*: "There is some evidence that we may have come to the end of the road as far as the scale of individual technological embodiments are concerned."
2. *Centralization*: "The trend towards centralization in modern technology is less clear and less certain than is sometimes asserted" (Brooks cited as examples cable TV, transportation, and alternative energy sources).
3. *Standardization*: "Enterprises that transcend national boundaries" disseminate . . . standardization on a world scale.
4. *Labor versus energy and materials*: "Much more innovative effort in the future will be directed at saving resources and energy [versus the past emphasis on labor-saving]."

Brooks also considers (a) decreasing consumer sovereignty, in the face of the increasing complexity of products; and (b) environmental pollution.

Government Signals

Government strategic signals are limited as to their positivity or negativity (see Table 5.4) because that decision depends not only on one's personal philosophy about the role of government in business, but also upon specific circumstances. For example, Johnson & Johnson's strategic managers may have been opposed philosophically to government regulation of business. Nonetheless, after 1982, when seven people died from taking some Johnson & Johnson Tylenol capsules that had been criminally adulterated with cyanide, the company issued a call for federal

TABLE 5.4 Selected government strategic signals	Category	Positive	Negative
	Business/government communication	Increases	Decreases
	Quality of governmental executives regulating one company/industry	Increases	Decreases

government standards for tamper-proof packaging. Since Johnson & Johnson was an industry leader in profitability, the tamper-proof packaging standard meant cost increases for all companies in the industry. Johnson & Johnson ultimately had a relatively more profitable position than its competitors.

Government regulation of big business can create barriers of entry to potential competitors and weaken the relative strength of those competing with industry leaders. Also, regulation has created new industries. For example, legislation to improve water quality has created a large pollution control industry.

Government regulation was a benefit to Sprint, MCI, and other long-distance telephone companies. Before deregulation, these companies leased long-distance lines from AT&T at the Federal Communication Commission's discount rates of up to 70 percent, and then resold the lines to corporate and private telephone users. After the deregulation of AT&T, this discount rate disappeared; long-distance companies now have to compete with AT&T on equal terms.

Federal government insistence on the reduction of health care costs led to maximum allowances for medicare payments, resulting in a number of strategic responses. Private, for-profit hospital corporations turned to health insurance, clinics, and acquisitions for growth. Medical insurers such as Blue Cross of Michigan and hospitals such as Houston's Ben Toub pushed hard for generic drugs — cheaper but chemically equivalent versions of brand-name pharmaceuticals.

The critical issues now confronting the high-tech manufacturers venturing into laser applications in medicine are the responses of the government and doctors. On the regulation side, the Food and Drug Administration must first approve the use of lasers in each and every type of operation. On the professional side, the doctors performing the thirty million surgical operations each year must decide if they prefer the laser or the scalpel.

The Process of Government. Once a decision is reached on whether a certain government act is a positive or negative strategic signal, the strategic manager then must interpret the significance of the positive opportunity or negative threat in light of the governmental process. Figure 5.4 summarizes federal government action.

Government regulation (the output of the governmental process) may affect the firm in the following ways.

What can go in the product
How the product is made
Who makes the product

FIGURE 5.4
Governmental
process

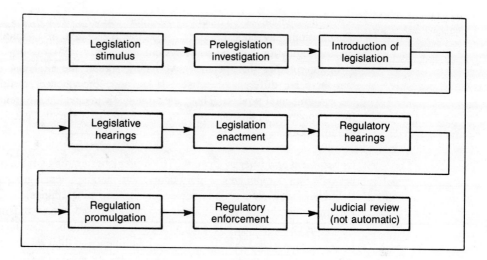

How much the product maker (and others) are paid

How the product is labeled

How the product is distributed

Who can (cannot) buy the product

How the product is priced

How the product is advertised

How the product purchase is financed

How financial results are reported

How financial results are taxed

How capital and debt are raised

How the work place is designed

How the firm affects the environment

How foreign competition affects the firm

Regardless of one's personal philosophy on regulation of business, one would conclude that the breadth of government regulation and the requirements for regulatory compliance are large. Some believe regulation is increasing.

As a specific government act moves from its stimulus stage through legislative hearings and into the regulatory stage — and possibly through the courts — the strategic manager must recognize that government reflects a process, not the desires of a "black box" or one specific interest group. An organization may choose to attempt to influence an important government act at the legislative phase by dealing with congressional representatives and their staff, or at the regulatory phase. The regulator's objectives may be substantially different from those of the legislator. Also, the actual impact of a government act on an organization can be influenced by the specific wording of the regulations (wherein the general legislative direction is converted into actual enforcement procedures and regulations). As a last resort, the organization may choose to challenge the legislation or its implementation (via specific regulations) in the court system.

In interpreting the specific government signal, the strategist must understand that there are different objectives, risks, and consequences at different stages of the governmental process. Thus, the strategist can develop different tactics, ranging from supportive and cooperative to hostile and adversarial, depending on the stage of the process.

Government and Interest Groups. The strategist examining government distinguishes between four components — politicians, bureaucrats, interest groups, and the media. Politicians seek election and reelection (among other things) by appealing to the maximum number of voters. Their appeals are based upon words and deeds, deeds including past assistance in transfering relative wealth between interest groups. Bureaucrats seek to increase the prestige and influence of their relative positions (among other things). They can accomplish this by taking actions and advocating programs that lead to more bureaucracy — more jobs and bigger budgets.

Interest groups naturally seek legislation in their own advantage. The larger the group, the less the per-member gain and the lower the per-member cost. Large groups tend to be relatively passive (except on significantly threatening issues). Small, concentrated interest groups often are most effective. An example is the lack of legislative results in Washington despite strong pockets of public support for gun control and prayer in the schools. With any one particular governmental issue, a strategic manager should assess not only an interest group's motivation (in connection with the issue), but should also consider how the issue affects the groups that are interested in the organization, including management, employees and unions, shareholders, creditors, suppliers, customers, competitors, communities, and governments. Are the interest groups allies, neutral observers, or adversaries?

The strategic manager also must recognize that public reality is what the media says it is. In the world of public reality, an event that is not covered by the media does not exist. In general, the more narrow, technical, or complex an issue, the less likely it is to exist as public reality.

The four components view of government can be extended, as in Working Concept 14.

| WORKING CONCEPT **14** STAKEHOLDER ANALYSIS | Stakeholder analysis focuses on the various parties — "stakeholders" — who have a stake in the outcome of an issue. For example, in an issue involving passage of an act to reduce foreign competition in a domestic industry, the stakeholders would include the following, along with companies facing similar situations for whom this issue might become a precedent. | Companies in the domestic industry
    employees
    managers
    shareholders
    creditors
Suppliers
Customers
Foreign competitors |

Stakeholder Analysis (continued)

Government employees
    diplomats
    economists
    trade and commerce
    congressional representative

Stakeholder analysis consists of (1) identifying the various stakeholders in an issue, (2) determining the cost-benefit impact on each stakeholder group from the alternative outcomes of the issue, (3) assessing the relative strength of each group, and (4) reaching conclusions as to the probable outcome.

MacMillan and Jones (1986) point out that the ideal is to manage all stakeholders over the long run, but that "few organizations have the resources required to manage all stakeholders during each and every strategic change." Therefore the firm must (1) identify stakeholders most affected by the strategic change, (2) develop political tactics to manage these stakeholders, or (3) modify the strategy if the stakeholder "cannot be managed." Understanding a policy's impact upon each stakeholder is essential, as is recognizing the different tactics required for internal versus external stakeholders. Competitors, for example, must be managed differently from employees or suppliers.

Chrysler's Lee Iacocca presented his view of the company's stakeholders in a speech in 1983, after Chrysler repaid the last of its government guaranteed loan:

What is often forgotten is the $2.2 billion that everybody else put up to keep the company together . . . all the guys who really had something at stake. So, our whole program was based on equality of sacrifice, because everybody offered up something — something important. First, we couldn't have made it without concessions from the members of the UAW. . . .

Next, our salary and management employees saw their numbers cut in half and those who stayed took cuts in pay and benefits. . . .

Next, our suppliers — all eleven thousand of them — rolled back prices, they bankrolled us by letting us pay them very slowly and even bought $75 million in debentures to provide us with capital. . . .

Next, our dealers really sacrificed — over 2,100 of them went out of business and the ones who survived lost lots of money for a couple of years running. But about four thousand of them are left — stronger than ever. . . .

Next, bankers helped save us during our darkest days, then supported our recapitalization program earlier this year. . . .

Then there were the state and local governments that helped us with loans and helped support our employees that were laid off. . . .

And then there is that unique institution, the Chrysler Guarantee Loan Board. . . .

Then there is one more big group [key members of the House and Senate], who had to stand up on the floor, and vote, and then convince the voters back home that they had done the right thing. . . .

And last, but maybe they should have been first, I want to thank the first one million people who bought our first million 'K' cars.

Social Signals   Looking for strategic signals that indicate changes in social values and expectations (see Table 5.5) is similar to looking for technology signals — it includes few objective and many subjective measures. In addition to economic data that indicate society's affluence, statistical data on population demographics and life styles, and specialized social studies, there are statistical measures of societal attitudes such as those on consumer attitudes published by the University of Michigan Division of Consumer Research. Many strategic managers follow the economic predictions of modelers such as the University of Pennsylvania Wharton group (national predictions) and the MIT Forester/Club of Rome analysis (global predictions).

TABLE 5.5
Selected social
strategic signals

Category	Positive	Negative
Consumer confidence	Increases	Decreases
Attitude toward business	Supportive	Antagonistic
Economic indicators	Increase	Decrease

Future Schlock. One substantial problem confronting the strategic manager is the reliability of these social projections. *The Christian Science Monitor* (6/7/84, p. 23) contrasted the Carter administration's "Global 2000" report showing a "more crowded, more polluted, less stable ecologically" world in which "people will be poorer," with the Simon and Kahn report presented at the 1983 American Association for the Advancement of Science, which concluded that the "world in 2000 will be less crowded, less polluted, more stable ecologically" with life "less precarious economically." *The Christian Science Monitor* concluded, "Beware the prophets of doom, and many other 'futurologists,' for that matter. Their projections of where the world is headed are often more a statement of political bias than a sound extrapolation of available data."

Some consultants and futurism experts provide subjective predictions of social trends; unfortunately for the strategic manager, this information is often contradictory. The full spectrum of predictions ranges from the pessimistic view of economists such as Veblen and Galbraith about the unending pressure for conspicuous consumption, to the optimism of New Age social scientists such as Ferguson who envision business executives leading the way to an Aquarian age of spirituality and higher consciousness.

One social commentator, Arcosanti's Paolo Soleri, looked to technology for predictions about society. By focusing on the technological trends of increasing complexity, miniaturization, and duration, Soleri (1983) suggested that the consequences of these trends would be (1) containment of habitat; (2) increasing ecological health of the city; (3) urbanization of marginal lands to preserve agricultural resources; (4) decrease in segregation of the individual; and (5) corresponding increase in an individual's participation in society, and thus in self-image and self-identification.

Prediction, Wishful Thinking, and Ideologies. The difficult aspect of the strategic manager's interpretation of social signals is in distinguishing between false prediction and fact, between wishful thinking and long-term trends. For example, in the early stages of the 1984 U.S. presidential campaign many believed a national industrial policy was imminent (including candidate Walter Mondale, who cited industrial policy as key to the election). National planning, however, turned out to excite voters and politicians much less than it did academicians and political consultants.

Political events are especially difficult to cite as trends of real societal shifts, not only due to the so-called "silent majority" but also due to the role of emotion and ideologies. Ideologies and views on emotional issues often are held by society only temporarily, as a way of screening out distressing (but real) information and reducing complexities to more manageable terms. Nonetheless, as our overview of basic fundamental values showed, societal values are characterized by change. Today's social values and expectations will inevitably evolve and change.

Consider the evolution of military thinking between the end of World War II and today. When the Cold War between the Soviet Union and the United States began, the dominant technological trend was toward high-tech superweapons and state-of-the-art, computer-based communication and control systems. The dominant Western ideology was that a global, unified Communist threat existed. The strategic conclusion based on this technology and ideology was a nuclear arms buildup and a minimization of conventional war capability.

Social scientists and military planners suggest that this strategic conclusion may well be in error. The unified conspiracy ideology has been questioned by differences and armed conflicts *between* Communist nations. Further, battlefield experience in Korea, Vietnam, Lebanon, and Iran suggests that military achievements are made more difficult by the delays and loss of impact due to circular communications between the field, the Pentagon, and the White House.

The strategist must periodically review social values in a systematic way for evidence of change. Change becomes strategic opportunity. Major league baseball is an industry that demonstrates the danger in not foreseeing the consequences of change. After a series of legal decisions in the 1970s made baseball players free agents, owners paid increasingly higher salaries to get top players. Between 1976 and 1984 the average player's salary increased seven times, from $51,000 to $329,000, while revenues increased only three times. Thirty-seven players made over $1 million in 1985; TV revenues have not saved the clubs. Two-thirds of the teams lost money; the teams as a whole have lost money since 1978 (*Fortune*, 4/15/85, pp. 17–21).

WORKING CONCEPT 15

THE PRECURSOR

One method of predicting social change is through the precursor society. Sweden is often cited as a precursor society for the United States, because its values and expectations provide a good indication of what American society will be like despite the differences between the Swedish and American experiences. (See Figure 5.5 for an illustration of the precursor concept.) The validity of Sweden as an indicator has just been reaffirmed by the crackdown on drunken driving in the United States, which occurred some three to five years after the same legislation passed in Sweden. Social scientists now are analyzing social trends in Sweden that include (1) a large percentage (40 percent) of public housing; (2) a large percentage (70 percent) of working women, resulting in changing attitudes toward women, most notably a low level of physical abuse; (3) low hospitalization costs achieved through a system similar to American Health Maintenance Organizations; (4) fully paid child-care leave (six months) for either parent; (5) procedures for worker ownership of part of the equity of businesses; (6) equal pay for equal work not only between sexes in one company but among all companies for the same job, as Swedish unions argue for wage levels by job function; and (7) formal organization of economic interest groups across society, such as landlords' unions as well as tenants' unions.

FIGURE 5.5
The precursor
society

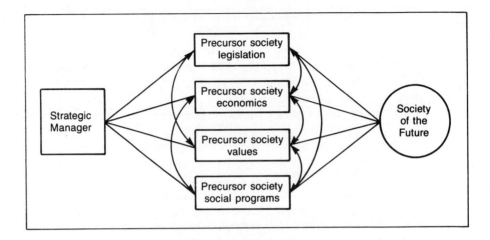

After completing an analysis of the external environment, the strategic manager prepares a summary of findings listing the positive signals that represent external opportunities and the negative signals that represent external threats. These forecasts represent only the beginning of the managerial process. Next comes strategic decision making and action; as the Noah Principle states, ''Predicting rain doesn't count; building arks does.''

Many observers of business (including the authors) have concluded that the more an organization engages in an analysis of the external environment, the more successful it will be. The more this analysis is a continuous process, the better it will be. Though this analysis (especially interpreting strategic signals and forecasting the consequences of those signals) is difficult and often lacks direction, the strategic manager knows what to look for, why to look for it, and what to do with the results. Perfect knowledge is impossible; the strategic manager seeks not to produce certainty but rather to reduce uncertainty.

Figure 5.6 shows the relationship between the firm and the external environment. One of the strategic manager's objectives is to move the firm to the right along this environment dependence spectrum. If the firm has sufficient resources and capabilities, the strategist may seek to shape and influence the environment, often through technology. On the other hand, a firm with limited resources and capability might have to adjust to the role of reacting to the environment.

Summarizing
Strategic
Signals — A
Swiss Example

In 1970 Hoffman-LaRoche, the Swiss pharmaceutical company, was the largest pharmaceutical manufacturer in the world. Its sales in 1970 were $840 million, compared with $670 million for Merck, the leading U.S. company. Hoffman-LaRoche had over thirty thousand employees, forty-two pharmaceutical plants, and two holding companies. F. Hoffman-LaRoche, a subsidiary in Basle, Switzerland, was responsible for Continental European, North African, and Middle Eastern business operations. SAPAC, a Canadian corporation headquartered in Uruguay, was responsible for

FIGURE 5.6
Environment
dependence
spectrum

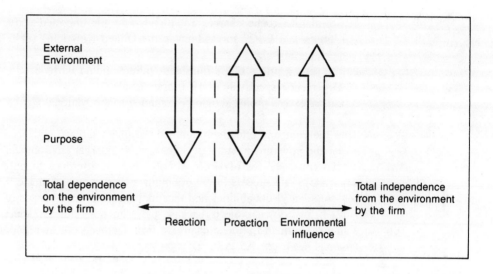

operations in all English-speaking countries, Asia, and South America. Two tranquilizers, Librium and Valium, represented almost three-fourths of company sales.

A summary of strategic signals regarding the firm's environment in 1970 might have included the following signals.

Positive Signals
    Expanding use (total customers; per customer)
    Strong competitive position (patent barriers to entry; little industry price competition; price small factor in purchase decision)
    Profitability (high margin products)
Negative Signals
    High technological risk (narrow product line)
    High level of regulation
    Adversarial social attitude (all health care costs; pharmaceutical industry)

Hoffman-LaRoche's strategic response to the external environment threats were effective with regard to technological risk. The company invested large sums in ongoing research in such areas as cancer and heart disease. Nonetheless, the company followed a less-than-effective strategy in the area of social values and government; its relatively passive strategies were inappropriate in view of emotional public attitudes about pharmaceuticals and in view of the highly regulated nature of the industry. Within a few years the company was under pressure to justify Librium and Valium prices in Australia, Canada, Germany, Holland, Sweden, and the United States. Further, the Monopolies Committee in England reported the following findings and recommendations to Parliament in 1973.

1. Hoffman-LaRoche charges £ 370 per kilo for imported active ingredients for Librium and £ 922 for Valium in the United Kingdom, yet £ 38 and £ 20 for the same in Italy.
2. The selling prices of Librium and Valium should be reduced to 40 percent and 25 percent respectively of 1970 price levels.
3. Earlier excess profits should be refunded to the National Health Service.

Thus the company effectively ignored the major threats evidenced by the negative social and government strategic signals in its external environment.

The consequences of Hoffman-LaRoche's indifference to public opinion were worsened by its success in the tranquilizer market, which made it (1) grow overly self-confident of its abilities and thus indifferent to the demands of the marketplace and (2) turn down projects because they did not offer the superstar potential of Valium. Hoffman-LaRoche chairman Fritz Gerber said, as reported by the *Boston Globe* (7/1/84, pp. A5–A7):

> *There was an arrogance with the success. LaRoche was taken by surprise and was not ready for it. This might have created some kind of over-built self-confidence. The company isolated itself, it became more conservative and probably quite litigious. . . .*
>
> *Once you have a best-seller that sells one million copies, a second book that sells ten thousand copies gets you no applause. Valium created a level of research expectation that was so high, we had a blank for new products.*

Between the mid-1970s and the mid-1980s, profits dropped from 16 percent to 4 percent, and the company fell from first to ninth place in total sales within the industry.

STRATEGY RESEARCH AND THE EXTERNAL ENVIRONMENT

Classic research studies of the external environment include those of Aguilar, Chandler, Emery and Trist, Klein, Penrose, and Porter.

Aguilar, in *Scanning the Business Environment* (1967), analyzed the environmental study patterns of 137 managers in forty-one companies. He concluded that different kinds of scanning — indirect viewing, conditioned viewing, informal, and formal — were appropriate in specific situations. He discovered that firms made few environmental study efforts because managers relied primarily on oral and personal contacts for data (although this varied significantly according to firm size and organizational level). In reaction to this, Aguilar urged strategic managers to establish procedures to ensure the timely identification of environmental change.

Chandler analyzed the relationship between the external environment and strategy in *Strategy and Structure: Chapters in the History of the American Industrial Enterprise* (1962). Studying in depth the histories of Sears, du Pont, General Motors, and Standard Oil of New Jersey, Chandler suggested that change in demand in a firm's market was the principal stimulus for change. Strategy was primarily determined by market and population trends in these case studies, which dated from the 1920s and 1930s.

Emery and Trist (1965) studied "The Causal Texture of Organizational Environments." They identified four causal textures: (1) a placid (stable, unchanging), randomized (randomly distributed resources) environment, in which strategy should be to perform at top standard; (2) a placid, clustered (concentrated resources) environment, in which strategy should be based on location to gain access to concentrated resources; (3) a disturbed environment, in which competitive power is a key focus of strategy; and (4) a turbulent environment, which requires a dynamic strategy that includes constant monitoring of opportunities and threats and developing appropriate response.

Klein, in a dissertation at Columbia entitled "Incorporating Environmental Examination into the Corporate Strategic Planning Process," (1973) showed how the external environment affected an oil company through the following three factors.

Government
  regulation of oil industry
  legislation regarding safety, environment
Technology
  energy research
  pollution control
  advances in materials, electronics
Competition
  product strategy
  location strategy
  investment strategy

Penrose provided insight into strategic opportunities in the external environment by means of her discussion of interstices in *The Theory of the Growth of the Firm* (1968). She concluded that growth is possible because of *interstices*, or spaces, between product markets. Interstices are caused either because large firms do not or cannot exploit them, because managers seek not profit maximization but rather absolute dollar profit levels, which causes managerial inefficiency (managerial slack). Or, interstices are caused because of macroeconomic growth attributable to population increases, technology advances, and productivity improvements.

Porter asserted in *Competitive Strategy* (1980) that a firm's study of the external environment usually is centered on the acts of competitors. Profits and the level of competition within an industry are determined by (1) current competition, (2) relative power of suppliers, (3) relative power of customers, (4) threat of substitutes, and (5) threat of new firms. The strategist should analyze the current state of, and the likely future trend in, these five factors.

Additional research in the external environment includes studies by the following authors.

Aharoni (1966), in studying the foreign investments of thirty-eight U.S. companies, concluded that

1. A strong force is necessary to trigger an organization into a new path of studying the external environment.
2. Such external studies are designed and carried out in a step-by-step process, so that negative conclusions after each step will terminate the study.

Cooper, DeMuzzio, Hatten, Hicks, and Tock (1974) studied firms responding to new product technology, and found that

1. The first introduction of the new product was often made by a firm outside the industry.
2. The old firms tried, many unsuccessfully, to participate in both the old and new technologies.
3. Those old firms with small market share were particularly unsuccessful with the new technology.

Coplin and O'Leary (1985) studied eighty-two countries to assess the risk levels for international business. They rated the countries in terms of the probability of political and social turmoil (China and Japan, low; Jamaica and Poland, moderate; Iraq and South Africa; high) and assigned "grades" for financial risk, investment risk, and exporting risk.

Dess and Davis (1984) studied Porter's generic strategies, such as low-cost producer and market niche. They measured two factors — strategic group measurement and organizational performance — to test the predictive capabilities of these "generic strategies as determinants of strategic group membership and organizational performance."

Diffenbach (1983) listed seven advantages of "corporate environmental analysis in larger U.S. corporations," including

1. Increased management awareness of changes
2. Better strategic planning and decision making
3. Greater effectiveness in government matters
4. Better industry and market analyses
5. Better results in foreign businesses
6. Improvements in diversification and resource allocation
7. Better energy planning

Notwithstanding these advantages, environmental analysis still must overcome difficulties of interpretation, inaccuracy, misperception, and short-term orientation, as well as the complex environments of diversified companies.

Fahey and Narayanan (1986) distinguished between (1) the at-hand task environment (customers, suppliers), (2) the industry environment, and (3) the broad macroenvironment. These experts urged a four-step process: (1) identify general signals of change, (2) monitor specific trends and patterns, (3) forecast future changes, and (4) assess the organizational implications of these environmental changes. Each step should interact with another in a dynamic process.

Gold (1983) reviewed empirical and theoretical studies of technology in U.S. industries. Gold pointed out that strategists must recognize technology not just in production machinery, but in (1) technical personnel's expertise, (2) production system structure and operation, (3) change limits of product design and mix, (4) labor organization and skills, and (5) new capital goods.

Leemhuis (1985), Shell's manager of corporate planning, described the use of scenarios to develop strategies. Scenarios, or "descriptions of a possible future [of evolving] social, political, economic, and technical developments," were used to reduce uncertainty in Shell's strategic decision making. Leemhuis urged using scenarios as part of informal, flexible planning. This proposal contrasts with the formal planning found in large companies like Shell "with heavy reporting requirements and bureaucratic overloads."

Leidecker and Bruno (1984) studied critical success factors (CSFs) in environmental analysis. They concluded that the starting points for identifying critical factors should be (1) major business activity, (2) large dollar amounts involved, (3) major profit impact, and (4) major changes in performance.

McNamee (1984) studied three types of matrices to determine their effectiveness in displaying competitive analysis. McNamee concluded that strategic managers will be aided by matrix displays of competitive analysis in an approach "complementary to the Product Market Portfolio."

Steele (1983) listed four common strategic errors regarding technology. First, firms fail to accept "good enough" technology and seek only the best possible technology; cutting-edge technology doesn't necessarily lead to economic success. Second, some firms assume that the majority of innovations are successful; many are not. Third, firms overlook extensions of current technology and seek revolutionary advances rather than evolutionary, economically feasible ones. Finally, top management must direct and control the technology effort in order to have a productive scientific resource.

Stubbart (1982) researched formal environmental scanning systems in three empirical studies. Stubbart concluded that he was "reluctant to encourage top managers of diversified firms to establish corporate level environmental scanning units." He found that organizations concentrate on "industry analysis" and not on "general environmental scanning," and are thus too narrow in scope.

Utterback and Abernathy (1974) studied technological innovations and the stage of corporate development in 120 firms that witnessed 567 successful innovations. The researchers found that

1. Innovation as a strategy was most important to Stage I entrepreneurial firms.
2. Stage I entrepreneurial firms introduced "original" innovations; Stage III divisionalized firms innovated through imitations and adoptions from suppliers.

EXECUTIVE COMMENTS

The basic strategy for corporate survival is to anticipate the changing expectations of society, and serve them more effectively than competing institutions. This means that the corporation itself must change, consciously evolving into an institution adapted to the new environment.

R. H. Jones, chairman of General Electric, 11/25/74.

You can observe a lot by just watching.

Yogi Berra

KEY TERMS

competition (page 96)

government (page 97)

identification of strategic signals (page 101)

interpretation of strategic signals (page 101)

markets (page 93)

society (page 97)

strategic signals (page 101)

technology (page 96)

BIBLIOGRAPHY

Abell, D., *Defining the Business: The Starting Point of Strategic Planning* (Englewood Cliffs, NJ: Prentice-Hall, 1980).

Abernathy, W., K. Clark, and A. Kantrow. "The New Industrial Competition," *Harvard Business Review* (September-October 1981), pp. 168–181.

Aguilar, F. J., *Scanning the Business Environment* (New York: MacMillan, 1967).

Aharoni, Y., "The Foreign Investment Decision Process," Division of Research, Harvard Business School, 1966.

Becker, L. C., *Property Rights: Philosophic Foundations* (London: Routledge & Kegan Paul, 1977).

Boulton, W., et al., "Strategic Planning: Determining the Impact of Environmental Characteristics and Uncertainty," *Academy of Management Journal,* (September 1982).

Bright, J. R., "Evaluating Signals of Technological Change," *Harvard Business Review* (January-February 1970).

Brooks, H., "Technology, Evolution and Purpose," in A. Teich, ed., *Technology and Man's Future* (New York: St. Martin's Press, 1981).

Chandler, A. D., *Strategy and Structure: Chapters in the History of American Industrial Enterprise* (Cambridge, MA: MIT Press, 1962).

Cooper, A. C., E. DeMuzzio, K. Hatten, E. J. Hicks, and D. Tock, "Strategic Responses to Technological Threats," *Academy of Management Proceedings* (Boston, 1974).

Coplin, W., and M. O'Leary, "The 1985 Political Climate for International Business," *Planning Review* (May 1985), pp. 36–43.

Dess, G. G., and P. S. Davis, "Porter's (1980) Generic Strategies as Determinants of Strategic Group Membership and Organizational Performance," *Academy of Management Journal* 27 (September 1984), pp. 467–488.

Diffenbach, J., "Corporate Environmental Analysis in Large U.S. Corporations," *Long Range Planning* 16 (June 1983), pp. 107–116.

Drucker, P., *Management: Tasks, Responsibilities, and Practices* (New York: Harper & Row, 1974).

Edmunds, S., "The Role of Future Studies in Business Strategic Planning," *Journal of Business Strategy* (Fall 1982).

Emery, F., and E. Trist, "The Causal Textures of Organizational Environments," *Human Relations* (August 1965), pp. 124–151.

Fahey, L., and V. K. Narayanan, *Macroenvironmental Analysis for Strategic Management* (St. Paul, MN: West Publishing, 1986).

Ferguson, M., *The Aquarian Conspiracy: Personal and Social Transformation in the 1980s* (Los Angeles: J. P. Tarcher, 1980).

Galbraith, J. K., *The New Industrial State* (Boston: Houghton-Mifflin, 1967).

Gold, B., "Strengthening Managerial Approaches to Improving Technical Capabilities," *Strategic Management Journal* 4 (October-December 1983), pp. 209–220.

Halle, D., *America's Working Man* (Chicago: University of Chicago Press, 1985).

Heilbroner, R., "Does Capitalism Have a Future?" *New York Times Magazine* (August 15, 1982).

Kantrow, A., "The Strategy-Technology Connection," *Harvard Business Review* (July-August 1980), pp. 6–21.

Klein, H. E., *Incorporating Environmental Examination into the Corporate Strategic Planning Process*, Dissertations, Columbia University, 1973.

Klein, H., and R. Linneman, "The Use of Scenarios in Corporate Planning — Eight Case Histories," *Long Range Planning* 14 (October 1981).

Kotler, P., *Marketing Management: Analysis, Planning, and Control* (Englewood Cliffs, NJ: Prentice-Hall, 1980).

Lebell, D., and O. J. Krasler, "Selecting Environmental Forecasting Techniques for Business Planning Requirements," *Academy of Management Review* (July 1977).

Leemhuis, J. P., "Using Scenarios to Develop Strategies," *Long Range Planning* 18 (April 1985), pp. 30–37.

Leidecker, J. K., and A. V. Bruno, "Identifying and Using Critical Success Factors," *Long Range Planning* 17 (February 1984), pp. 23–32.

McCormick, R. E., and R. D. Tollison, *Politicians, Legislation and the Economy: An Inquiry into the Interest Group Theory of Government* (Boston: Martins-Nijhoff, 1981).

MacMillan, I. C., and P. E. Jones, *Strategy Formulation: Power and Politics*, 2nd ed. (St. Paul, MN: West Publishing, 1986).

McNamee, P., "Competitive Analysis Using Matrix Displays," *Long Range Planning* 17 (June 1984), pp. 98–114.

Meadows, D. H., et al., *The Limits to Growth: A Report for the Club of Rome's Project on the Predicament of Mankind* (New York: Universe Books, 1972).

Miles, R., *Coffin Nails and Corporate Strategies* (Englewood Cliffs, NJ: Prentice-Hall, 1982).

Moore, W. L., and M. L. Tushman, "Managing Innovation over the Product Life Cycle," in M. L. Tushman and W. L. Moore, eds., *Readings in the Management of Innovation* (Boston: Pitman, 1982).

Penrose, E., *The Theory of the Growth of the Firm* (Oxford, England: Blackwell, 1968).

Porter, M. E., *Competitive Strategy* (New York: Free Press, 1980).

Porter, M. E., "The Contributions of Industrial Organization to Strategic Management," *Academy of Management Review*, vol. 6, no. 4 (1981), pp. 609–620.

Porter, M. E., "How Competitive Forces Shape Strategy," *Harvard Business Review* (March-April 1979), pp. 137–145.

Soleri, P., "Excerpts from Arcosanti: An Urban Laboratory," *ReVision* (Fall 1983).

Steele, L., "Manager's Misconceptions About Technology," *Harvard Business Review* (November-December 1983), p. 133.

Stubbart, C., "Are Environmental Scanning Units Effective?" *Long Range Planning* 15 (June 1982), pp. 139–145.

Ulrich, D., and J. Barney, "Perspectives in Organization: Resource Dependence, Efficiency, and Population," *Academy of Management Review*, vol. 9, no. 3 (July 1984).

Utterback, J. M., and W. J. Abernathy, "A Test of a Conceptual Model Linking States in Firms' Process and Product Innovation," Harvard Business School Working Paper 74–23, Boston, 1974.

Veblen, T., *The Theory of the Leisure Class*: *An Economic Study of Institutions* (New York: Viking Press, 1899).

Wheelwright, S., and S. Makrodakis, *Forecasting Methods for Management* (New York: Wiley, 1980).

Zentner, R., "How to Evaluate the Present and Future Corporate Environment," *Journal of Business Strategy* (Spring 1981).

APPENDIX: THE INTERNATIONAL BUSINESS ENVIRONMENT

International businesses, or multinational firms, are those in which the strategist makes decisions and seeks opportunities from a worldwide viewpoint. What the U.S. multinational companies do explains what the U.S. business economy does. The multinational companies in the *Fortune* 500 account for approximately two-thirds of the output and employment and three-fourths of the profits of U.S. business.

The complexity of its external environment distinguishes the multinational corporation from other firms. In analyzing the external environment and looking for positive signals of strategic opportunities and negative signals of strategic threats, the multinational's strategic manager studies environments that may differ in important ways from those of the home country. These critical differences increase as the strategist moves further and further away from the North American, industrialized-nation experience into countries whose economic systems, infrastructures, and ethical and philosophical traditions are unfamiliar.

The multinational's strategic manager faces complexities that may include

Markets
    significantly earlier life cycle stages
    limited avenues of product promotion and advertising
    reduced consumer expectations (Western necessities versus Third World luxuries)

    lower service levels

    little or no consumer credit

    few distribution options

    less price flexibility

Competition

    new ways of competing due to different business ethics, practices

    limited competition

Technology

    lagging technical capabilities

    technology transfer pressures and opportunities

Government

    regional economic associations (i.e., European Economic Community)

    increased government role, often through unions

    currency controls and exposures

    international political situation

Society

    little data on trends

    different rates of change and growth

    different attitudes toward materialism

    great divergence of personal values of host country managers and organizational
        priorities

HOST COUNTRY POWER

The position of the host government is of special concern to the strategic manager. The relative strength and influence of the government and the multinational depend on the contributions of each. The multinational may contribute investment capital, potential exports that will earn currencies, products, and technology. The host country may be a source of scarce resources, new markets, and a labor supply. The multinational strategist must understand the relative contributions of the corporation and the host government.

    The strategic trend of the relationship between the multinational and the host country favors the host country as more multinationals offer more technology and investment opportunities. The continuing labor cost gap between nations, the greater number of multinational companies and "superpowers," and the increasing scarcity of some resources (e.g., bauxite, uranium, and molybdenum) also boost the relative power of the host country.

    Consider the significance of Japanese automobile manufacturers building manufacturing and assembly plants in Brazil or China rather than in the United States or Canada. The government of Brazil, facing high external debt and a dependency on imported oil, naturally will be more cooperative than the U.S. government that is faced with the protectionist demands of U.S. automobile producers.

As the host country power grows, the host country probably will reduce investment incentives, increase performance requirements, or both. Investment incentives include such acts as tax holidays, credit to subsidiary companies, and even outright cash grants. Frequently encountered performance requirements are local content (a percentage of the product must be produced within the host country), local equity (Mexico has required Mexican ownership of 51 percent of the equity of "foreign" corporations), export percentage requirements, and limits on local currency borrowings. Some of these performance requirements may be exactly what the multinational corporation would do anyway, such as local content requirements when the corporation is seeking scarce local resources.

MULTINATIONAL STRATEGY AND HOST COUNTRY POWER

The activities of Anaconda, ITT, and Kennecott in Chile illustrate the changing relationship of host country and the multinational.

Political Background

Chile, as did many other developing nations after World War II, experienced substantially growing economic nationalism during the 1950s and 1960s. A concurrent trend was an increase in social demands and expectations. With the social changes came the emergence of socialist and communist groups, who were met by the subsequent alliance of the liberals and conservatives.

The Communist party was outlawed in 1947, although the Communists had three elected cabinet ministers in the government in 1946. Communists were stricken from the electoral roles as the government in power moved toward the right, partially in order to obtain aid and development capital from the United States. During that period the Chilean conservatives held themselves out as the saviors of "Western Christian civilization"; the liberals, in announcing the outlawing of the Communist party and the expelling of the Communist ministers, said that those ministers "were instruments of a worldwide plan to deprive the United States of primary materials in the event of war."

In the 1958 election the conservative Alessandri received 32 percent of the vote, the radical Allende 29 percent, and the liberal Frei 21 percent. Frei threw his support to Alessandri, and in 1964 Frei, running as the combined conservative and liberal candidate, received 56 percent of the vote. In 1970, however, the radical Allende received 36 percent, higher than either the conservative Alessandri or the liberal (Christian Democrat) Tomic, Frei's successor. The final choice was then up to the Chilean Congress.

Exhibit 1 details some of the World Bank statistical estimates of Chile and selected neighboring "middle income developing nations."

The Copper Industry

The international copper industry is oligopolistic at the mining stage, and only slightly less so at the processing (smelting and refining) and fabricating stages. The major U.S. copper producers (Anaconda, Kennecott, and Phelps Dodge) account

EXHIBIT 1
World Bank
statistics

	Argentina	Chile	Peru	Venezuela
Population	25,700,000	10,500,000	15,800,000	12,500,000
Area (sq. kms.)	2,767,000	757,000	1,285,000	912,000
GNP per capita (U.S. $, mid-1970s)	$1,550	$1,050	$800	$2,570
GDP growth 1960–1970	4.2%	4.2%	5.4%	5.9%
Percentage GDP in industry 1960–1970	38%	38%	29%	22%
Population growth 1960–1970				
total	1.4	2.1	2.9	3.4
urban	2.3	3.7	4.3	4.9

for about 70 percent of domestic U.S. production. The other major global producers include the Roan-American Metals group, the Anglo-American group Union Miniere, and International Nickel.

There has been an increasing trend toward dilution of this oligopolistic concentration, due to new copper finds in Africa, Canada, and the South Pacific, and to backwards integration by the fabricators. Also, aluminum as a substitute for copper creates a constantly increasing threat to the industry.

Chilean copper has represented 15 to 20 percent of the total world copper production since World War II. In Chile, Anaconda operated the world's largest open-pit copper mine, Chuquicamata, which it purchased in 1923. Its annual output was over 200,000 metric tons. In Chile, Kennecott operated the world's largest underground copper mine, El Teniente, with an annual output of 150,000 metric tons. Kennecott had purchased El Teniente from the Guggenheims in 1915. Copper was and is an important resource to Chile. Kennecott and Anaconda copper production recently has represented between 7 and 20 percent of Chile's gross domestic product. Tax revenues paid by these two companies have represented between 10 and 40 percent of government expenditures; copper exports have represented between 30 and 80 percent of hard currency earnings. Exhibit 2 provides further measures of the relationship between Anaconda, Kennecott, and Chile.

The post–World War II Chilean government's position on copper mining has been that the foreign companies should (1) expand local employment and purchases, (2) refine more in Chile instead of the normal practice of refining in the United States, (3) develop more Chilean managers and copper technicians, and (4) raise prices. The government created a copper department in the 1950s (*Departmento del Cobre*), staffed with business, engineering, and legal personnel.

The push for higher prices often was resisted by the multinational companies, due to the system of "producer's prices." Producer's prices represented an attempt by copper miners and fabricators to remove uncertainty and fluctuation from copper prices. Basically, these producer prices were price and volume contracts between miners and fabricators; on the surface they were annual contracts, but they contained clauses (evergreen provisions) for perpetual renewal. The vast majority of copper tonnage was controlled by these contracts; only a small volume of copper moved

EXHIBIT 2
Anaconda and
Kennecott in Chile

	1945–1955	1955–1965	
Anaconda, Kennecott profits	$275,000,000	$465,000,000	
Chile direct taxes	$328,000,000	$909,000,000	
Investment			
Anaconda	$137,000,000	$212,000,000	
Kennecott	13,000,000	40,000,000	
total investment	$150,000,000	$252,000,000	
		Chile operation	Total global operations
Pretax income per sales $			
Anaconda		47¢	23¢
Kennecott		59¢	34¢
Return on assets			
Anaconda		11.5%	5%
Kennecott		29.5%	10.5%

Note: All amounts in U.S. dollars.

through the open markets of the New York Commodity Exchange and the London Metals Exchange. In essence, this system of producer prices meant that the miner would give up "windfall" profits in periods of higher demand in exchange for "normal" profits in periods of lower demand. To a Chilean government official, the producer price looked artificially low when the copper exchange markets enjoyed high prices in periods of increasing demand.

Chile felt especially exploited when the United States tried to freeze copper prices during the Korean War. Chile insisted that the frozen producer price arrangements be set aside and that Chilean copper be sold through open copper markets. Another U.S.-related historical event that resulted in increased economic nationalism within Chile was the Kennedy-inspired Alliance for Progress. Chilean conservatives responded most unfavorably to the Alliance's call for rapid advances in land reform.

By the mid-1960s Anaconda's Chilean mines produced one-half of total company production and about two-thirds of total company earnings. Anaconda's upper management had moved to the top along a path that included management responsibilities in Chile. For Kennecott, the reverse was true. El Teniente produced less than one-third of total production and less than one-eighth of total earnings.

Between 1930 and 1965, Anaconda had a net capital investment in Chile of approximately $100 million; Kennecott had a net capital disinvestment of $5 million. After World War II, Kennecott undertook no exploration or development projects; Anaconda opened two new mines and built a large plant.

Theodore Moran summarized the situation facing the copper companies, confronted by the slogan "El Cobre es Chileno," in his book *Copper in Chile: Multinational Corporations and the Politics of Dependence* (Princeton University Press, 1974):

Between 1945 and 1970 the Chileans closed in on the foreign-dominated copper industry in their country . . . [this period saw] the interaction of two systems — a system of multinational copper companies operating under unstable conditions of imperfect competition, and a system of domestic interest groups in Chile trying to respond to rising demands for national development and national welfare — both struggling to take advantage of each other and reduce each other to manageable proportions.

MULTINATIONALS AND STRATEGIC MANAGERS

ITT in Chile

Following a decade of growth through diversification and acquisition, ITT in 1970 was one of the biggest multinational corporations in the world. With worldwide sales of $7 billion, it was among the ten largest U.S. multinationals; like other U.S. firms, it faced the threat of expropriation by developing nations. In September 1970, ITT's chairman and chief executive officer, Harold S. Geneen, faced the threat of nationalization of ITT's Chilean telephone system by the government of Salvador Allende.

Geneen was born in England in 1910 to a Russian father, a director of tourist concerts, and an English mother, a light-opera singer. His parents emigrated to the United States; because of their early separation, Geneen spent his youth in boarding schools and camps. His father went bankrupt in the 1926 Florida land bust. Leaving school at age sixteen, Geneen worked at the stock exchange as a page, witnessing the great crash of 1929. While taking classes in accounting at New York University, he worked with the accounting firm of Lybrand, Ross and Montgomery. His special aptitude with figures led him to executive positions at Bell & Howell, Jones and Laughlin, and Raytheon. Twice married, most recently to his ex-secretary at Bell & Howell, Geneen is childless but, as one observer noted, "his life is his company." In ITT's 1967 Annual Report Geneen described management as "a philosophy of aggressive *anticipation* of goals and problems and of effective advanced counteractions to insure our attainment of final objectives."

Pessimistic about long-term international opportunities, Geneen undertook a series of acquisitions in the U.S.. including Sheraton Hotels, Continental Banking, Avis, Levitt Homebuilders, and the Hartford Life Insurance Company. ITT's management system was based on careful review of business plans and budgetary controls. Internationally, the company developed governmental connections by various means; Latin American critics frequently accused ITT of bribery. ITT had 400,000 employees worldwide and 200,000 stockholders. In 1970 only three of the three thousand ITT executives were women.

In his book *Managing* Geneen describes a typical work day of ten to twelve hours, filled with staff meetings: "The only way I knew how to judge people at ITT was by the test of performance." In this atmosphere of applied pressure, insiders joked that one characteristic of ITT executives was insomnia. During a prolonged staff meeting, the overhead lights began to flicker. "Hal, even the lights are getting tired," one executive commented to Geneen. He replied, "Only the lesser lights."

By 1970 ITT had gained twenty-five years of experience in expropriation. Its subsidiary in Cuba was nationalized by Castro without compensation. Peron had compensated ITT for its Argentine subsidiary, nationalized in 1946. Peru's compensation of $18 million was tied to a reinvestment in Peru of $8 million, which was done through a Sheraton hotel in Lima. Brazil had paid ITT $20 million for the Brazilian operating company during the mid-1960s. By 1970, ITT operated telephone systems in Puerto Rico, Chile, and the Virgin Islands. ITT Chile employed six thousand workers and was valued by ITT at $150 million. The terms of the concession included payment to ITT in gold.

Anaconda in Chile

In 1969 Anaconda's stock had a market value of $1.4 billion. Its leadership had been through a series of three similar personalities — Clyde Weide, Charles Brinckerhoff, and Jay Parkinson. An industry observer commented that these three were "so bedazzled by the huge returns Chile yielded that they were blinded to the hazards of rising nationalism."

In 1969, a year in which 75 percent of Anaconda's profits were from Chile, Chairman Brinckerhoff said, "You can be absolutely certain that we have never considered for a moment that we couldn't live without the Chileans." Brinckerhoff's successor, Jay Parkinson, presented a company goal that he called "a five-hundred-year plan." Anaconda's managerial style was described by industry observers in *Forbes* (1/15/72) as

> a patrician stance and an attitude of affluence that is its corporate style of life . . . in true 19th century fashion, Anaconda runs its worldwide enterprises out of its richly paneled offices on the fringe of Wall Street, [complete with] male secretaries and uniformed attendants.

The Anaconda board of ten directors had four outside members, but "the real power was vested in an executive committee composed exclusively of company executives."

Anaconda faced the Chilean crisis from an almost colonialist, old-fashioned, narrow perspective. The leadership never thought of contingencies or change, but planned for a "constant" five hundred years.

Kennecott in Chile

Kennecott earned 11 percent of its 1969 profits from Chile. Its president was fifty-eight-year-old Frank Milliken, a tough-minded mining engineer. An industry spokesperson observed that Frank Milliken and Kennecott management "[do not] shy away from knockdown, drag-out fights with the government. Frank Milliken fought for years a federal order to divest Kennecott's wire and cable subsidiary . . . [Milliken] . . . recognized a full decade ago that the loss of the Chilean properties could only be postponed, not averted."

Kennecott's diversification activities had not been successful under Milliken. A 1950s excursion into South African gold resulted in a $36 million write-off in 1960; and a molybdenum mine in British Columbia was written off in 1970 for $23 million.

MULTINATIONAL STRATEGIES

The differences between the strategic managers Geneen, Parkinson, and Milliken and the relative economic power of Chile versus the companies naturally led to differences in company strategy. ITT's strategy was forceful and aggressive, if less than ethical. Anaconda was passive, or reactive, and relied on moral codes of conduct. These codes were inappropriate in the face of Chile's increased power, which grew due to Chile's increased technological knowledge and Anaconda's loss of power following its committed investment. Kennecott's strategy was active, tying Chile to a series of contracts that gave Kennecott 49 percent of a $300 million book value company versus 100 percent of a $70 million book value company. Kennecott made all the contractual relationships binding under New York law, and made allies of the U.S. government and Japanese and Italian interests.

ITT's Actions in Chile

In 1964 Frei, a Christian Democrat, was elected president of Chile. ITT had offered to provide campaign funds to Frei through CIA director John McCone. In 1965 McCone became a director of ITT, while continuing to serve as a secret consultant to the CIA.

In the September 1970 election, the Marxist-Socialist Salvador Allende received 36 percent of the vote, more than his rightist and Christian Democrat rivals, Alessandri and Tomic. Without an absolute majority, the choice of president was to be made by the Chilean congress seven weeks after the election. Geneen and others were convinced expropriation would follow an Allende victory.

As a congressional committee investigating multinationals in the 1970s disclosed, ITT and Geneen took the following steps prior to and after the election.

1. In July 1970 Geneen offered William Broe, the CIA's head of clandestine services for Latin America, "a substantial amount" for the campaign fund of the conservative Alessandri. This offer occurred at a meeting set up by McCone with his successor at the CIA, Richard Helms.

2. After the September 4th election, Geneen offered $1 million to create an anti-Allende coalition. This offer was transmitted by McCone to Helms and Henry Kissinger, who were to respond if the CIA decided to create such a coalition. McCone said he heard no more about such a plan.

3. Broe visited ITT's headquarters late in September with a plan to create economic instability in Chile through sabotage — delay of bank credit, withdrawal of technical help, and late shipments of goods and spare parts. ITT contacted a number of companies doing business with Chile from a list of companies provided by Broe, but Geneen concluded that the plan would fail because they could not trust the other companies.

4. After Allende's election by Congress on October 24, ITT applied persuasion and pressure on Secretary of State Rogers, Kissinger, and others in Washington to adopt an anti-Allende plan, later formalized into an eighteen-point program to see that Allende did not get through the next six months. The plan included economic pressure, fomenting discontent among the Chilean military, and encouraging support for the conservative right.

Copper Strategies

Anaconda, reasoning that it had been and was now a "good corporate citizen" of Chile, relied on continual lobbying with Chilean government officials, emphasizing its investment and development record. It also emphasized the inviolability of its corporate sovereignty.

Kennecott, having discovered that El Teniente's resources were much more vast than originally estimated in the early 1960s, negotiated the following deal with Frei's government in 1964.

1. Kennecott sold 51 percent interest in El Teniente, which had a book value in total of $70 million, to the Chilean government.
2. The purchase price was to be based on a doubling of book value and would total $80 million.
3. The newly composed El Teniente would modernize ($200 million of investment) and would almost double its capacity.
4. Modernization and expansion costs would be funded as follows:
   (a) $110,000,000 from the Export-Import Bank, partially "arranged" by Alliance for Progress officials.
   (b) The Chilean payment of $80 million, loaned back to the joint venture by Kennecott.
   (c) A Chilean government additional investment of $28 million.
   (d) The sale of future copper production to Japanese and European customers for $45 million.
5. The loan of $80 million (see point 4b) was guaranteed by the United States Agency for International Development (AID).
6. The loan of $110 million and the Chilean payment of $80 million (see points 2 and 4a) were to be guaranteed unconditionally by the Chilean state.
7. Collection rights on the Japanese and European contracts for $45 million (see point 4d) were sold to a Banca Commerciale Italiana consortium and to a Mitsui & Company consortium.
8. Kennecott would manage the joint venture for ten years for a fee.
9. The agreement was to be executed in, and made subject to the laws of, the State of New York.

As the 1970 Chilean election campaigns began organizing in the late 1960s, it was clear that Anaconda could expect increased political pressure. The leftist Allende, the centrist Tomic, and the rightist Alessandri — along with Cardinal Silva Henriquez and other Church leaders — were all advocating nationalization.

Anaconda refused to make a "Kennecott" deal with Chile, resisting any Chileanization or a Chilean 51 percent control with compensation. Anaconda instead asked to be fully nationalized with full compensation. In 1969, shortly before the end of Frei's term of office, an Anaconda nationalization-with-full-compensation plan was announced. Anaconda sold 51 percent of Chuquicamata and El Salvador mines to Chile for $197 million, to be paid in twenty-four payments over twelve years.

On July 16, 1971, in response to now-President Allende's legislative plans, the Chilean Congress passed a constitutional amendment nationalizing the Chilean subsidiaries of Anaconda and Kennecott. Compensation was offset in total by a deduction for "excessive profits" by the U.S. companies. The Chilean tribunal ruled Anaconda and Kennecott had made $774 million in excess profits since 1955. Theodore Moran: "A high Kennecott official in Santiago reflected: 'Nationalization was inevitable. It was only a question of time!' " An Anaconda legal adviser noted that the company was now on the receiving end.

Copper Aftermath

Despite Allende's pledge of "Ni un centavo!" the pressures on Chile from the United States, Europe, and Japan, plus Kennecott's legal acts including attachment writs against Chilean national aircraft landing in New York, resulted in Allende's government assuming and honoring all El Teniente's obligations except the ten-year management clause. Anaconda, on the other hand, was nationalized with no hope of compensation. The entire Anaconda top management was fired by the directors; the company, as Moran describes, tried to "do their best to forget about Chile."

While Kennecott collected $67 million from the U.S. government agency that insured the money lent by Kennecott to Chile, and while Kennecott seized shipments from El Teniente to Europe, Anaconda's chairman Parkinson (sixty-three), president John Hall (fifty-four), and senior vice president Charles Schwab (fifty-six) were swept out of office. A vice chairman of Chase Manhattan Bank, John Pace, was brought in as Anaconda president. Pace cut headquarters staff from 488 to 180, reduced total employment from 36,000 to 31,000, and eliminated 11 vice presidents.

Anaconda's 1969 stock market value of $1.4 billion dropped to $260 million in late 1971, a year that saw the company post a $357 million loss ($302 million of which was a write-off of its Chilean investment) — a loss of $15.30 per share against a stock price of $19.00. Shareholders also tried to "do their best to forget about Chile."

Chilean Lessons

Anaconda's limited perspective and ITT's manipulative managerial philosophy resulted in both firms' failure to note the strategic changes in the relative power of Chile vis-à-vis the multinational. Kennecott, on the other hand, took practical steps in recognizing the strategic shifts that occurred due to changes in power.

INTERNATIONAL BUSINESS LIFE CYCLE

Strategists react not only to power shifts but also to new international investing options, such as joint ventures, and to changes in international life cycles. Garland and Farmer (1986) described a product life cycle model for international business linking demand with strategic comparative advantage and highlighting the causative factors of firm level (versus national level) of competition.

Phase One   During the first stage of the product life cycle, the innovating firm produces and markets solely in the home market. At the moment when the products are introduced commercially, costs and prices are high. The innovating firm, however, typically benefits from real or perceived monopolistic advantages (if the product is sufficiently different from other existing products), and the initial buyers are relatively insensitive to price. If the product catches on, the market expands rapidly, eventually providing increasing economies of scale, lower unit costs, and further market expansion. This success encourages competitors, especially as production becomes more standardized. The market eventually becomes saturated and profits decline notably, for competitive reasons.

Phase Two   Vaster markets and greater economies of scale can be gained by exporting, however, and here begins phase two of the product life cycle. The assumption is that an imperfect market exists for knowledge and technology, and that the original advantage held by the innovator in the home market can be duplicated abroad. The U.S. producer typically has sought markets in Canada and Europe for two basic reasons: (1) they are large enough to be quite attractive; and (2) the demand patterns among industrialized countries are fairly similar, which precludes having to adapt the product substantially for the foreign market. Success in exporting to foreign markets prolongs the life of the product. Competitors eventually emerge — domestic firms in the targeted export market — but at first these competitors are noncompetitive due to normal start-up problems and to lack of economies of scale.

Phase Three   Eventually, foreign producers gain a substantial advantage by refining their production techniques and by gaining scales at least sufficient to cause a disadvantage to the original exporter, who has the added costs of distant transportation and communication. Cultural distance also becomes a factor, since foreign domestic companies are much more familiar with the market than foreign multinationals. Often, as in the case of the Japanese auto companies now investing in the United States, the foreign government will undertake protectionist actions in order to facilitate development or enhance the competitiveness of local producers. When these factors in aggregate become serious enough to affect exports adversely, phase three of the product life cycle emerges, in which the exporting firm shifts its strategy by locating production facilities abroad in the markets that have been served by exports up to this point. This pattern, until quite recently, has been dominated by U.S. multinational corporations, whose technological lead over the firms of war-devastated Europe and Japan was substantial for the two decades following World War II.

Phase Four   For those products that are particularly labor intensive and require mass manufacturing technologies, a final phase in the product life cycle allows the original, innovating firm to cease all production in the typically high-wage domestic market (and often also in the foreign markets that it first entered via exports and then production). Phase four also allows the firm to serve the home market through imports from those foreign subsidiaries located in low-wage areas abroad. These new production locations are typically in the most rapidly developing of the Third World countries such as Brazil or Singapore, where low labor costs are combined with sufficient infrastructure and generally excellent productivity levels.

These external complexities of evolving product life cycles and shifting host country power mean that the firm must commit extra resources to understand the environment. The multinational corporation must have a larger staff — especially in legal and financial areas — than the firm doing business in one location.

Some experts argue that the "global village" caused by worldwide communication creates a global market opportunity the strategist cannot ignore. Marketing expert Theodore Levitt commented in *Fortune*, "The new Republic of Technology homogenizes world tastes, wants, and possibilities into global market proportions, which allows for world-standardized products" (11/12/84, pp. 78, 80). Nonetheless, in the same issue of *Fortune*, Philip Kotler suggested, "There are only a very few products, if any, that you can safely standardize. I really think the whole global marketing craze is just a ploy by advertising agencies to get new business."

What is the likely trend of international strategic management? Garland and Farmer concluded that the "increasingly restrictive measures of host governments . . . and the substantially deteriorating foreign investment climate" mean two things for tomorrow's international strategist. First, the international strategic manager must "reappraise . . . overall strategy" because of the changed environment. Second, the manager will find it "more difficult . . . to globally integrate . . . functions and activities" in environments that "inevitably dictate suboptimizing behavior."

BIBLIOGRAPHY

Garland, J., and R. N. Farmer, *International Dimensions of Business Policy and Strategy* (Boston: PWS-KENT, 1986).

Geneen, H., and A. Moscow, *Managing* (Garden City, NY: Doubleday, 1984).

Moran, T., *Copper in Chile: Multinational Corporations and the Politics of Dependence* (Princeton, NJ: Princeton University Press, 1974).

Sampson, A., *The Sovereign State of ITT* (Briarcliff Manor, NY: Stein & Day, 1980).

FORMULATING STRATEGY

Life can only be understood backwards, but it must be lived forward.
Søren Kierkegaard

There is no Model of Strategy and there is no strategy without a model.
Medicine Dog

Chapter 6 builds upon the twin foundations of (1) the three steps of strategic analysis —
defining purpose, determining distinctive competence, and identifying opportunities
and threats — and (2) the levels of strategic management — functional, business,
and corporate. On this twin foundation, this chapter constructs the framework of
the strategic decision process using the tools of strategic management, including
product portfolio, industry, and competitive analysis. Next, this chapter illustrates
strategy formulation by looking at examples of successful strategic alternatives in
situations such as those of the new business, vertical integration, diversification,
turnaround, and withdrawal. Finally, this chapter measures and evaluates the results
of strategy formulation.

THE STRATEGIC DECISION PROCESS

Strategic decisions, or the formulation of strategy, consist of selecting those opportunities and threats indicated by strategic signals in the external environment (see Chapter
5) for which the enterprise has a distinctive competence (see Chapter 4). The distinctive
competence is based upon using the enterprise purpose (see Chapter 3) as the selection
criteria.

In commonsense terms, the strategic decision process consists of performing
those alternative strategic acts that allow you to use your strengths to attain your
purpose. Strategy formulation is thus a simple concept to describe, but a difficult
one to apply. The factors that make this application difficult include the breadth
and uncertainty of the external environment, the complexity of identifying distinctive
competence, and the multiple and potentially conflicting forces that comprise enter-

prise purpose. It is easy to understand why only a small minority of firms and strategic managers are satisfied with their strategy formulation.

EXAMPLE: *Formulating Strategy*

Black & Decker, the manufacturer of power tools, saw a substantial external environment threat to its 50 percent share of the total world market for power tools. Its Japanese competitor, Makita Electric Works, in three years during the early 1980s had gained a share equal to Black & Decker's in industrial power tools, and was expected to introduce a line of consumer power tools. Makita had a cost advantage over Black & Decker and had competed primarily on price, to date. Further, Black & Decker felt that the power tool market had limited growth potential. Black & Decker also felt that international markets were growing increasingly similar.

Black & Decker's distinctive competence in the internal environment included its quality reputation. Its internal earning base was limited, however; the firm earned only $44 million on $1 billion in sales in 1983. In 1982 the firm lost $77 million.

Black & Decker formulated a strategy for achieving its purpose of growth and profitability through acquisition. In 1984 it acquired General Electric's worldwide small appliance business. Top management believed that the joint product lines of power tools and small appliances, both based on small motor technology, would provide the firm with sufficient revenues to fight competition. Black & Decker could increase sales by 50 percent just through the acquisition, which was made by issuing stock to G.E. and thus leaving cash flows free to fight competition through plant modernization.

Black & Decker also felt it could take advantage of the increasingly similar global markets by standardizing both its manufacturing and distribution worldwide for both power tools and small appliances. This strategy formulation was produced by a number of observations: (1) a perceived external environmental opportunity of worldwide market similarities, (2) a perceived threat of the competitor Makita, (3) an internal competence based on a reputation for quality, and (4) an enterprise purpose of growth.

It is important to recognize that neither Black & Decker in this example, nor the strategic manager in general, need evaluate *all* the strategic options and alternatives facing the enterprise. Each earlier step of strategic analysis has served as a filter for reducing the number of options and increasing the strategic manager's ability to make well-reasoned, subjective judgments.

WORKING CONCEPT 16

THE STRATEGIC DECISION PROCESS

The strategic decision process, illustrated in Figure 6.1, consists of the strategic manager (1) selecting those opportunities and threats in the external environment to which to respond based upon (2) the firm's distinctive competence and (3) enterprise purpose.

Strategic managers draw three conclusions from this process. First, the process makes sense; selecting opportunities for which you have competence in order to achieve your purpose means doing what you are good at in order to get what you want.

Second, processes are ongoing. The strategic process is dynamic: new opportunities arise; new competencies develop; new

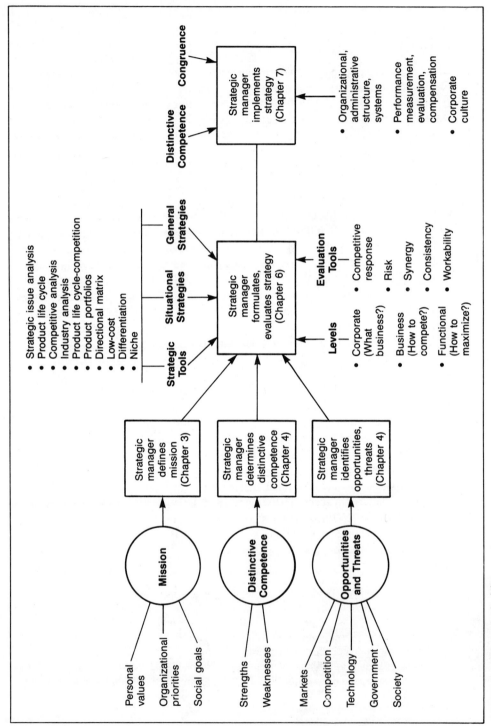

FIGURE 6.1 Strategic decision process

The Strategic Decision Process (*continued*)

strategies are formulated. Managers reassess performance and implemented strategies, and then they make changes. Performance assessment and evaluation provide new data to this dynamic process.

Finally, the process depends on all of its parts. Each step of the process must be undertaken, although identifying opportunities may require more resources than needed for defining purpose. Omitting strengths, threats, or social goals can result in a disastrous strategy.

DECISION LEVELS

Do the functional, business, and corporate strategists make decisions in the same way? Both commonsense and practical experience indicate that the answer is no. In general, functional managers pay particular attention to distinctive competence; business managers emphasize external opportunities and threats; and corporate managers focus on enterprise purpose.

Functional Decisions

A firm evaluates a functional manager by using a system that emphasizes such things as output, efficiency, and quality. These short-run measures can be affected most quickly by building on the firm's strengths and by correcting functional weaknesses such as production bottlenecks or ineffective marketing campaigns. The functional manager sees only a part of the whole picture; he or she concentrates on immediate results from a limited view of strengths and weaknesses, or distinctive competence.

Business Decisions

The business strategist has a broad view that encompasses all the functional areas of a business *and* the external environment, especially the marketplace. The business ultimately succeeds or fails based upon its reception in the market. Thus the business-level executive tends to rely on functional managers for short-term operating efficiency and effectiveness, and concentrates on the mid-term reaction of the market to both the firm's products and to competition.

Corporate Decisions

The corporate executive in the multinational, diversified corporation may know only the highlights of its short-term operating strengths and weaknesses. Corporate knowledge of business strategy includes awareness of the most important trends in the marketplace and of quantitative budgets, forecasts, and periodic financial results. The corporate executive cannot be expected to understand the details of the external environment of multiple international markets and multiple products. Rather, the corporate strategist seeks to maximize the attainment of long-term organizational priorities, such as maximizing shareholder wealth and developing managerial ability while exercising social responsibility through employment opportunities.

Because of (1) emphasis on short-term results and (2) limited perspective, the functional manager concentrates on increasing those strengths and overcoming problems, or correcting those weaknesses, that underlie the distinctive competence. The business strategist relying on subordinates — functional managers and supervisors — studies the product market external environment. The corporate executive adjusts the long-term direction of the firm to achieve enterprise goals.

Many things affect the relative validity of these differences in managers: individual ability and initiative of the manager, com-plexity of technology, and breadth and depth of product lines, to name a few. For example, an ambitious, capable functional manager in a multinational, Stage Three corporation would have a long-term perspective that includes both social goals and a wide range of organizational priorities. Nonetheless, in most instances the levels of strategy affect the degree of emphasis within the strategic decision process. Thus, useful insight and practical guidelines can be gained from a model or Working Concept of this relationship, such as is suggested by Figure 6.2.

FIGURE 6.2
Strategic decision process and strategic levels

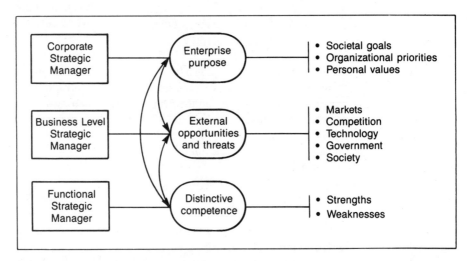

STRATEGIC MANAGEMENT TOOLS

When moving from functional strategy to corporate strategy, managers make strategic decisions that increasingly focus on external opportunities and enterprise purpose. Similarly, managers employ tools that range from the product life cycle (functional level) to product portfolios (business level) to industry and strategic issue analysis (corporate level). This general model for using strategic tools must not obscure the important fact that any one manager may indeed use any strategic tool, just as any one manager may focus on distinctive competence, external opportunities, or enterprise purpose.

The strategic manager can use one of seven methods or tools of strategic management. These methods include

1. Product life cycle
2. Porter's Determinants of Competition
3. Product portfolios
4. Product life cycle–competition matrix
5. Directional policy matrix
6. Industry analysis
7. Strategic issue analysis

Product Life Cycle

The functional manager uses the product life cycle to (1) focus attention on the all-important product market; (2) recognize the changing functional needs of promotion, production, and distribution; (3) forecast profits; and (4) measure performance. Working Concept 10 (Chapter 4) describes the product life cycle tool.

Porter's Determinants of Competition

The business-level manager uses Porter's model of the five determinants of competition for either (1) "positioning the company so that its capabilities provide the best defense against the competitive force" or (2) "influencing the balance of forces through competitive moves, thereby improving the company's position" (Porter 1979, p. 143). As Porter pointed out, Dr. Pepper chose to position itself against the Coke- and Pepsi-dominated industry by stressing its unique — if narrow — product line. Porter included marketing innovations that differentiate product and capital investments and that alter barriers to entry as ways the firm can influence the balance of competitive forces.

Porter (1979) also has shown how competition increases in an industry due to threats of new entrants or substitute products, or due to the economic power of customers and suppliers. These four forces affect the moves and countermoves — the fifth determinant of the levels of competition — of specific rival firms.

After analyzing competitive levels by Porter's methods, as described in Chapter 5, the strategic manager can choose specific strategic steps from among the preemptive opportunities presented in Table 6.1.

These preemptive moves primarily make up functional- and business-level strategies. Working Concept 12 (Chapter 5) describes Porter's model in detail.

TABLE 6.1
Preemptive
opportunities

Critical competitive force à la Porter	Preemptive opportunity
Suppliers' power	1. Research new raw materials, components
	2. Secure access to supply
	(a) long-term contracts
	(b) production equipment link
	(c) logistics domination
Buyers' power	1. Segment
	2. Build brand loyalty
	3. Secure key accounts
	4. Link to customers by service, training
	5. Dominate distribution logistics
Product substitution	1. Expand product scope
	2. Introduce new products
	3. Develop dominant design
New entrants	1. Expand capacity
	2. Integrate vertically
	3. Research production process
Competitor's moves, countermoves	1. Any and all of the above

WORKING CONCEPT 18

PRODUCT PORTFOLIOS

Product portfolio analysis, pioneered by the Boston Consulting Group (BCG), uses a matrix to examine products and markets, with market growth (business growth rate) as one axis and relative market share (relative competitive position) as the other. Figure 6.3 presents one version of this product analysis. Products with high relative market share in high-growth businesses are "stars"; those with low relative market share in low-growth businesses are "dogs." High market share assumes high profits through economies of scale. "Cash cows" are high market share products in low-growth businesses, and thus represent high profit. Cash cows are the stable earnings base that supports the firm. Uncertainty surrounds "question marks," those products with low share of high-growth businesses. The Boston Consulting Group's experience suggests that the organization should liquidate the dogs and use the cash resources generated by the cash cows to turn the most promising question marks into

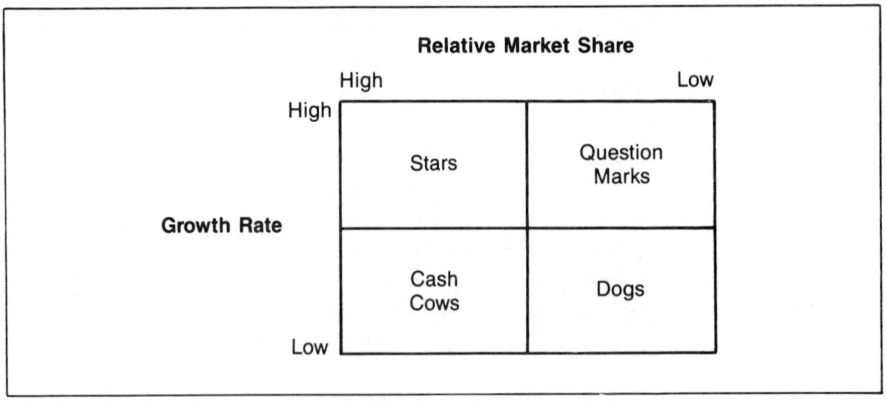

FIGURE 6.3
BCG's product
portfolio matrix

Product Portfolios (continued)

stars. The remainder of the question marks should be divested.

The market share assumptions underlying the product portfolio technique were supported by the PIMS research.

PIMS

The longitudinal data of over 1,700 businesses make up the PIMS (Profit Impact of Market Strategies) data base (Schoeffler et al., 1974). The findings reported in the "PIMS Newsletter" of the Strategic Planning Institute in Cambridge, Massachusetts, and in strategy literature include the impact of market share on profitability. Other important variables include investment intensity, a variable frequently ignored in strategic models (a product portfolio dog coupled with low investment could be a star in terms of return-on-investment); purchase frequency; product quality; research effort; capacity utilization; and relative price.

The PIMS data base is not without its limitations. First, the PIMS "businesses" are all portions of major diversified corporations. Thus, Stage One and Stage Two firms are not present. Secondly, businesses that perform better than average tend to stay in the PIMS data base; below-average firms tend to leave PIMS. Although PIMS has been in effect since 1970, only one hundred businesses have entered data for more than eight years. Less than six years' worth of data has been entered by 1,100 businesses, and less than four years' data has been entered by 200 businesses.

Further implications of the product portfolio, and the resulting strategies of "build, hold, and harvest," were discussed by Gupta and Govindarajan (1984). The limitations as well as the uses of portfolio analysis were described by Haspelslagh (1982) and Channon (1979).

PROBLEMS WITH PRODUCT PORTFOLIOS

Specific problems with product portfolios were discussed by Professor Day (1977) of the University of Toronto in his research paper "Diagnosing the Product Portfolio." First, the assumption that market share is a proxy for relative profit performance may not be true in many circumstances, such as when "one competitor has a significant technological advantage (resulting in a different cost reduction/experience curve)" or "profitability is highly sensitive to the rate of capacity utilization, regardless of size of plant." Day also points out that the pursuit of market share can be disastrous when financial resources are inadequate or when antitrust action results. Also, the definitional problems in product portfolios are substantial, as Day demonstrates by asking "what share of what market," raising segmentation, geographic, potential versus actual, and other measurement problems.

EXAMPLE: *Product Portfolios*

Gillette's strategy of diversification is an example of a portfolio management approach. Faced with declining sales in the early 1980s, Gillette sought new businesses to add growth to its stable, highly profitable (cash cow) razor blade core business. Gillette chairman C. M. Mocker told the *Boston Globe* (10/2/84, p. 53): "It's what we call an aggregation strategy. We can make minor investments in several companies in the field and as these companies develop we can take advantage of those that perform favorably and ignore those that do not."

Haspelslagh (1982) pointed out that one problem in the portfolio planning technique is "the difficulty of generating new internal growth opportunities." Wheelwright (1984) elaborated on this idea and warned that the "portfolio-based content approach . . . values management for cost reduc-

---

Product Portfolios *(continued)*

tion'' rather than for long-term technological competitive advantage.

Tom Peters and Nancy Austin, in *A Passion for Excellence*, argued that quality is the determining factor in portfolio planning, and that concentration on increasing market share by getting cost down might reduce quality and service.

The business-level strategist uses product portfolio analysis to study both the firm's and competitors' portfolios. In addition to suggesting how resources might be allocated among the firm's products, the analysis can show the strength of its competitive position. Competitive position is one dimension of the fourth strategic tool, the product life cycle–competition matrix.

WORKING CONCEPT 19

PRODUCT LIFE CYCLE–COMPETITION MATRIX

Charles W. Hofer (1977) developed conceptual constructs for formulating corporate and business strategies (also the name of his article). As Figure 6.4 shows, one of these constructs plotted the product life cycle with the relative strength of the firm's competitive position. Four products at various life cycle stages (Product 1 at development, Product 2 at growth, Product 3 at maturity, and Product 4 in decline) have different competitive positions. Products 2, 3, and 4 lack the competitive strength of Product 1. Hofer used circle size as an indication of total industry sales, and showed share of the market through a parenthesis inside the circle.

The life cycle focuses attention on the developing Product 1 and the growth Product 2; but market share (25 percent for Product 1 versus 7 percent for Product 2) and the stronger competitive position of Product 1 suggest that Product 1 should receive managerial attention and support. The product life cycle–competition matrix also leads to the conclusion that Product 3, because of its large market share, should be ''milked'' as a cash cow and its resulting funds used for Product 1. The company should minimize investment in Product 3 and should harvest and drop Product 4, it being weak competitively and with little market share. Perhaps Product 2 should also be neglected, unless its competitive position can be strengthened.

Competitive capabilities, or business strength, underlie the directional policy matrix, as well as the product life cycle–competition matrix.

WORKING CONCEPT 20

DIRECTIONAL POLICY MATRIX

The directional policy matrix extends the product portfolio matrix and makes it more qualitative. The result, as developed by companies such as General Electric and McKinsey & Company, is shown in Figure 6.5.

Will all strategic managers reach the same conclusions when they evaluate the product markets in the crosshatched area in Figure 6.5 between ''Invest'' and ''Divest''? Personal values and attitudes will lead one manager to invest based upon high firm strength, and another to invest based upon high industry attractiveness.

Risk can be added as another factor in the strategic manager's evaluation of the

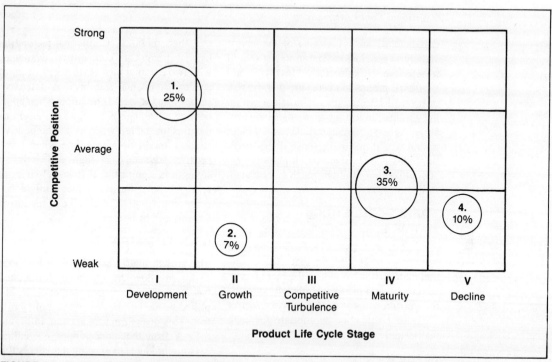

FIGURE 6.4   Product life cycle–competition matrix

Adapted from Hofer, C. W., "Conceptual Constructs for Formulating Corporate and Business Strategies (Boston: Harvard Case 9-378-754, p. 3).

FIGURE 6.5
Directional policy
matrix

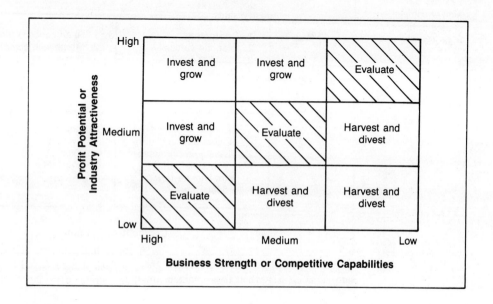

Directional Policy Matrix (continued)

crosshatched area, and also of the invest and divest conclusion. The strategist should review the ''Evaluate,'' ''Invest,'' and ''Divest'' groups to make sure that the risk or level of uncertainty is consistent within the groups. Investing in a high-industry-attractiveness, medium-business-strength option would not make sense if the medium-industry-attractiveness, high-business-strength option would be much more certain in its outcome.

MARKET-COMPETITION MATRIX

Figure 6.6 presents Christensen, Berg, and Salter's model (1976) of a market-competition matrix. It incorporates the rate of market growth and the firm's relative competitive position into a two-by-two matrix suggesting strategies appropriate for each matrix unit.

SPACE MATRIX

Rowe, Mason, and Dickel (1982) developed a matrix tool, known as a *space ma-*

trix, that combined two internal factors (financial strength and competitive advantage) with two external factors (industry strength and environmental stability). A defensive strategy might seem appropriate when competitive advantage is low and the environment is unstable, whereas a competitive strategy might be appropriate when competitive advantage is high and industry strength is significant. If financial strength is high, the defensive strategy might become conservative, while the competitive strategy might become aggressive.

GROWTH MATRIX

The growth matrix used by Ansoff (1965) to describe how strategy can be formulated based upon products and markets is a simplified version of the directional policy matrix. This growth matrix appears in Figure 6.7. A firm that concentrates on selling existing products to existing markets is following a *market penetration* strategy. If a firm sells existing products to new markets it is using a *market development* strategy;

FIGURE 6.6
Market-competition strategic choice matrix

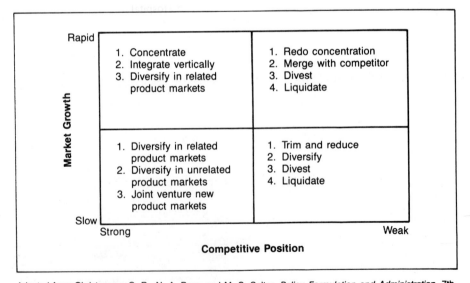

Adapted from Christensen, C. R., N. A. Berg, and M. S. Salter, *Policy Formulation and Administration*, 7th ed. (Homewood, IL: Richard D. Irwin, 1976), pp. 16–18.

Directional Policy Matrix (continued)

and if it sells new products to existing markets it is following a *product development* strategy. *Diversification* strategy involves selling new products to new markets. The four boxes in the matrix — or growth vector, as Ansoff calls it — in Figure 6.7 represent four possible sources of growth.

EXAMPLE: *Product Development*

The health care industry provides an illustration of the attractiveness of bringing new products to existing customers, or product development. The five major industry components — hospitals, nusing homes, home health care, health maintenance organizations (HMOs), and medical equipment — all saw the importance of expanding the products and services to their customers, so that the patient or customer could have "one-stop health shops." Individual companies tried expansion, joint ventures, horizontal integration, and acquisition in order to become the integrated health care company that would be the health care leader in the 1990s. Thus Hospital Corporation of America and Baxter Laboratories both pursued a merger with American Hospital Supply Corporation in 1985; and Whittaker bought an HMO, Health Plan of Virginia, to go with its newly purchased International Diagnostic Technology and General Medical (hospital supplies) subsidiaries.

Schering-Plough's strategy, as described in *Business Week* (8/20/84, p. 122), can be viewed as a balancing of market penetration with product development. As Schering-Plough's consumer businesses (Maybelline, Dr. Scholl, and St. Joseph aspirin) grew slowly but steadily, research funds of $170 million (about 10 percent of sales) were spent on biotechnology, chemical synthesis, and new drugs. While total employment fell by 3,000, the research staff grew by 30 percent to 1,400 during the 1983–1984 period.

In the mid-1980s, the new management at ITT turned away from the diversification strategy that had been pursued for twenty years and pursued a market development strategy. ITT entered a new market in the United States, telecommunications, based upon ITT's telecommunication systems already in place in Europe. As ITT brought its Modular System 12 products to the new U.S. market, the vice president of research said, "We've won every technical shoot-out we've entered" (*Business Week*, 10/22/84, p. 116).

EXIT STRATEGY

On the other side of Ansoff's growth matrix is divesting. Not all products reach stardom nor are all plans successful. The firm needs

FIGURE 6.7
Ansoff's growth matrix

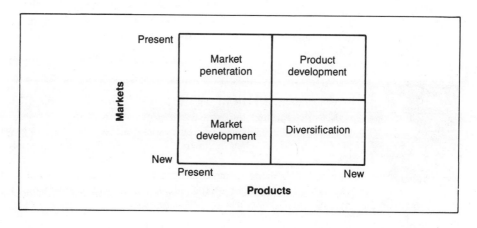

Directional Policy Matrix (continued)

an exit strategy for declining products and failed plans. An exit strategy formulates a way for the firm to divest a product and exit a market while minimizing adverse consequences such as customer relationships and closing costs. The U.S. farm equipment industry in the mid-1980s provides a good example of the necessity of following exit strategies, as companies such as International Harvester divest themselves of farm equipment businesses.

Many U.S. farmers, adversely affected by grain embargos, economic recessions, declining exports, a drop in debt capacity, and high interest rates, began to postpone or eliminate altogether their purchases of farm equipment. Tractors replaced every five to seven years during the 1970s were being held eight to ten years or longer during the 1980s.

The plant capacity expansion of J. I. Case, Deere, International Harvester, Ford, Allis-Chalmers, Massey Ferguson, and others resulted in overcapacity. By the 1980s the large (over 100 horsepower) tractor market had capacity for sixty thousand units and demand for thirty-five thousand. Japanese manufacturers dominated the small (under 40 horsepower) tractor business. Massey Ferguson turned to the Canadian

government for a massive refinancing. International Harvester, in an exit strategy move that many industry analysts expected to be repeated within the farm equipment industry, sold its farm equipment business to its competitor, J. I. Case.

The growth matrix helps the strategic manager to organize the alternative opportunities for which the firm has distinctive competences. Some opportunities are for market penetration (existing products, existing markets), others are for product development (new products, existing markets), and still others are for market development (existing products, new markets) — all of which build on the firm's experience with existing products or existing markets. If the strategic manager decides to pursue growth through diversification, then he or she can find no past experience — no "common thread," in Ansoff's terms — since the firm will be dealing in both new products and new markets. All other things being equal, diversification must offer greater opportunities than the three other options on the matrix, for diversification is the path of the greatest risk. The firm will accept this higher risk with diversification only in order to earn higher returns.

The business-level executive concentrates on the profit potential in the directional policy matrix; the corporate strategist is concerned with industry attractiveness. Industry analysis provides the corporate strategist with the tool necessary to determine industry attractiveness.

WORKING CONCEPT **21**

INDUSTRY ANALYSIS

Hofer and Schendel (1978) suggested five steps to determining the attractiveness of an industry. Industry analysis seems especially appropriate when reviewing more than one industry.

First, the strategic manager determines what criteria are appropriate for judging a

particular industry. The strategist selects from among many options: (1) relative profitability; (2) level of government regulation; (3) competitive pressures; (4) product market size; (5) growth rates; and (6) the cost-volume-profit relationship, including capital, marketing, labor, and materials costs.

Industry Analysis (continued)

After selecting some appropriate criteria, the manager next assigns a weighting factor or priority ranking to each criterion. Then, he or she collects data about each criterion. As a fourth step, the manager analyzes the data and determines an appropriate measure for the criteria. This measure can be quantitative or subjective ("attractive, neutral, unattractive").

As a fifth and last step, the strategist compares the weighted ranking with the opinions of other managers and experts. This final step serves as a check against incomplete data or inappropriate criteria, which might be indicated by a big difference between the weighted ranking and expert opinion.

Porter (1980) adds a method of analyzing industries in his "strategic mapping" described in *Competitive Strategy: Techniques for Analyzing Industries and Competitors*. Figure 6.8 presents a strategic map with twin dimensions of distribution channels and quality/reputation. Various companies divide the total market into strategic groups, including electric saws

FIGURE 6.8
Strategic mapping: U.S. chain saw industry

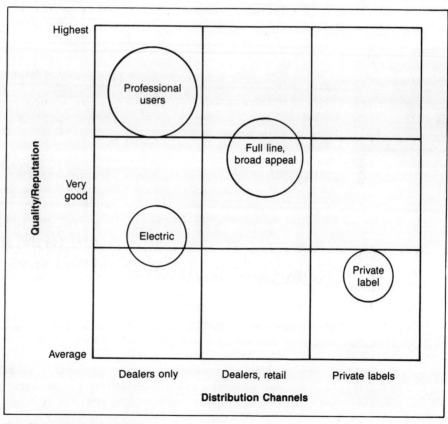

Note: Circle size equals market share.
Adapted from Porter, M.E., *Competitive Strategy: Techniques for Analyzing Industries and Competitors* (New York: Free Press, 1980), p. 153.

Industry Analysis (continued)

only (Skil), professional user manufacturers (Stihl), private labelers (Remington), and those competing in broad markets with full lines (McCulloch, Homelite).

Robinson and Pearce (1985), in a study of ninety-seven manufacturers in six industries, found five clusters of strategy that relate to Porter's strategy groups: (1) efficiency and service, (2) service/high-priced markets and brand/channel influence, (3) product innovation/development, (4) brand identification/channel influence and efficiency, and (5) no clear strategic orientation.

The corporate strategist uses industry analysis to determine which directions the firm will pursue to satisfy enterprise purpose. The executive may also face a specific strategic issue, such as the trend in energy price, social change, or the threat of entry into an industry. Strategic issue analysis provides a tool for studying a specific strategic issue.

WORKING CONCEPT 22

STRATEGIC ISSUE ANALYSIS

Strategic issue diagnosis (Dutton et al. 1983), or strategic issue analysis (King 1982), is the examination of an external environment strategic signal or group of related strategic signals. Strategic issues, although uncertain, are important topics that require analysis.

King (1982) presents one example of a strategic issue — Will a new company enter our industry? — and shows how to use strategic issue analysis to break the strategic issue down into its component parts in order to reach a conclusion. In the new entry example, King suggests considering the component parts of "economies of scale, product differentiation, capital requirements, cost advantages independent of size, access to distribution channels, and government policy."

King described ways of using strategic issue analysis to find the stimulus to action. When Dutton et al. researched strategic issue diagnosis, they emphasized that the strategist uses strategic issue diagnosis to stimulate the strategic process, so that these environmental signals become a part of proactive strategic management.

Strategic issues should be thought of as strategic signals, and strategic issue analysis as one term to describe the process of determining the positive or negative characteristics of strategic signals. Strategic issues thus become opportunities or threats.

In reviewing the seven tools of strategic management, we have found that certain tools are used primarily, although certainly not exclusively, by either functional, business-level, or corporate strategic managers. For example, corporate strategists may use Porter's determinants of competition to estimate future potential of industries. Figure 6.9 summarizes the tools and levels of strategy.

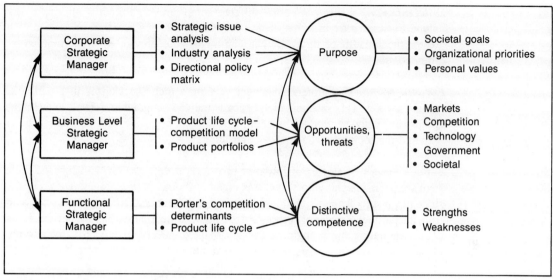

FIGURE 6.9 Strategic tools and levels

EXAMPLES OF STRATEGY FORMULATION

This next section of Chapter 6 gives examples of formulated strategy. These examples include Porter's broad, general (or generic) strategies and more specialized strategies for specific situations.

Porter's Generic Strategies   Harvard Business School professor Michael Porter (1980) identified three generic or basic categories of strategy: (1) low-cost producer, (2) differentiation, and (3) focused niche.

Low-Cost Producer. The business level strategist trying to be the lowest-cost producer considers such options as

Investing in plant and equipment
Riding the experience curve to economies of scale
Stringent cost control and minimization
Marginal contribution analysis and aggressive pricing to build volume

This general category of strategy seems appropriate for commodity products and high price elasticity markets.

Differentiation. A firm can pursue differentiation through a product offering that is unique to the market in terms of design, special features, quality, or service. The greater the breadth of buyer purchase motives, the greater the opportunities for differentiation.

Focused Niche. The strategic manager seeking a niche specializes in a particular product market. This specialization or focus may be geographic, related to customer groups, or related to product function. The smaller company with limited resources may find the focused niche strategy appealing.

Situational Strategy

Porter's generic strategies of low-cost producer, differentiation, and focused niche stem from his insights into ways to compete. Another way to categorize groups of strategies results from a situational perspective. Situational strategy categories stem from the particular stages of corporate development, i.e.; (1) starting the new business; (2) concentrating on a single business; (3) integrating vertically; (4) diversifying; or seeing a faltering business in a critical phase of either (5) turnaround or (6) divesting and/or exiting.

Starting the New Business. Hofer and Schendel (1978) emphasized two major strategic efforts each new business will have to make if it is to survive. First, the firm must acquire sufficient resources to support its growth from entrepreneur's idea up to profitable operating levels. The new firm's most critical resource is often financial. Second, the firm must prepare itself for a period of competition. It must develop strengths, and thus create the beginning — albeit a flexible and immature one — of a distinctive competence.

Concentrating on a Single Business. Successful single businesses have the common strategic characteristic of a strong distinctive competence. This distinctive competence may be focused on technology, as in the case of Polaroid, or on the customer, as in the example of McDonald's. It allows the firm to grow through market penetration or product development. Polaroid moved from instant black-and-white photography to "35-millimeter quality" color photographs. McDonald's became a global fast-food enterprise.

Integrating Vertically. Firms pursue backward and forward vertical integration strategies to ensure supply and distribution channels, and to try to capture the profit margins from suppliers and customers. Harrigan (1985) studied the linkage between corporate strategy and vertical integration in the make-or-buy decisions of 192 firms in sixteen industries. She found an explanation for the intra- and interindustry differences in their demand certainty. The more certainty existed, the more vertical integration; the less industry volatility, due to relatively higher concentration and exit barriers, the more firms turned to vertical integration. Harrigan pointed out that the chief executive officers must support synergy in integration: "No synergy exists . . . unless executives consciously enforce policies causing SBUs to (1) communicate; (2) share inputs, outputs, R&D, or other useful attributes and capabilities; or (3) cooperate in some other useful manner.''

Diversifying. Firms diversify as they seek those growth and profit opportunities that are unavailable in single concentration or vertical integration strategies. A firm can diversify through internal research and development or corporate venturing (Burgelman 1985), through joint ventures, or through the acquisition of other firms. Benefits to diversifying include reduced risk (by broadening the base of activity) and greater rewards.

Strategic managers can pursue additional growth and profit opportunities in businesses related to their own through technology, products, or markets; or they can pursue opportunities in unrelated businesses. Sears diversified from retailing to insurance (through Allstate Insurance) and to real estate and financial services, but also built upon its retail customer market base in its diversification activities. ITT, on the other hand, diversified from the telephone and communications field into unrelated activities such as insurance, hotels (through Sheraton), and car rentals (through Avis).

The unrelated diversification strategy can be selected by those managers seeking not only greater growth and profit potential, but also those managers who believe the corporate management resources exist to supervise operating subsidiaries through financial portfolio management techniques and capital budgeting procedures. Few strategists try to manage unrelated subsidiaries at the business level; instead, they rely on financial controls at the corporate strategic level. Even fewer strategists succeed in operating unrelated businesses.

The critical strategic principle to remember in diversification, then, is that strategic implementation is just as difficult — if not more difficult — as strategy formulation. The diversified strategist must rely on key executives within the diversified, decentralized subsidiary. Strategic management succeeds or fails based upon the effectiveness of linking *planning* and *action*. Table 6.2 below summarizes managerial resources and diversification strategies.

Turnaround Strategies. The company facing financial pressures and profit squeezes selects a turnaround strategy. These strategies fall into general categories described by Hofer (1980), including (1) reducing and controlling costs, (2) increasing revenues, (3) withdrawing resources from profit drains and allocating resources to profit potentials, and (4) replacing strategic managers. A company can try one or more of

TABLE 6.2 Diversification strategies		**Related diversification**	**Unrelated diversification**
	Managerial Resource	Operating company technology, product-market skills	Holding company financial control and capital budgeting
	Diversification Method	Internal venturing and research, joint venture, merger	Acquisition

these strategies to turnaround a faltering business, but Hofer emphasizes that most successful turnarounds have included replacing top management. In 1985 Apple Computer relieved its founder, Steve Jobs, of most if not all of his strategic duties; other troubled computer companies like Wang, Data General, and Digital Equipment Corporation concentrated on employee layoffs.

Hall, in "Survival Strategies in a Hostile Environment" (1980), found a zero survival rate in eight industries. He concluded that turnaround efforts had arrived too late, since rivals were too strong and/or resources were too scarce for survival.

Caterpillar Tractor stressed cost reduction in its mid-1980s turnaround strategy. After losing more than $1 billion in three years, Caterpillar cut its work force by one-third, subcontracted production, and reduced manufacturing capacity so that costs were cut by 22 percent in 1985 (*Business Week*, 11/15/85, p. 41).

Divest and Exit. What does the strategic manager do with the "dog" business? Abell (1978) presented four options: (1) close the gap, (2) shift to selected market segments where a fit occurs, (3) cut back and milk the business, and (4) exit through liquidation or sale. Optimally, the failing business can be sold to some other firm that can produce a successful turnaround with its own capabilities and/or new synergies.

Harrigan (1982) analyzed firms in declining industries and marginal firms in nondeclining industries. Although these firms should be expected to divest and exit, the exit strategy was affected by

1. Economic exit barriers, such as losses on disposal of assets and expenses of unfunded pension obligations and other severance costs.
2. Noneconomic exit barriers, including fear of communicating a poor management image to customers and shareholders.

Harrigan concluded that exit barriers, especially asset disposal variables, were substantial. Firms pursuing a low-cost producer strategy built upon capital investment thus would encounter more exit and divesting difficulties than firms pursuing differentiation or focused niche strategies.

Exit strategies are those strategies that suggest when the firm should stop following growth and profit objectives. In other words, exit strategies are strategic plans for withdrawing from product markets. Such exit contingency plans are most effective if they include implementation guidelines. The strategic manager should not only propose carrying out a new venture that is expected to earn a return of, for example, 18 to 24 percent on investment, but should also plan that the firm withdraw from the new venture if returns of less than, for example, 12 percent are experienced. Finally, the manager should suggest alternative plans for withdrawal, such as liquidating, licensing, or selling the venture.

In January 1985, after trying diversification, General Mills was disillusioned. General Mills kept its Betty Crocker, Wheaties, and Gorton Seafood operations, but announced that its Izod and Parker Brothers subsidiaries were for sale. Commenting on General Mills's exit strategy, an industry observer noted in *Business Week*: "One thing the management group prides itself on is that they don't let the problem areas run for long" (2/11/85, p. 31).

Furchgott's, the Jacksonville, Florida, department store operator, saw its exit strategy collapse because of poor implementation. Furchgott's agreed in principle to sell its businesses to Stein Mart Inc., a discount department store. Nonetheless, Regency Square Mall, the operator of the premier mall where Furchgott's had a store, announced that it would not accept Stein Mart as a Regency Square operator. Furchgott's filed for Chapter 11 bankruptcy protection in January 1985 only hours after Stein Mart announced it was terminating acquisition negotiations.

Other Strategies

Other researchers have described variations on the basic low-cost producer, differentiation, or focused niche strategies for low market share businesses (Hammermesh et al., 1978); high market share businesses (Bloom and Kotler, 1975); global enterprises (Harrell and Kiefer, 1981); firms in stagnant (Porter 1976), unstable (Fredrickson and Mitchell, 1984), or decline industries (Harrigan 1984); and firms seeking growth (Kierulff 1981).

One path to growth is through the new venture division of the large, diversified company, such as General Electric. Burgelman (1985), in researching management of the new venture division, urged the large firms to "structure themselves for dealing for *more*, rather than less, autonomous behavior." Earlier (1983), Burgelman had presented a "process model of internal corporate venturing in the diversified major firm." Cooper (1978) noted that "an increasing number of corporations have developed new venture departments." These various strategies provide organized ways in which to view strategic options, as in Table 6.3. David (1986) has provided

TABLE 6.3 Strategic categories overview	Categories	Context/Content
	Porter's generic strategies	
	low cost producer	Commodity, economies of scale
	differentiation	Product uniqueness
	focused niche	Limited resources
	Situational strategy	
	new business	Build resources, strengths
	single business	Distinctive competence
	vertical integration	Certainty, little volatility
	diversification — related	Growth through operating management
	diversification — unrelated	Growth through portfolio management
	turnaround	Increase revenue, reduce cost, change allocations and management
	divest and exit	Sell, minimize exit barriers

additional guidelines for selecting integration, penetration, market and product development, diversification, and exit strategies.[*]

Forward Integration

When an organization's present distributors are especially expensive, or unreliable, or incapable of meeting the firm's distribution needs

When the availability of quality distributors is so limited as to offer a competitive advantage to those firms that integrate forward

When an organization competes in an industry that is growing and is expected to continue to grow markedly. This is a factor because forward integration reduces an organization's ability to diversify if its basic industry falters.

When an organization has both the capital and human resources needed to manage the new business of distributing its own products

When the advantages of stable production are particularly high. This is a consideration because an organization can increase the predictability of the demand for its output through forward integration.

When present distributors or retailers have high profit margins. This situation suggests that a company could profitably distribute its own products and price them more competitively by integrating forward.

Backward Integration

When an organization's present suppliers are especially expensive, or unreliable, or incapable of meeting the firm's needs for parts, components, assemblies, or raw materials

When the number of suppliers is few and the number of competitors is many

When an organization competes in an industry that is growing rapidly. This is a factor because integrative strategies (forward, backward, and horizontal) reduce an organization's ability to diversify in a declining industry.

When an organization has both the capital and human resources needed to manage the new business of supplying its own raw materials

When the advantages of stable prices are particularly important. This is a factor because an organization can stabilize the cost of its raw materials and the associated price of its products through backward integration.

When present suppliers have high profit margins, which suggests that the business of supplying products or services in the given industry is a worthwhile venture

When an organization needs to acquire a needed resource quickly

[*] List © Fred R. David, *Fundamentals of Strategic Management* (Columbus, OH: Merrill, 1986). Reproduced by permission. Adapted from David, F. R., "How Do We Choose Among Alternative Growth Strategies?" *Managerial Planning* 33, no. 4 (January-February 1985), pp. 14–17, 22.

Horizontal Integration

When an organization can gain monopolistic characteristics in a particular area or region without being challenged by the federal government for "tending substantially" to reduce competition

When an organization competes in a growing industry

When increased economies of scale provide major competitive advantages

When an organization has both the capital and human talent needed to successfully manage an expanded organization

When competitors falter due to a lack of managerial expertise or a need for an organization's particular resources. Note that horizontal integration is not appropriate if competitors are doing poorly because overall industry sales are declining.

Market Penetration

When current markets are not saturated with your particular product or service

When the usage rate of present customers can be increased significantly

When the market shares of major competitors have been declining while total industry sales have been increasing

When the correlation between dollar sales and dollar marketing expenditures has historically been high

When increased economies of scale provide major competitive advantages

Market Development

When new channels of distribution are available that are reliable, inexpensive, and of good quality

When an organization is very successful at what it does

When new untapped or unsaturated markets exist

When an organization has the needed capital and human resources to manage expanded operations

When an organization has excess production capacity

When an organization's basic industry is rapidly becoming global in scope

Product Development

When an organization has successful products that are in the maturity stage of the product life cycle. The idea here is to attract satisfied customers to try new (improved) products as a result of their positive experience with the organization's present products or services.

When an organization competes in an industry that is characterized by rapid technological developments

When major competitors offer better quality products at comparable prices

When an organization competes in a high-growth industry

When an organization has especially strong research and development capabilities

Concentric Diversification

When an organization competes in a no-growth or slow-growth industry

When adding new, related products significantly enhances the sales of current products

When new, related products can be offered at highly competitive prices

When new, related products have seasonal sales levels that counterbalance an organization's existing peaks and valleys

When an organization's products are currently in the decline stage of the product life cycle

When an organization has a strong management team

Conglomerate Diversification

When an organization's basic industry experiences declining annual sales and profits

When an organization has the capital and managerial talent needed to compete successfully in a new industry

When an organization has the opportunity to purchase an unrelated business that is an attractive investment opportunity

When financial synergy exists between the acquired and acquiring firm. Note that a key difference between concentric and conglomerate diversification is that the former should be based on some commonality in markets, products, or technology; whereas the latter should be based more on profit considerations.

When existing markets for an organization's present products are saturated

When antitrust action could be charged against an organization that has historically concentrated on a single industry

Horizontal Diversification

When revenues derived from an organization's current products or services would significantly increase by adding new, unrelated products

When an organization competes in a highly competitive and/or a no-growth industry, as indicated by low industry profit margins and returns

When an organization's present channels of distribution can be used to market the new products to current customers

When the new products have countercyclical sales patterns compared to an organization's present products

Joint Venture

When a privately owned organization forms a joint venture with a publicly owned organization. The advantages to being privately held include close ownership. The advantages to being publicly held include access to stock issuances as a source of capital. Sometimes the unique advantages of being privately and publicly held can be combined synergistically in a joint venture.

When a domestic organization forms a joint venture with a foreign company. Joint venture can provide a domestic company with the opportunity for obtaining local management in a foreign country, thereby reducing such risks as expropriation and harassment by host country officials.

When the distinctive competencies of two or more firms successfully complement each other

When a project is potentially very profitable, but requires overwhelming resources and risks (e.g., the Alaskan pipeline)

When two or more smaller firms have trouble competing with a large firm

When an organization needs to introduce a new technology quickly

Retrenchment

When an organization has a clearly distinctive competence, but has failed to meet its objectives and goals consistently over time

When an organization is one of the weakest competitors in a given industry

When an organization is plagued by inefficiency, low profitability, poor employee morale, and pressure from stockholders to improve performance

When an organization has failed to capitalize on external opportunities, minimize external threats, take advantage of internal strengths, and overcome internal weaknesses over time. That is, when the organization's strategic managers have failed (and possibly been replaced by more competent individuals).

When an organization has grown so large so quickly that major internal reorganization is needed

Divestiture

When an organization has pursued a failed retrenchment strategy to accomplish needed improvements

When a division, in order to be competitive, needs more resources than the company can provide

When a division is responsible for an organization's overall poor performance

When a division does not fit with the rest of an organization. This can result from radically different markets, customers, managers, employees, values, or needs.

When a large amount of cash is needed quickly and cannot reasonably be obtained from other sources

When government antitrust action threatens an organization

Liquidation

When an organization has pursued unsuccessful retrenchment and divestiture strategies

When an organization's only alternative is bankruptcy. Liquidation represents an orderly and planned means of obtaining the greatest possible cash for an organization's assets. A company can legally declare bankruptcy first and then liquidate various divisions to raise needed capital.

When the stockholders of a firm can minimize their losses by selling the organization's assets

EVALUATING STRATEGY

Although the strategic manager uses many tools and examples when formulating strategy, the strategic formulation process also requires subjective interpretation and judgment. Fortunately, the strategic manager can use five criteria to assess the results of the strategic formulation process: (1) competitive response analysis, (2) risk, (3) synergy, (4) consistency, and (5) workability. The manager should review the formulated strategy in terms of these criteria not just while the strategy is formulated, but at periodic future intervals. As David (1986) asserts, "success today is no guarantee for success tomorrow."

Competitive Response Analysis

First the strategic manager asks if the formulated strategy is appropriate in view of the firm's strengths and weaknesses versus those of *potential* competitors. In preparation, the manager has searched the environment for competitive threats. Now that the strategy is formulated — be it market development via globalization by Black & Decker, cementing existing supplier relationships by Arrow Electronics, divestiture and diversification by Trans World, or product development from a customer base by Sears — the manager must analyze not the present competitive threats but the future responses of competitors.

Competitors rarely do nothing in response to another firm's market and product development activities. The more competitors exist, the slower the total industry's growth, the lower the industry's profits, and the more standardized the industry's products — then the more likely it is a competitor will make significant responses to another's activities. The strategic manager must plan for competitors' responses.

The strategist selling in relatively competitive markets finds it useful to develop a series of countermoves, as contingency plans against a spectrum of possible competitive responses. In designing these countermoves, the manager assesses the strategy;

poor strategy formulation leaves the manager in situations with few, if any, options. More effective strategy gives the manager feasible countermove alternatives, allowing the manager to guide the firm into a flexible position, not into a dead end. Competitive response is comparable to a chess game. All plans, initial moves, and strategy must be based in part on the opponent's countermoves.

Competitive response analyses, then, consist of (1) anticipating competition's probable response to your strategic moves and (2) assessing your strategy according to the feasibility and quality of your available counterresponses to competition's moves. The more feasible a firm's counterresponses, the more effective the strategy formulated. The less threatening competition's response, the more effective the firm's formulated strategy.

EXAMPLES: *Competitive Response*

For a long time Anheuser-Busch, the leading U.S. brewer, was an industry follower. Perhaps its plodding Clydesdales were appropriate symbols for its slow and deliberate competitive responses. Anheuser-Busch waited four years to enter the national low-calorie beer market, during which time Miller's Lite beer became the second-best-selling beer after Budweiser. However, Anheuser-Busch's competitive response pattern changed 180 degrees after the Lite experience. In the summer of 1984, after only brief market tests, Anheuser-Busch's Clydesdales burst from the starting gate with the national introduction of the first low-alcohol beer, LA.

The St. Louis newspaper market has seen a series of strategic actions and competitive responses. After buying the conservative morning newspaper, the *St. Louis Globe-Democrat*, in early 1984, the new owner followed a market penetration strategy that built upon the paper's conservative reader base by including strongly conservative editorials. The competition, the more liberal *St. Louis Post-Dispatch*, which had only been the leader in its circulation race with the *Globe-Democrat* since 1982, switched from being an afternoon paper to a morning paper, thus more directly competing with the *Globe-Democrat*. Three months later the *Globe-Democrat* owners responded with a new afternoon paper, the *St. Louis Evening News*. Meanwhile, the *Post-Dispatch* added more stories to its paper and stepped up promotion efforts.

Sears, Roebuck was the big unknown in competitive response analysis in the credit card industry in 1985. Citicorp, with about ten million cardholders, was aggressively pursuing not only bank cards but its own Choice, Diners Club, and Carte Blanche cards. American Express was defending its share of fifteen million cardholders. But both Citicorp and American Express watched anxiously as Sears tested various forms of credit cards, and pondered its move from its base of sixty million Sears cardholders.

Two interesting aspects of competitive response analysis are the variables of experience and origin. How the industry responds the first time to a competitive move may be quite different from how it responds at subsequent times. And competitors can act differently based on who initiates competitive acts. For example, the 1982–1983 price cuts in the airline industry were started by the "old guard" companies, notably Pan Am. Most big airlines responded by across-the-board fare cuts, and for a time travelers could go just about anywhere for ninety-nine dollars. In the fare war of 1984, however, People Express and Braniff initiated the fare cuts. This time the big airlines, principally United and American, matched fare cuts on crucial routes, but raised fares on nondiscounted routes. Further, the big airlines placed significant limits on peak-hour discount seats.

Competitive response analysis is further complicated by companies' differing responses. During the early 1980s some tobacco companies (R. J. Reynolds, Brown & Williamson) cut cigarette prices. Liggett & Myers continued its commitment to "generic" cigarettes. Phillip Morris, on the other hand, pursued aggressive advertising and marketing tactics, experimenting with new, higher-capacity packages and other marketing innovations. The range of possible competitive responses, then, can make contingency strategies a necessity.

Risk

The strategic manager asks if the expected return from the formulated strategy is worth the risk. Although competition's countermoves represent one aspect of risk, the strategic manager must consider the following six other dimensions of risk, which represent measures of vulnerability.

Technological (How limited is our technological base?)

Product/market (How narrow is our product line and how few markets do we serve?)

Financial (How flexible is our financial structure and how many financial options do we have? What will be the short- and long-term effects on earnings?)

Managerial (Can management effectively carry out the strategy?)

Production (What percentage of capacity is committed to the formulated strategy?)

Environmental (Are there undesirable consequences for either society or government?)

The opposite of vulnerability and risk is opportunity. The strategic manager must be assured that the potential returns from the formulated strategy outweigh these risks.

EXAMPLES: *Risk and Timing*

One aspect of risk is timing. Generally, the sooner the firm takes strategic action, the greater the risk. Waiting for more information and more confirmation of environmental trends is generally less risky, but greater rewards often exist for those who take early advantage of environmental opportunities. Quinn (1980) saw "logical incrementalism" as one strategy for change. A cautious attitude can represent bad timing if technological progress and competitive response make waiting risky. Anheuser-Busch adopted a cautious attitude toward light beer and watched Miller's Lite capture an enviable share of the market. Having learned its lesson, Anheuser-Busch aggressively introduced its low-alcohol L.A. brand in 1984. IBM's view of the advisability of "being first" is seen in its delayed introduction of personal computers.

In the early 1970s Mars's Snickers became the number 1 candy bar, pushing out Hershey. Snickers plus M&Ms gave Mars half of the top 10 U.S. candy bars, with Hershey holding the other half of the top 10. An industry observer commented in *Fortune* on Hershey's sense of timing and competitive response: "It took the

Hershey people seven or eight years to realize that Mars was not going to go away. Then it took them another five years to get their act together'' (7/8/85, p. 53).

The proactive view of timing held by Leslie Wexner, head of The Limited, was described in *Fortune* by a division executive: "It'll be 11:30 at night, and we're figuring out how to market $1.99 panty hose, and suddenly Les is thinking five and ten years out, and encouraging everyone else to do the same" (8/19/85, p. 157).

There are many aspects of risk. So far we have focused on the location and source of risk in the dimensions of risk, including (1) competition, (2) technology, (3) product market, (4) financial, (5) managerial, (6) production, and (7) environmental. Three other elements of risk are inherent in risk itself, just as important as the sources or timing of risk. Just as the strategic manager should not focus on only one measure of performance, so should the manager not assess and evaluate only one source or element of risk. The three elements of risk are

1. *Information*: Strategic risk originates from a lack of perfect information with which to make a strategic decision.
2. *Innovation*: Strategic risk or risk-taking means taking an innovative course of action. Risk, then, is built into entrepreneurship.
3. *Variability*: Risk means revenues and profits will vary. Strategies have a range of possible outcomes.

By examining these three elements of risk, the strategist will make conclusions about ways to reduce uncertainty and/or the necessity for contingency planning.

Synergy

In reviewing the selected strategy, the strategic manager looks for synergy. *Synergy* is the idea that the whole is greater than the sum of its parts, or that 2 + 2 equals more than 4. Synergy as it relates to strategy means that the formulated strategy results in an interaction of enterprise resources, producing total benefits greater than those that could be produced by the independent use of those resources.

Sears, Roebuck saw synergistic opportunities in the merger of its loyal customer base and convenient locations with financial and real estate services. Harlequin saw a combined benefit greater than the sum of each part in the addition of Western novels and science fiction to its production and distribution systems for romance literature. Synergy often is achieved by either applying distinctive competence to a related activity (market or product development within the growth matrix) or through using a few resources many times, resulting in efficiencies similar to those generated by economies of scale.

EXAMPLE: *Synergy*

Greyhound pursuit of synergy is reflected in its acquisitions. In February 1985 Greyhound announced its purchase of the consumer products of Purex Industries, products such as Purex bleach and Brillo soap pads. Greyhound already counted Parson's ammonia, Dial soap, and various antiperspirants among its consumer products. In the words of a Wall Street analyst, quoted in the *Christian Science Monitor*: "[The two groups] are both doing the same thing — their products are right next to each other on the shelf; they'll be able to combine their distribution systems. One plus one will make three, eventually'' (3/1/84, p. 11).

The absence of apparent opportunities for synergy suggests that the manager should rethink the strategic match for such opportunities, but it does not mean the formulated strategy is likely to be ineffective. Rather, the presence of apparent opportunities for synergy suggests that the strategy will be effective. Kitching (1967) showed how elusive synergy could be, and why mergers ''miscarry.''

Consistency

As a fourth quality check, the strategic manager asks if the formulated strategy is consistent with itself and with the organization's purpose and environments. Specifically, the test of consistency means assuring that the strategic path selected is appropriate for and consistent with (1) enterprise purpose, (2) the strengths and weaknesses of the internal environment, and (3) the opportunities and threats of the external environment.

Frohman and Bitondo (1981) studied the consistency between technology and strategy. They stressed the need for coordinating business strategy and technical planning. With the significant benefit of hindsight, inconsistencies in strategy formulation become apparent. Howard Head's refusal to expand his ski-making technology beyond metal skis to include fiberglass resulted in strategic risk inconsistent with the enterprise purpose of high growth. Harlequin's attempted transfer of its romance novel skills to science fiction novels proved inconsistent with the intellectual demands of the external environment's science fiction markets.

Workability

The strategist must determine if the strategy is workable and practical for the firm; in other words, if the strategy will succeed. The test of workability is a test of the likelihood that the strategic objectives will be achieved.

Examples of the unworkability of strategies abound. Aside from current examples, a list of unworkable strategies includes the World Football League, the League of Nations, the national dreams of world domination, and the domination of commodities by speculators. Paul et al. (1978) commented on workability in describing ''the reality gap'' in strategic planning. Linneman and Kennell (1977) pursued the practical and the workable in their ''shirt-sleeve approach'' to long-range plans.

AN OVERVIEW OF STRATEGY FORMULATION

To summarize the process of strategy formulation and to introduce the general topic of organizational structure discussed in Chapter 7, Figure 6.10 presents a schematic showing how (1) the levels of strategy interact and (2) the tools of strategic management fit within a strategic planning system or organizational structure. Subsets of this planning process include capital investment and operating budgets, which usually are planning cycles that follow strategic planning, although they may coincide with strategy formulation.

Figure 6.10 assumes a diversified, divisional firm. At earlier stages of corporate

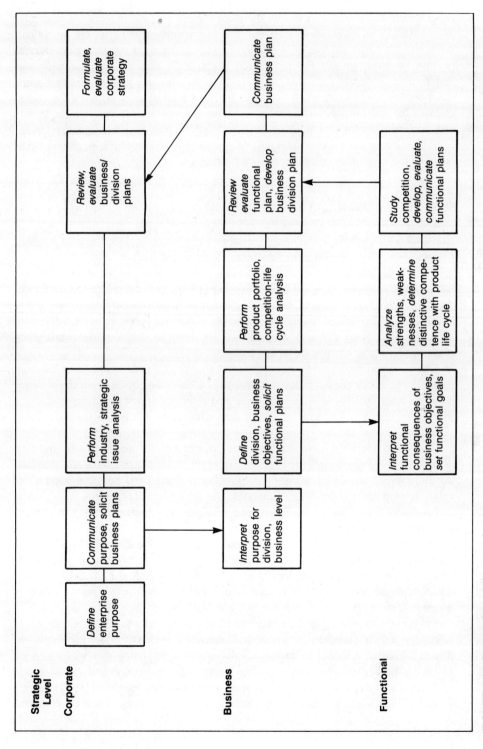

FIGURE 6.10 Strategy formulation overview

development the levels, and indeed the steps themselves, are reduced significantly. The critical factor in Figure 6.10 is the flow of information between the functional, business, and corporate levels. While the functional manager normally concentrates on that function, so that the production manager focuses on production matters and receives external data that is likely to center around production, that same functional manager interprets the broader business level plans in terms of the consequences for that function. The functional manager provides feedback on the threats and opportunities for that function as it follows the proposed business level plan.

Similar communication — analysis, interpretation, and feedback — should occur between the corporate- and business-level strategist.

STRATEGY FORMULATION RESEARCH

Classic research efforts in the area of strategy formulation include those of Argenti, Chamberlain, Cyert and March, Lindblom, Simon, and Steiner.

Argenti, in *Systematic Corporate Planning* (1974), not only addressed the procedures of corporate strategy formulation, but also urged the strategic manager to ensure that the formulated strategy took advantage of major opportunities and defended against major threats. He also stressed that the strategist should make contingency plans in the face of significant strategic threats.

Chamberlain presented his concept of "counterpoint" in *Enterprise and Environment* (1968). While the operating manager tries to maintain equilibrium, the strategic manager must pull the firm through time and space to deal with strategic changes in the environment. The strategist must deal with disequilibrium in the move from point to counterpoint.

Cyert and March presented a bargaining model which underlies the formulation of strategy in *A Behavioral Theory of the Firm* (1963). Organizational slack, conflicting objectives, sequential attention to functional goals, and personal aspirations result in adaptive, "satisficing" strategies.

Lindblom's message is similar to that of Cyert and March. Lindblom argued, in "The Science of 'Muddling Through'" (1959), that the scientific, management view of strategy formulation — the rational, comprehensive method of agreeing on purpose and selecting from alternatives based on purpose — was often not appropriate or was not done. Rather, Lindblom said, decision makers follow a successive limited comparison method in strategy formulation, which involves achieving a consensus on means, not ends. This method occurs especially in complex situations.

Simon (1964) investigated problem-solving models and goals. In one sense, his work represents a synthesis of scientific and behavioral models of strategy formulation. Simon presented a model of problem solving and formulation that was based on searching for feasible alternatives, given a known set of constraints and requirements.

Steiner's study, *Pitfalls in Comprehensive Long-Range Planning* (1972), is rich in observations about dangers and problems in strategic planning. These observations encompass organizational and procedural dangers, but also address strategy formulation itself, warning of (1) top management allowing focus on current operating problems to invalidate strategic decisions and (2) using intuition instead of the strategic decision process in strategy formulation.

Current significant research efforts in strategy formulation include works by the following authors.

Abbanat (1967), focusing on the strategies formulated by small companies competing against larger firms, reached two conclusions. (1) Small companies look for interstices; that is, for market gaps and untried products ignored by the larger companies. (2) Small companies compete by unconventional (customization, improved service) means, often attracting technicians who appreciate the environment of the small firm.

Chaffee (1985) pointed out that definitions of strategy may be based on one or another of three models of strategy:

1. *Linear*: Integrated decisions, actions, or plans that will set and achieve viable organization goals.
2. *Adaptive*: Environmental assessment of internal and external conditions that leads to the organization adjusting to a viable match between opportunities and capabilities.
3. *Interpretive*: The organization attracts individuals in a social contract or a collection of cooperative agreements.

Chaffee concluded that the lack of consensus on a definition of strategy is due to its multidimensional and situational characteristics.

Dutton, Fahey, and Narayanan (1983) researched SID (Strategic Issue Diagnosis) as both a planning trigger or stimulus and an implementation planning tool. These three researchers showed how SID can "mobilize behavioral and political forces toward action," presenting an input-process-output model of strategic issue diagnosis. Strategic issue diagnosis is a focused analysis of one strategic signal, or a group of interrelated signals.

Glueck (1976), building on Hofer's categories and a wealth of business articles from the 1930s to the 1970s, reclassified Hofer's twenty-eight challenges-responses into four broad strategies — growth, stability, retrenchment, and combination. Glueck found that trade (wholesale and retail) and consumer goods companies generally follow growth strategies; natural resources and construction companies generally follow stability strategies; and conglomerates generally follow retrenchment strategies. Glueck also discovered that most firms followed stability strategies in the thirties, growth strategies in the forties, combination strategies in the fifties, and retrenchment strategies in the sixties and seventies.

Gutmann's project (1964) analyzed fifty-three firms that had experienced high growth. Gutmann concluded that high-growth firms concentrate on a few product-market segments rather than covering many segments. Gutmann also observed that while half of the high-growth firms made acquisitions, they did not experience growth significantly greater than firms that did not follow the acquisition path.

Hanna (1969) studied three companies that each operated in several industries. He found that the multi-industry company strategies followed not only a corporate purpose but overall growth policies, financial policies, and organizational policies. He also noted that these companies paid more attention to these policies than to an analysis of existing products and markets.

Hofer categorized twenty-eight external challenges and threats and a matching set of strategic responses to these challenges. This initial effort reached general conclusions, and was further developed by Glueck. Part of Hofer's major contribution was his categories of challenges and responses, developed by studying four hundred challenges-responses contained in business articles over a twelve-year period.

King (1982) researched a methodology for integrating strategic issues analysis into the planning process, based upon a joint manager-analyst team approach. He recommended (1) identifying the strategic issue, (2) developing a formal statement of that issue, (3) developing a preliminary issue model, (4) critiquing and revising the model, (5) gathering data, and (6) using the model in the planning process.

Kitching (1967), in his study of sixty-nine of the mergers by twenty-two firms, reached two conclusions. (1) Acquisitions were most successful in instances of financial synergy; somewhat successful in marketing synergy instances; and least successful in cases of production and technology synergy. (2) Unsuccessful acquisitions resulted from the acquired company's top management's refusal to change strategies.

Rumelt, by examining 250 companies in 1949, 1959, and 1969, identified strategy types (single businesses, dominant-vertical firms, conglomerates, and so on) and five administrative structures (geographic, holding companies, product division, functional, and functional with subsidiaries). Rumelt reached two important conclusions. (1) Science firms used diversification to correct declining current businesses; nonscience firms did not. (2) Firms diversified to achieve EPS gains, but did not achieve real long-term improvements.

Schendel, Patten, and Riggs (1974) reached three conclusions after studying corporate turnarounds in fifty-four companies. (1) Overall strategy changes were necessary to reverse earnings declines. (2) Eighty-one percent of the turnaround companies changed management. (3) Marketing changes, plant additions, product and geographic diversifications, and efficiency programs were utilized more than divestiture in the successful turnaround strategies.

Weber (1984) asked, How does the strategic manager deal with uncertainty? To answer, Weber analyzed managerial uncertainty and found two kinds of ambiguity: uncertainty ''about the gaps between what they want to achieve and what they have or expect to achieve'' and uncertainty ''about their steps to close the gaps.'' Weber advocated a dialectic process, ''heuristics for achieving synthesis.'' Weber also proposed "challenging conditions with counterconditions" so that "new concepts or new data" emerge, resulting in a synthesis.

Wheelwright (1984) studied the difference between strategy using analytical concepts, as at Texas Instruments, and an incremental-value–based approach, as at Hewlett-Packard. Wheelwright commented on the differences in resulting strategy regarding the product life cycle, cost and pricing strategies, production plans, and portfolio balance. Wheelwright concluded that each firm must carefully select its strategy planning approach, since each approach has significant strengths and weaknesses.

EXECUTIVE COMMENTS

Strategy formulation is explicitly addressed within Searle at both the corporate and product line group levels. It is the intent of the process to stimulate congruence of strategy formulation efforts throughout the firm. In slightly different terms, we view formalized planning primarily as a managerial communications system and *process — and not as a separate functional exercise.*

> R. C. Lancey, Searle executive (in Schendel & Hofer, 1979)

The really pressing problem [at Gulf Oil is] "How do we know good strategy when we see it?"

> B. C. Ball, Jr., Gulf Oil executive (in Schendel & Hofer, 1979)

To use some of International Harvester's terminology, there are some key vulnerabilities . . . in strategic and policy research such as . . . the basic assumption of rationality. Many times business decisions are made or are impacted significantly by forces which objectively and according to competitive theory are not rational.

> R. O. Aines, International Harvester executive (in Schendel & Hofer, 1979)

KEY TERMS

competitive analysis (page 160)

consistency (page 164)

directional policy matrix (page 144)

growth matrix (page 146)

industry analysis (page 148)

product portfolios (page 142)

risk (page 162)

strategic issues (page 150)

strategic levels (page 139)

strategy formulation (page 136)

synergy (page 163)

BIBLIOGRAPHY

Abbanat, R. F., "Strategies of Size," D.B.A. dissertation, Harvard Business School, 1967.

Abell, D. F., "Strategic Windows," *Journal of Marketing* (July 1978), pp. 21–26.

Ackoff, R., "On the Use of Models in Corporate Planning," *Strategic Management Journal* (October-December 1981).

Andrews, K. R., *The Concept of Corporate Strategy* (Homewood, IL: Richard D. Irwin, 1980).

Ansoff, H. I., *Corporate Strategy: An Analytical Approach to Business Policy for Growth and Expansion* (New York: McGraw-Hill, 1965).

Argenti, J., *Systematic Corporate Planning* (New York: Wiley, 1974).

Astely, W. G., "Toward an Appreciation of Collective Strategy," *Academy of Management Review* (July 1984).

"Black & Decker's Gamble on 'Globalization,' " *Fortune* (May 14, 1984), pp. 40–48.

Bloom, P., and P. Kotler, "Strategies for High Market Share Companies," *Harvard Business Review* 53 (November-December 1975), pp. 63–72.

Bower, J. L., *Managing the Resource Allocation Process: A Study of Corporate Planning and Investment* (Cambridge, MA: Division of Research, Graduate School of Business Administration, Harvard University, 1970).

Burgelman, R. A., "Managing the New Venture Division," *Strategic Management Journal* 6 (January-March 1985), pp. 39–54.

Chaffee, E. E., "Three Models of Strategy," *Academy of Management Review* 10 (1985), pp. 89–98.

Chamberlain, N. W., *Enterprise and Environment: The Firm in Time and Space* (New York: McGraw-Hill, 1968).

Chandler, A. D., Jr., *Strategy and Structure: Chapters in the History of the Industrial Enterprise* (Cambridge, MA: M.I.T. Press, 1962).

Channon, D. F., "Commentary," in D. E. Schendel and C. W. Hofer, eds., *Strategic Management* (Boston: Little, Brown, 1979), pp. 122–133.

Christensen, C. R., N. A. Berg, and M. S. Salter, *Policy Formulation and Administration*, 7th ed. (Homewood, IL: Richard D. Irwin, 1976).

Christopher, W., "Achievement Reporting — Controlling Performance Against Objectives," *Long Range Planning* 10 (October 1977), pp. 14–24.

Cooper, A. C., "Strategic Management: New Ventures and Small Business," in C. W. Hofer and D. E. Schendel, eds., *Strategy Formulation* (St. Paul, MN: West Publishing, 1978).

Cyert, R. M., and J. G. March, *A Behavioral Theory of the Firm* (Englewood Cliffs, NJ: Prentice-Hall, 1963).

David, F. R., *Fundamentals of Strategic Management* (Columbus, OH: Merrill, 1986).

Day, G. S., "Diagnosing the Product Portfolio," *Journal of Marketing* 41 (April 1977): pp. 29–38.

Dutton, V. E., L. Fahey, and V. K. Narayanan, "Toward Understanding Strategic Issue Diagnosis," *Strategic Management Journal* 4 (October-December 1983), pp. 307–323.

Fredrickson, J. W., and T. R. Mitchell, "Strategic Decision Processes: Comprehensiveness and Performance in an Industry with an Unstable Environment," *Academy of Management Journal* 27 (June 1984), pp. 399–423.

Frohman, A. L., and D. Bitondo, "Coordinating Business Strategy and Technical Planning," *Long Range Planning* 14 (December 1981), pp. 58–67.

Ginter, P. M., and A. C. Rucke, "Can Business Learn from Wargames?" *Long Range Planning* 17 (June 1984), pp. 123–128.

Glueck, W. F., *Business Policy, Strategy Formation, and Executive Action* (New York: McGraw-Hill, 1976).

Gupta, A. K., and V. Govindarajan, "Build, Hold, Harvest: Converting Strategic Intentions into Reality," *Journal of Business Strategy* 4 (March 1984), pp. 34–47.

Gutmann, P. M., "Strategies for Growth," *California Management Review* (Summer 1964), pp. 31–36.

Hall, W. K., "Survival Strategies in a Hostile Environment," *Harvard Business Review* 58 (September-October 1980), pp. 75–85.

Hammermesh, R. G., M. J. Anderson, Jr., and J. E. Harris, "Strategies for Low Market Share Businesses," *Harvard Business Review* 56 (May-June 1978), pp. 95–102.

Hanna, R. G. C., "The Concept of Corporate Strategy in Multi-Industry Companies," D. B. A. dissertation, Harvard Business School, 1969.

Harrell, G. D., and R. O. Kiefer, "Multinational Strategic Market Portfolios," *MSU Business Topics* (Winter 1981), pp. 5–15.

Harrigan, K. R., "The Effect of Exit Barriers Upon Strategic Flexibility," *Strategic Management Journal*, vol. 1 (1980), pp. 165–176.

Harrigan, K. R., "Exit Decisions in Mature Industries," *Academy of Management Journal* 25 (December 1982), pp. 707–732.

Harrigan, K. R., "Vertical Integration and Corporate Strategy," *Academy of Management Journal* 28 (June 1985), pp. 397–425.

Harrigan, K., and M. Porter, "End-Game Strategies for Declining Industries," *Harvard Business Review* 61 (July-August 1983).

Haspelslagh, P., "Portfolio Planning: Uses and Limits," *Harvard Business Review* 60 (January-February 1982), pp. 58–73.

Hedley, B., "Strategy and the Business Portfolio," *Long Range Planning* 10 (February 1977), pp. 9–15.

Henderson, B., "The Application and Misapplication of the Experience Curve," *Journal of Business Strategy* (Winter 1984).

Hofer, C. W., "Conceptual Constructs for Formulating Corporate and Business Strategies" (Boston: Harvard ICCH 9-378-754, 1977).

Hofer, C. W., "Some Preliminary Research on Patterns of Strategic Behavior," *Proceedings of the Business Policy and Planning Division of the Academy of Management*, Academy of Management, August 1973.

Hofer, C. W., "Toward a Contingency Theory of Business Strategy," *Academy of Management Journal* 18 (1975), pp. 789–810.

Hofer, C. W., "Turnaround Strategies," *Journal of Business Strategy* 1 (Summer 1980), pp. 19–31.

Hofer, C. W., and D. Schendel, *Strategy Formulation: Analytical Concepts* (St. Paul, MN: West Publishing, 1978).

Hussey, D. E., "Strategic Management: Lessons from Success and Failure," *Long Range Planning* 17 (February 1984), pp. 43–53.

Katz, R. L., *Management of the Total Enterprise* (Englewood Cliffs, NJ: Prentice-Hall, 1970).

Kierulff, H. W., "Finding the Best Acquisition Candidates," *Harvard Business Review* 59 (January-February 1981), pp. 66–68.

King, W. R., "Using Strategic Issue Analysis," *Long Range Planning* 15 (August 1982), pp. 45–49.

Kitching, J., "Why Do Mergers Miscarry?" *Harvard Business Review* 45 (November-December 1967), pp. 84–101.

Lindblom, C. E., "The Science of 'Muddling Through,'" *Public Administration Revew* (Spring 1959), pp. 79–88.

Linneman, R. E., and J. D. Kennell, "Shirt-Sleeve Approach to Long-Range Plans," *Harvard Business Review* 55 (March-April 1977), pp. 141–150.

McGinnis, M. A., "The Key to Strategic Planning: Integrating Analysis and Intuition," *Sloan Management Review* (Fall 1984), pp. 45–52.

MacMillan, I., "Preemptive Strategies," *Journal of Business Strategy* (Fall 1983).

Mintzberg, H., and J. A. Waters, "Tracking Strategy in an Entrepreneurial Firm," *Academy of Management Journal*, vol. 25, no. 3 (1982), pp. 465–499.

Paul, R. N., N. B. Donovan, and J. W. Taylor, "The Reality Gap in Strategic Planning," *Harvard Business Review* 56 (May-June 1978), pp. 124–130.

Peters, T., and N. Austin, *A Passion for Excellence* (New York: Random House, 1985).

Porter, M. E., *Competitive Strategy: Techniques for Analyzing Industries and Competitors* (New York: The Free Press, 1980).

Porter, M. E., "How Competitive Forces Shape Strategy," *Harvard Business Review* 57 (March-April 1979), pp. 137–145.

Porter, M. E., "Please Note Location of Nearest Exit: Exit Barriers and Planning," *California Management Review* 19 (Winter 1976), pp. 21–25.

Quinn, J. B., *Strategies for Change: Logical Incrementalism* (Homewood, IL: Richard D. Irwin, 1980).

Robinson, R. B., Jr., and J. A. Pearce, III, "The Structure of Generic Strategies and Their Impact on Business-Unit Performances," Academy of Management Proceedings 1985, pp. 35–39.

Robinson, S. J. Q., R. E. Hitchens, and D. P. Wade, "The Directional Policy Matrix: Tool for Strategic Planning," *Long Range Planning* 11 (June 1978), pp. 8–15.

Rothschild, W. E., "Surprise and the Competitive Advantage," *Journal of Business Strategy* 4 (Winter 1984), pp. 10–18.

Rowe, H., R. Mason, and K. Dickel, *Strategic Management and Business Policy* (Reading, MA: Addison-Wesley, 1982).

Rumelt, R., "Diversification Strategy and Profitability," *Strategic Management Journal* (October-December 1982).

Rumelt, R., *Strategy, Structure and Economic Performance* (Cambridge, MA: Harvard University Press, 1974).

Schendel, D. E., and C. W. Hofer, eds., *Strategic Management: A New View of Business Policy and Planning* (Boston: Little, Brown, 1979).

Schendel, D. E., R. Patten, and J. Riggs, "Corporate Turnaround Strategies," Academy of Management, Seattle, August 1974.

Schoeffler, S., R. D. Buzzell, and D. F. Heany, "Impact of Strategic Planning on Profit Performance," *Harvard Business Review* 54 (March-April 1974), pp. 137–145.

Scott, B. R., "Stages of Corporate Development" (Boston: Intercollegiate Case Clearing House, 9-371-294, 1971).

Seeger, J. A., "Reversing the Image of BCG's Growth/Share Matrix," *Society of Management Journal* (January-March 1984).

Simon, H. A., "On the Concept of Organizational Goals," *Administrative Sciences Quarterly* (June 1964), pp. 1–22.

Steiner, G., "Formal Strategic Planning in the U.S. Today," *Long Range Planning* 16 (June 1983), pp. 12–18.

Steiner, G., *Pitfalls in Comprehensive Long Range Planning* (Oxford, OH: Planning Executives Institute, 1972).

Taylor, B., "Strategic Planning — Which Style Do You Need?" *Long Range Planning* 17 (June 1984), pp. 51–62.

Thompson, J. D., *Organizations in Action* (New York: McGraw-Hill, 1967).

Weber, C. E., "Strategic Thinking — Dealing with Uncertainty," *Long Range Planning* 17 (October 1984), pp. 60–70.

Wheelwright, S. C., "Strategy Management and Strategic Planning Approaches," *Interfaces* 14:1 (January-February 1984), pp. 19–33.

Williams, J. R., "Technological Evolution and Competitive Response," *Strategic Management Journal* (January-March 1983).

Woo, C. Y., and A. Cooper, "The Surprising Case for Low Market Share," *Harvard Business Review* 60 (November-December 1982), pp. 106–113.

CHAPTER 7

IMPLEMENTING STRATEGY

*Strategy formulation emphasizes the abilities to conceptualize, analyze, and judge.
. . . Implementation depends upon the skills of working through others, instituting
internal change, and guiding . . . activities. . . . Implementing strategy poses
the tougher management challenge.*

A. A. Thompson and A. J. Strickland, *Strategic Management*

This chapter defines the two components of implementation, namely, organization
structure and motivation systems. It then presents two criteria for the implementation
decision: distinctive competence and congruence.

The strategic manager implements strategy by selecting organizational structure,
control, measurement, and reward systems from a range of alternatives. In addition
to being a resource allocator (see Working Concept 6), the manager may need to
serve as negotiator, disturbance handler, or innovator. The manager uses certain
criteria to select specific implementation steps from the range alternatives, including
(1) distinctive competence and the fit between strategy and structure and (2) congruence.

NO RIGHT ANSWER

This chapter reviews the wide range of structural, systematic, and procedural organizational alternatives that confront the strategic manager trying to implement strategy.
The problem of choosing from among multiple alternatives is complicated further
by variables connected with the new strategy, the current structure, and leadership
style.

The type of strategy selected and the degree of change between the new and
current strategy influence the choice of organizational alternatives. The organization's
current state, and the types of organizational problems encountered by the strategic
manager, affect the manager's choice. Implementation alternatives differ depending
on whether the firm's leader is a visionary, an autocrat, a liaison/coordinator, a

"hands-on" coparticipant, or a consensus builder. This vast range of interacting and important variables offers the strategic manager many different solutions. Each situation has several "right answers." Emphasizing that simplicity is the key to good management, Peter Drucker concluded, "The simplest organization structure that will do the job is the best one."

IMPLEMENTATION DEFINED

The implementation of strategy occurs when the strategic manager selects a specific organizational structure and motivation system and allocates specific organizational resources to help create them. The manager selects these specific organizational resources and steps, which include managerial planning and control systems, administrative structure and hierarchies, and performance measurement and incentives, based upon strategic congruence and distinctive competence.

IMPLEMENTATION ILLUSTRATED

The strategic manager creates structures and systems that are supportive of and consistent with his or her formulated strategy. The basic requirement of the action and resource-allocation phase of strategy implementation is that action and allocation be determined by the formulated strategy. Strategy determines structure and its resulting systems, as Chandler (1962), Galbraith (1977), and others have asserted.

The strategic manager who pursues growth by developing a new product must create an organizational structure and supporting systems consistent with new product development. Aspects of such a consistent structure might include

Incentive systems for those sales personnel who contribute new product ideas

A strong product R&D staff supported by adequate budgets and a creative environment with minimal bureaucracy

Active scanning and analysis of customer needs and industry trends, including joint research projects with suppliers and customers

Because these motivation systems and information systems are a logical extension of the formulated strategy, they fully support that strategy. In the mid-1980s Peugeot acquisitions resulted in an inconsistent structure of duplicated production facilities — Peugeot, Citroen, and Talbot — which worked against the strategy of worldwide competition by preventing the achievement of economies of scale.

Table 7.1 suggests other structures and systems compatible with differing (market development and diversification) growth strategies. Because each strategic situation is different, however, these suggestions are general and tentative. They appear here to illustrate the process of implementation and resource allocation. A specific illustration of different organizational structures at different times (General Electric) was presented in Chapter 1 (pages 12–14).

TABLE 7.1 Organization systems and structures	Structure or system component	Formulated strategy	
		Market development	*Diversification*
	Management structure	Centralized, at least in marketing and market research	Decentralized, to bring decision makers closer to opportunities
	Compensation systems	Based on sales	Based on stock performance
	Information systems	Highlight new markets and market shares	Show performance within the different product/ market groups, intergroup differences

STRUCTURE AND SYSTEMS COMPONENTS

What alternative organizational structures and motivations systems are available to the strategic manager? Table 7.1 suggests that they include management or administrative structure, information systems, and compensation systems. They also include performance measurement and nonmonetary aspects of organizational structure.

Administrative Systems

Administrative systems, or management structures, fit within a spectrum that has centralization on one end and decentralization on the other. The strategic manager selects certain alternatives based upon his or her formulated strategy. A centralized managerial structure is a well-defined, hierarchical reporting structure which reduces participation in strategic planning and decision making as one moves further down the management hierarchy. Such a structure might be appropriate for a company with limited products or markets, a developing company, or an organization that needs to respond quickly to threats.

As a firm decentralizes, more managers participate in strategic decision making as more decentralized divisions, and thus more divisional managers, are added to the firm. Diverse product markets require decentralized structures or else elaborate bureaucratic hierarchies, with their attendant problems of slow response time and high overhead. Nonetheless, the different divisions of decentralized companies duplicate such services as accounting and personnel. The decentralized strategic manager also may focus too much on the decentralized unit, never seeing the forest for the trees.

Two administrative systems, matrix organizations and strategic business units, were designed to have the breadth of the decentralized structure while achieving the fast response and strategic concentration of the centralized organization.

Matrix Organizations. A matrix organization is a two-tiered management structure that focuses on the manager. The strategic manager in the matrix organization has one responsibility to a product/market or project group, but that same strategic manager also has additional long-term responsibilities to a functional group. For example, a manager might be responsible for a personal computer product line while also planning for miniaturized printed circuits.

Matrix units help the manager to get the best of both worlds; that is, the special expertise and economies of scale of functional management with the new product innovation of product managers. However, Galbraith (1971) and Davis and Lawrence (1978) pointed out the problems of matrix organizations. Knight (1980) argued that the seven theoretical advantages of matrix organizations — (1) efficient use of resources, (2) flexibility in conditions of change and uncertainty, (3) technical excellence, (4) ability to balance conflicting objectives, (5) freedom of top management for long-range planning, (6) improving motivation and commitment, and (7) giving opportunities for personal development — must be weighed against four major problems — (1) controlling conflict, (2) achieving balance, (3) minimizing stress, and (4) incurring increased administrative and communication costs.

Strategic Business Units (SBUs). A strategic business unit is also a two-tiered management structure, but rather than focusing on the manager it revolves around groups of products and markets. All decentralized business components dealing with similar product markets are grouped together at the highest levels of the organization only, not at the level of the individual manager, into strategic business units. Individual management units and operating divisions dealing with ground weapons development or two-way military communication systems can be joined at the level of top management into a defense SBU. Hall (1978) described SBUs as "the hot new topic in the management of diversification." SBUs were covered in Working Concept 3 (pages 12–14).

Lawrence and Lorsch (1967) studied two aspects of administrative systems in depth: differentiation and integration. *Differentiation* is the degree of difference in attitudes and behavior of functional groups within the organization, including differences between managers as to goals, time frames, formality, and interpersonal relationships. *Integration* is the degree of collaboration and coordination among the functional groups and managers. A key factor in controlling organizational integration is in resolving conflicts effectively. The degrees of change, uncertainty, and stability in the external and internal environment determine the appropriateness and importance of differentiation and integration. Figure 7.1 presents some of the integration options against a spectrum of complexity and, presumably, expense.

Information Systems

An information system can fit into any number of categories, such as the extent and type of computerization, the relationship between the system and the organizational structure, or the costing and accounting techniques underlying the system. Strategists need to know whether the information system is primarily for one of three categories: (1) control, (2) planning, or (3) a combination of the two. Computerization, organization linkage, and costing methods are techniques used within these three important categories.

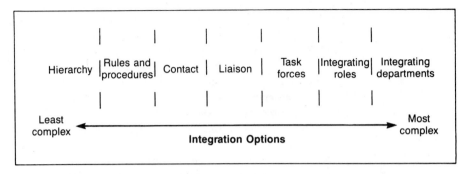

Source: Adapted from J. Galbraith and D. Nathanson, "The Role of Organizational Structure and Process in Strategy Implementation," in D. Schendel and C. Hofer, eds., *Strategic Management* (Boston: Little, Brown, 1979).

Control Systems. Control information systems measure and report current data from within the internal environment of the firm. Management reports might show the variance between standard costs and actual production costs; or they might report on the overhead costs of production and administrative departments. Control systems primarily function as the strategic manager's method of reviewing the efficiency of the internal environment. They are generally appropriate for formulated strategies of achieving lower costs to meet competition and/or to achieve growth, as lower production costs result in lower sales prices and thus higher volume. The marketplace is presumably stable for a firm using a control system; and the firm concentrates on production.

Planning Systems. Planning information systems are directed primarily toward the external environment; they are more concerned with estimating or detecting trends and problems than with measuring current performance data. Planning information systems might present reports showing simulations of what happens if a company takes actions 1, 2, or 3; if competitors take actions X, Y, or Z; and if the economic cycle is stagnant or experiencing slow growth. The planning reports might project various industry and economic data, including customers' and competitors' inventories and orders; or they might extrapolate foreign currency trends and the resulting currency exposures. Planning information systems are more appropriate for the strategic manager facing turbulent market conditions and complex environments.

Combination. This planning versus control dichotomy illustrates how the information system is determined by the manager's strategic objectives. In the vast majority of situations, the strategic manager utilizes a combination of planning and control reports, which emphasize current performance and project the consequences of this performance for the future. Managers use measurements of less than expected efficiency in order to stimulate corrective actions by management; they use projections of tomorrow's external environment in order to plan for modifications of today's operations. Thus, most information systems generally include both control and planning functions. The strategic manager knows which functions to stress based upon the formulated strategy and the selected strategic objectives. In reviewing the information systems during the implementation of strategy, the strategic manager asks two questions. (1) Is the control function of the information system consistent with and adequate for our formulated strategy? (Hobbs and Heany [1977] told how to "couple strategy to operating plans.") (2) Is the planning function of the information system consistent with and adequate for our formulated strategy? The strategic manager considers the present and future dimensions of both planning and control needs, encompassing both the internal and external environment.

Vancil (1973) explored what kind of management control a firm needs. Sihler (1971) gave pointers toward a better management control system. Christensen (1987) concluded,

> It is virtually impossible to make meaningful generalizations about how proper standards might be set in particular companies. It can be said, however, that in any organization the overall strategy can be translated into more or less detailed future plans (the detail becoming less predictable as the time span grows longer), which permits comparison of actual with predicted performance.

Compensation and Measurement Systems

After determining the appropriate administrative structure and the information content and flow within that structure, the strategist must turn to measuring and compensating for performance. Performance incentives include not only monetary items such as raises and bonuses, but less tangible compensation such as the physical work place and the firm's style and atmosphere (also called the *corporate culture*). Knowing the strategic objectives, the strategist decides what mix of the various performance, compensation, and intangible incentives will motivate the organization's employees. The spectrum of options includes the following incentives.

1. *Performance measurement unit*: The strategic manager might measure output and performance at the individual level at one end of the spectrum, or for the total organization only at the other end of the spectrum, or at intermediary stages such as production location or sales group.

2. *Performance measurement basis*: Measurement can be based on a long-term perspective or on the very short term. The measure itself can be quantitative or qualitative — the latter frequently stated in terms of tasks or objectives. Performance measurement will change from the personal, subjective criteria of the entrepreneur, to technical and cost criteria for functional managers, and to return and market criteria for diversified, decentralized managers.

3. *Performance and compensation linkage*: The extremes of the options range from compensation based completely on performance, as in an escalating commission plan, to compensation unrelated to any performance measure.

4. *Performance evaluation method*: The strategic manager has a range of options from a highly formalized, completely documented system of periodic peer and supervisory review, to an informal, catch-as-catch-can evaluation plan.

5. *Compensation*: Will compensation be limited to monetary rewards, or should it include a related plan of levels of office size and furnishings, praise, memberships, insurance benefits, vacation, travel allowances, stock options, and other nonmonetary benefits?

6. *Corporate culture*: Top management can create an atmosphere and operating style ranging from totally threatening and ruthless to totally supportive, nurturing, and forgiving. Leadership style can be based on persuasion or on commands. The organization form can be tight or loose ("mechanistic" or "organic" [Burns and Stalker, 1961]). Some firms, such as Procter & Gamble, are known for their corporate culture and atmosphere of internal competition; others, such as the oft-cited Japanese enterprises, intentionally create a nonthreatening environment in which each person has long-term job security.

In extreme situations, such as the start-up or bankruptcy phases of a business, the strategic manager might choose extreme positions within these six preceding implementation options. Since relatively few extreme situations exist, most managers find themselves using a combination of options that center at about the middle of the option spectrum. They make their decisions based on the relative importance of the human resource factor in attaining strategic objectives, and upon the values of key managers.

Leontiades (1981) advised on how to choose the right manager to fit the strategy. Tichy et al. (1982) analyzed strategic human resource management. Christopher (1977) suggested ways to control performance against objectives that would result in "achievement reporting."

The strategic manager considers the total strategic situation; he or she does not rely merely on a few progress and performance measures. Financial managers might measure earnings growth, price multiples, and return statistics, but strategic managers view these as superficial symbols of environmental forces that must be analyzed and understood. Sales managers might study unit and dollar growth rates, but strategic managers assess the change in relative strength of competition and in market demand and technology.

Holistic Measures. Strategic evaluation of progress encompasses all aspects of the organization seen from the perspective of the chief executive. The strategic manager has a holistic perspective; he or she is concerned with the total system's progress, not with unidimensional measurement of one or a few parts of the whole. The following list presents holistic measures of strategic progress.

1. *Stage of completion*: How complete is the strategic activity that is being measured?
2. *Timing*: Is the activity on schedule?
3. *Resources*: Is the activity within budget?
4. *Modification*: Is the activity that is being measured achieving the strategic objective, or is some modification desirable?

Limited or unidimensional measures can result in undesirable behavior by those managers being measured. Managers might focus on short-term rather than strategic objectives; short-term measures such as quarterly profits do not measure strategic progress.

General Electric's multiple criteria for performance evaluation provides an example of an evaluation system that avoids the unidimensional or the suboptimizing measure. G.E.'s eight criteria include (1) balance between long-term and short-term objectives, (2) public responsibility, (3) productivity, (4) product leadership, (5) personnel development, and (6) employee attitudes — along with the more frequently encountered criteria of market position and profitability. The effective strategist recognizes not only the necessity for multiple measures of progress, but also the danger of short-term perspectives and the problem of means becoming ends.

Short-Term Perspective. Companies frequently assess performance and progress by measuring

Production
    capital/labor/material mix
    costs
    efficiency/output
    value added
Marketing
    sales growth
    market share
    margins
Finance
    stock price
    net profit
    earnings per share
    return ratios (assets, investment, equity, sales)
    liquidity
    leverage

The short-term perspective of these measures blurs their effectiveness as strategic evaluation tools. Strategy takes a long time to formulate and implement. Strategic frameworks are long term, but these measures are short term. The strategist studies trends in these measures, not the measures themselves.

A Long-Term Financial Measure. Many researchers have concluded that the stock exchange is an efficient capital market that incorporates economic data in an efficient way. From this conclusion, the strategist who works in a firm whose shares are traded on the stock exchange is provided with a measure of strategic performance, or relative earnings multiple (REM).

Securities sell on the stock exchange at an average multiple of earnings, called the *price-earnings ratio* or the *earnings multiple*. This earnings multiple is calculated by dividing current earnings per share into the stock price. A stock earning $2 per share and selling for $16 would have an earnings multiple of 8.

REM, the relative earnings multiple, compares the earnings multiple with the average stock market multiple, and quantifies this comparison by calculating a ratio of actual earnings multiple to the average earnings multiple.

$$\text{REM} = \frac{\text{Actual earnings multiple for stock}}{\text{Average stock market earnings multiple}}$$

If the stock market on average values shares at 8 times earnings, and our stock is trading at an earnings multiple of 10, our REM is 1.25 (10 ÷ 8). If our stock is trading at an earnings ratio of 6, our REM is 0.75 (6 ÷ 8).

The longer-term perspective of the stock exchange gives the strategic manager an outsider's evaluation of strategy that many believe is based upon an efficient capital market. REM can be even more insightful if the strategist uses as the denominator not the average stock market multiple, but averages for specific industries and companies, including competitors. REM should be calculated for a firm's competitors as well as for the firm itself; those REM trends should be studied by the strategist.

For example, on April 8, 1980, the Seagram Company sold its oil and gas subsidiary, Texas Pacific Oil, to Sun Company. Seagram had entered the oil and gas business in 1953; by 1979 oil and gas revenues were $190 million versus $2,363 million for spirits and wine, and oil and gas assets were $498 million versus $1,939 million for spirits and wine assets. Each 1979 dollar of oil and gas assets produced $0.38 of revenue, while each dollar of spirits and wine assets produced $1.22 of revenue for Seagram. Thus one could conclude that Seagram was more productive, and presumably more profitable, in its core business, spirits and wine. Further, this sale to Sun was for the equivalent of twelve dollars a barrel for oil in the ground, about three dollars a barrel more than the previous record payment by Shell for Belridge Petroleum in 1979.

Table 7.2 shows that Seagram's REM was greater than that of the Sun's, and that it increased relative to Sun's REM in the quarter of the sale and in the next quarter.

	Price earnings multiple		Standard & Poor's composite price earnings multiple	REM		Ratio Seagram to Sun's REM
TABLE 7.2 Relative earnings multiple, Seagram and Sun						
Quarter ending	*Sun*	*Seagram*		*Sun*	*Seagram*	
December 1979	7	13	7.4	0.94	1.75	1.86
March 1980	6	13	6.7	0.90	1.94	2.17
June 1980[a]	6	14	7.6	0.79	1.84	2.33
September 1980	6	15	8.7	0.69	1.72	2.50

[a] Oil and gas sale in April 1980.

Means and Ends. The act of measuring performance can result in the organization focusing on the measure while excluding or ignoring the strategic ends. Thus a cost-reduction target that is the *means* to a competitive advantage might result in ABC firm treating cost reduction as an *end*. While ABC firm achieves cost reductions, XYZ company might introduce a product improvement that renders ABC's lower-cost product obsolete. Thus the means of cost reduction completely obscures the end of competitive advantage. The strategist, forewarned of the serious problems inherent in the substituting means for ends, monitors the evaluation system to ensure that means support, not replace, ends. Multiple measures are most helpful in this regard.

Verifying Assumptions. Measuring progress is only one part of strategic reporting and evaluation. Not only does the strategist need to know how well the firm is moving toward its objectives, but he or she also has to ensure that the original judgments made in formulating these objectives are still valid.

The strategic manager makes assumptions and judgments and reaches conclusions about both the internal and external environments based on perceptions of trends and opportunities. Strategic evaluation also includes reviewing these environments to ensure that these assumptions are still valid and that perceived trends are still in evidence. Most practitioners suggest that this review should be made as part of a recurring strategic planning cycle. Many firms utilize an annual planning cycle. Merchant (1982) studied and reported on planning cycles and on the control function of management.

In addition, it is recommended that new perspectives be added to this review effort by assigning strategic managers who did not participate in the original review. This strategic manager asks

1. What significant assumptions and judgments were reached about opportunities and threats in the external environment?
2. What conclusions were reached about strengths and weaknesses in the internal environment?
3. Are these assumptions, judgments, and conclusions still valid?

Contingency Planning. Recognizing the difficulty in accurately predicting strategic progress, many practitioners of strategy suggest that the original implementation plans, schedules, and budgets should be made on a contingency basis; the strategic manager should develop not one but several contingency plans. The importance of contingency planning is determined by the relative difficulty in predicting strategic progress. Contingency plans are also more appropriate over longer planning cycles. The harder it is to predict consumers' and competitors' moves, and the longer the term of the strategic plan, the more beneficial contingency planning will be.

Whether the strategic manager has one or a series of contingency implementation plans, it is clear that evaluating progress means redoing the strategy implementation phase of the strategic process. And verifying assumptions means redoing the strategy formulation phase of the strategic process. Thus, the strategic process is dynamic; the periodic evaluation of earlier strategic formulation and implementation sends messages that may restart the strategic process. Evaluation provides the feedback to the total system. Strategic feedback is the life force of the dynamic strategic process.

EXAMPLES: *Measurement*

AMF faltered when its strategic feedback collapsed. The oil boom that AMF counted on, which earned it operating revenues of $63 million in 1981, turned into an oil bust. In 1983 the energy services division lost $24 million. In an interview with *Business Week*, a former AMF manager said, "The strategic planning was fine, but when the facts dictated that the thinking should change, it didn't." (8/12/85, p. 50).

One interesting variable in the strategic feedback and reporting system is the receptivity of the strategic manager. In reporting that Texas Instruments was "Shot Full of Holes and Trying to Recover," *Business Week* (11/5/84, p. 82) explained that strategic feedback collapsed as the weight of "the domineering styles of Chairman Mark Shepherd, Jr. and President J. Fred Bucy often intimidated product managers, who told them what they wanted to hear — not what was really going on. For example, neither learned of the home computer problems until the company was drowning in inventory." *Fortune* also commented on this phenomenon of strategic receptivity in "No More Mickey Mouse at Disney" (12/10/84, p. 57), describing Walt Disney's successor E. C. Walker as follows:

> *Subordinates feared Walker as a tyrant, quick to ridicule underlings in public and impervious to any point of view but his own. He made decisions according to what he thought Walt would have done. As a result the company steadily lost touch with modern taste, growing as hermetic as a religious sect or a communist cell. Executives clinched arguments by quoting Walt like Scripture or Marx, and the company eventually supplied a little book of the founder's sayings.*

Unfortunately, bad news often does not rise to the top. One task of the strategic manager is to ensure that the underlying spirit of the evaluation system is one that encourages the reporting of all news — bad and good. *Forbes* (3/26/84, p. 102) reported G.E. Chairman Welch's determination to tolerate mistakes and to report failures: "To prove he means what he says, Welch has been loudly rewarding some near-misses. When a $20 million project was scrapped because of a change in the market, Welch promoted the manager and gave him a bonus."

EXAMPLE: *Implementation and Corporate Culture*

A critical factor in the selection of these implementation options is not only the option itself but the degree of change between the proposed option and the existing implementation selection. Changing the system of performance measurement in an organization can produce shock waves; challenging or changing corporate culture can be especially difficult. *Fortune* reported on the difficulty in challenging corporate culture, especially in the case of Seiko, a firm with a corporate culture dating from 1881 (11/12/84, pp. 44–54). One grandson of Seiko founder Kintaro Hattori preferred to concentrate on the comfortable world of the watch industry. The other grandson, who preferred the challenges of high technology and computers, slowly tried to act as the general leading the firm into the diversification, high-tech battle, through internal "prolonged combats of courtesies."

Similarly, in describing the efforts of PPG's new chairman to cut costs, revitalize existing problem businesses, and expand the company, *Business Week* (11/12/84, p. 128) noted that "his toughest job is ridding the company of its cautious culture. Traditionally, PPG has preferred studying moves rather than making them and penalizing risk-takers rather than rewarding them."

One symptom of change in the corporate culture is executive turnover. Noting that twelve managers had left Hewlett-Packard in just six months, *Business Week* (11/5/84, p. 76) found the cause to be a change in marketing culture, from a "technology-driven, engineering-oriented culture, in which decentralization and innovation were a religion and entrepreneurs were the gods." In the same issue, *Business Week* commented that eleven of thirty-four vice presidents had left Digital Equipment as the company sought to replace the "rampant chaos" of entrepreneurial individuals with a "marketing-oriented, team spirit."

SELECTION CRITERIA

Although many solutions exist to any implementation situation, two factors help the strategic manager choose among implementation alternatives. The first factor is distinctive competence, to ensure a fit between structure and strategy. The second factor is congruence.

Distinctive Competence

As shown in Figure 7.2, the strategic manager bases the formulated strategy on the firm's distinctive competence. Distinctive competence, as described in Chapter

FIGURE 7.2
Determinants of distinctive competence

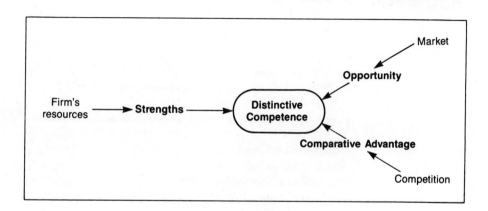

4, matches the firm's strength with both a market need, which represents an opportunity for the firm, and with a comparative advantage over competition, which represents a relative advantage of the firm compared to competition.

The manager selects implementation alternatives that will support and strengthen the distinctive competence and thus will ensure that structure fits strategy. The manager selects implementation alternatives that build upon the firm's strength, seize the market opportunity, and capitalize on the firm's comparative advantage. If a firm has a distinctive competence in high technology, for example (as is true in the U.S. large computer industry), it will select organization structures and control systems that encourage innovation and research. Its measurement and reward systems will provide incentives for engineering breakthroughs. This firm's corporate culture will include professionalism and a respect for science.

Congruence   Jay Galbraith (1977), building upon the major foundation of Lorsch and Morse (1974), showed that a firm needs congruence between (1) structure, (2) people, (3) rewards, and (4) information and decision processes in order to implement strategy successfully. Both Galbraith and Lorsch linked the degree of congruence to the level of the firm's performance.

The strategic manager considers the congruence or fit between each new implementation alternative being evaluated and those alternatives already selected. The law of congruence requires each alternative to be a part of the whole solution if it is to be successful. Galbraith (in Schendel and Hofer, 1979) argued, ''The firm should match its structure to its strategy, match all the components of the organization with one another, and match the strategy with the environment.''

WORKING CONCEPT 23

IMPLEMEN-TATION SELECTION MODEL

In implementing strategy, the strategic manager selects from a spectrum of alternatives: administrative structure, information, measurement, and compensation systems (see Figure 7.3). The first criterion each alternative must satisfy is that it be consistent with the distinctive competence; in other words, that it supports or strengthens that distinctive competence. Secondly, each alternative must be consistent with the others; in other words, there must be a fit between, or congruence among, the alternatives.

This selection model underscores the fact that strategy is an art. The model proposes two criteria, both of which are subjective. Decision rules and operating policies may give an impression of scientific management, but the objective scientist must yield to the subjective artist — that is, the strategic manager.

Galbraith (in Schendel and Hofer, 1979) stressed that ''congruence among organizational structure, processes, and systems is the important factor, not fit with the environment.'' Nonetheless, Galbraith (1977) also pointed out that time complicates matters: congruence must be balanced between the short run and the long run. He

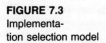
FIGURE 7.3
Implementa-
tion selection model

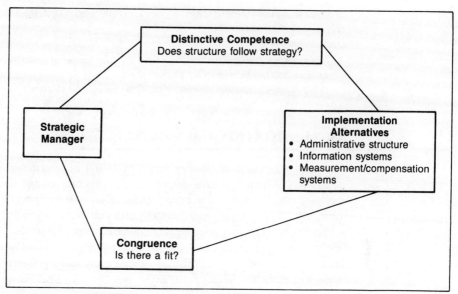

provided the illustration of excellent congruence in the Swiss watch industry, which was built to produce mechanical watches. This same strong short-run congruence, however, kept the Swiss manufacturers from switching to electronic watch technology.

Competition is also an important variable in congruence. Galbraith noted that the degree of congruence becomes increasingly important as the degree of competition increases. At the extreme, the monopolistic firm's performance may vary little with changes in congruence. Galbraith concluded, "Only under competitive conditions does a mismatch between strategy and structure lead to ineffective performance."

In summary, although many solutions exist to each implementation situation, the manager answers two questions: (1) Does this alternative support my distinctive competence? and (2) Is this alternative congruent with my structure, systems, and decision processes?

DIFFICULTIES IN IMPLEMENTING STRATEGY

Implementing strategy and managing change is difficult at best. Not only do a multiplicity of solutions exist, but the strategic manager also confronts the natural resistance to change. Machiavelli warned the Prince that "there is nothing more difficult and dangerous, or more doubtful of success, than an attempt to introduce a new order of things . . . enemies [are] all those who derived advantages from the old order of things, while those who expect to be benefited by the new institutions will be but lukewarm defenders."

Business Week (8/19/85, p. 35) described the implementation difficulties that surrounded Beatrice, whose management ranks were "decimated" as it tried to recover from the "headstrong" James L. Dutt, who "systematically berated" executives:

"The longer you got with a guy like Dutt, the longer it takes to solve problems" [*an analyst said*]. *The photos of Dutt that once hung in every Beatrice office are already being removed. But the imprint of his tenure won't be so easy to erase.*

IMPLEMENTATION AND STRATEGIC LEVELS

The implementation of strategy flows from and is determined by the formulation of strategy, which is in turn shaped by the opportunities and threats of the external environment, the distinctive competences of the internal environment, and purpose (mission). A well-implemented strategy also will include specific strategic objectives.

As the strategic manager determines objectives and implements strategy, he or she also will have reviewed the seven dimensions of managerial action that the management consultants McKinsey & Company call the *Seven S model*: Strategy, Structure, Systems, Skills, Staff, Style, and Shared values. In strategic implementation, the seven dimensions of managerial action are common to all levels of strategy. The corporate strategist might spend more time on strategy and structure, and the functional strategist more time on skills; still, the seven dimensions and the implementation activity are a critical part of levels of strategy. Since an ideal organization design and rules for matching structure to strategy do not exist, implementation offers a great deal of opportunity for creativity on the part of all strategic managers.

AN IMPLEMENTATION ILLUSTRATION

The issues confronting the university-owned bookstore were presented in Appendix C to Chapter 2. The decades-old monopoly of the University of New Hampshire (U.N.H.) bookstore had been ended by the competition for the student book market instituted by local stores.

The economics of the situation were that (1) the U.N.H. bookstore was an auxiliary enterprise under state law, which meant any surplus could only be reinvested in the specific enterprise, i.e., the bookstore and (2) the profit and cash flow, each averaging about $50,000, had changed to a loss of $75,000 and a cash drain of about $100,000. The bookstore manager, John Maier, had been trying to build business by offering more trade books and soft goods and by advertising to the general public. Some cost control measures had been taken, including eliminating eight clerical employees.

A gubernatorial efficiency commission had made many recommendations to the university, including leasing the bookstore to a private operator. The bookstore manager and staff responded through a public relations campaign directed at trustees, students, faculty, university administration, and the media, emphasizing the lack of service that leasing to an independent operator would mean.

The case analysis in Appendix D of Chapter 2 suggests that different levels of strategic perspective can be used in analyzing this case. From the corporate-level, the U.N.H. president felt that leasing for "real" dollars (i.e., dollars that can be used outside of the bookstore), was preferable to deficit operations, and to a bookstore staff that is vocal in the media. The "collegiality" objective of the university, however, should not conflict with any presidential actions.

From the point of view of the business level, John Maier needed to shift from a service objective to a profit objective, while maintaining or increasing support from within the university "family" of trustees, administration, faculty, and students. The administration's support was critical; the "captive" student market was also significant.

At a functional level within the bookstore, such as that of the employee in charge of soft goods, the functional strategy needed to support the store's profit objective. The functional employee would seek to increase efficiency and to generate new business.

The following text outlines specific steps that might serve to implement strategy.

Corporate Strategy

The corporate strategy (embodied by the U.N.H. president) might require conversion to an independent, private bookstore lease while maximizing consensus and minimizing resistance to "top-down" management.

Administrative Structure. Delegate discussion and the generation of recommendations (but not final decisions) to an ad-hoc committee of trustees, faculty, students, and administration. Administration representatives should be well-respected, forceful individuals.

Information and Culture. Provide the committee with a brief but dramatic overview of the "big picture" — the university's commitment to education, along with its limited resources and alternative priorities (health care, residences, computer systems, and library). Create a culture that promotes university-wide perspective and the university family as a whole, not isolated (problem) areas such as the bookstore.

Procedures. Push for early resolution, with the decision announcement made when classes are not in session to minimize adverse reaction. Contribute a portion of the lease income to "Motherhood and Apple Pie" use, such as the acquisition of new library materials.

Business Strategy

The business strategy (embodied by the bookstore manager) might require support within the administration, not as controversial agent but as one trying to support education by means of service (special book orders and out-of-print services, streamlined semester start-up procedures, other university textbook lists for faculty), and, if possible, by pointing out problems at other leased locations for other schools. The business strategy will stress trying to "buy time" in order to reverse profitless operations, stressing the need for a longer-term view and the development of managerial abilities.

Administrative Structure. Streamlining the organization is necessary during this "survival" period; a hierarchy is essential to this process. A functional (soft goods versus school textbooks versus popular textbooks versus operations) structure must give way to efficiency and overlapping responsibilities.

Information and Culture. The trustees and administrators must not be viewed as "the enemy"; the manager must disseminate information down through the organization about administrative achievements regarding the main objective, education. All information from the bookstore to the outside, including the media, must come through the manager. The manager should stress the "big family" and "big picture" as part of the bookstore culture. Operating results should highlight the profit centers and problem centers.

Procedures. Rather than being a part of the problem by attacking the power structure, the manager should try to use the distinctive competence — the tie-in to the student body. Campaigns such as "Save the Bookstore" and "Show Your Loyalty" should stress patronizing the bookstore — rather than local competition — because "it's our store." A student committee might investigate making the store a student cooperative, especially if co-op fees can be directed to the university, not just to the bookstore.

Functional Strategy

The functional strategy (embodied by the soft goods manager) might require increasing efficiency through better resource utilization and decreased costs, postponing all nonessential expenditures, and generating new revenue.

Administrative Structure. Part-time and work-study students presumably will be less expensive to hire, although the functional manager then must make employee supervision and responsibility levels (approvals, controls) part of the structure.

Information and Culture. Operating statements should stress the areas of revenue and expense that the functional employee can influence and control. Competition between functions should be minimized, however, and cooperation stressed.

Procedures. Techniques to increase the number of purchases per visit should be developed, including traditional tactics such as loss leaders, suggestion selling, and merchandise layout to encourage impulse buying. Areas of major student purchases (music, fads, and games) should be offered. Pricing of identical items must be competitive.

STRATEGY IMPLEMENTATION RESEARCH

While Machiavelli and other political theorists have given advice and prescribed actions for implementing strategy, the classic research in implementation includes studies by the following authors.

Lorsch and Lawrence (1972), in *Organizational Planning* and elsewhere, studied the degree of specialization or differentiation within the organization's structure and systems. The greater the differentiation, the greater the need for integration by the strategic manager. Further, the degree of differentiation was caused by and followed from the degree of uncertainty in the environment. The more environmental uncertainty existed, the more the strategist would need differentiated structure and systems.

Other researchers include **Galbraith,** whose *Organization Design* (1977) continued Lorsch's work and stressed the importance of congruence. **Thompson** (1967) described organization's responses to domains that were either competitive — built on distinctive competence — or concentrated — gaining power from sources. **Burns and Stalker** (1961) identified "organic" structures appropriate for high rates of change, and "mechanistic" structures suitable for stable markets.

Current significant research projects in implementation include works by the following authors.

Alexander (1985), in surveying ninety-three firms, found that the ten most frequently encountered implementation problems were (1) more time to implement than allocated, (2) unanticipated major problems, (3) ineffective activity coordination, (4) attention distracted by competing or crisis activities, (5) insufficient employee capabilities, (6) inadequate training and instruction to lower levels, (7) uncontrollable external factors, (8) inadequate departmental manager leadership, (9) poorly defined implementation steps, and (10) inadequate monitor information system. Alexander urged that the good implementation idea be supported by detailed planning, adequate communication, sufficient resource support, and employee commitment to the idea.

Argyris (1982) described ways of changing managerial systems and styles from a "win/lose single-loop" model to a "win/win double-loop" model. These suggestions included switching from advocacy to inquiry and public testing, and switching from unilateral face-saving to learning situations. The consequences of such a switch would be more "effective problem solving" and less "self-dealing, error escalating processes."

Bower (1970), after studying strategy planning for three years in a large firm, made two conclusions. (1) Structure may determine strategy, in that the organization's structure (hierarchies, systems) determines what projects will be studied and how they will be studied. (2) Bargaining and persuasion are an important part of both project definition and project implementation.

Collier (1984) described eight strategic principles of implementation: (1) the chief executive officer commitment, (2) proper strategic management organization, (3) credible strategic plans, (4) functional action plans supporting the strategy, (5) realistic and goal-supporting resource allocations, (6) strategy-compatible organizational culture and manager psychology, (7) effective monitoring and early-warning system, and (8) rewards for operating managers for implementation success.

Heany and Vinson (1984) used the strategy-technology connection as a central part of their study of new product development. They concluded that the difficulty of linking business goals and technical goals was a major contributor to product innovation problems. Strategy formulation and implementation should improve communication and encourage initiative and responsibility so that the general manager and the new product staff can combine business and technical goals.

Hirschleim (1983), in researching information and control systems, concluded that the data base was a "neglected corporate resource" important to strategic planning. Hirschleim described ways in which strategic managers could use the data base.

Horovitz (1984), searching for new perspectives on strategic management, reported on an intellectual and a social process in strategy implementation and strategy formulation. The intellectual process of implementation is the "fitted management design" wherein organization structure and information and control systems are designed rationally. The social process of implementation is "people activation," wherein the strategist gains commitment from others.

Huber and Power (1985) studied accuracy in strategic reports. They presented "guidelines for increasing . . . accuracy" in "retrospective reports of strategic level managers."

Jaeger and Baliga (1985) studied the Japanese experience with control systems and strategic adaptation. They analyzed the potential strategic costs and benefits of culture (Japanese) versus formal/bureaucratic (traditional American) control systems. They concluded that an ideal situation would be a "swing back and forth as necessary between bureaucratic and cultural control systems."

Kantrow (1980) stressed the importance of having the implementation structure encompass technology: "Technology should be viewed as a central part of business thinking at all levels and not as a kind of a line phenomenon to be held at arm's length by all but R&D engineers."

MacMillan and Jones (1984) studied ways of "designing organizations to compete." They concluded that the strategic manager must answer seven questions to implement strategy:

1. What is the organization's strategy?
2. How will we know that the strategy has been accomplished?
3. How will the strategy affect competitors?
4. What major task groupings represent feasible design alternatives?
5. What linkages are necessary between groupings?
6. What support systems are needed?
7. What execution problems can be anticipated?

Mitroff and Kilmann (1975) showed how firms can recognize and take advantage of differing managerial perspectives on the "ideal" organization. They grouped managerial perspectives into four categories: (1) sensing-thinking, (2) sensing-feeling, (3) intuition-thinking, and (4) intuition-feeling.

Naylor (1985) studied the strategic process at General Motors and recommended implementation and planning with the acronym STRATEGY: S — Stick to it; T —

Think it through; R — Risk, responsibility, and reward; A — Awareness of self and competition; T — Talking to each other to communicate strategy; E — Evaluating each step; G — Growing your people; and Y — Yes-I-Can winning attitude.

Pearce (1983) studied financial measures of strategic performance, analyzing reporting orientation and reporting on "the relationship of internal versus external orientations to financial measures" of strategy.

Peters and Waterman (1982) identified forty-three "excellent" companies, and tried to evaluate the strategies that accounted for the excellence. Their "attributes" of excellent strategies included

1. Bias for action
2. Staying close to the customer
3. Autonomy and entrepreneurship
4. Simple form, lean staff
5. Stick to the knitting (staying with the distinctive competence)

Rockart and Scott Morton (1984), both M.I.T. researchers, stressed the need to consider information technology not only as a way of supporting business strategies but as a means of creating opportunities for new business strategy. Because data processing has become information technology — robotics, decision support systems, data bases, communications networks — technology should be driving management's processes. Information, after all, is power.

Rockart and Treacy (1982) focused on the CEO and information technology in their study of how "The CEO Goes On-Line."

Stopford and Wells expanded the stages of corporate development in their 1972 model, which included international divisions based upon a study of U.S. firms expanding abroad.

Vancil et al. studied strategic planning systems and performance for seventy-six companies from 1969 to 1972 (their series of planning studies was subsequently discontinued). Reports on this Formal Planning Systems Research Project at the Harvard Business School include "Setting Corporate Objectives" (Aguilar 1971) and "The Successful Use of Computer Models in Planning" (Hammond 1972).

EXECUTIVE COMMENTS

One of General Motor's most important characteristics [is] its effort to achieve open-minded communication and objective consideration of facts.

Alfred P. Sloan, Jr., *My Years with General Motors*

A good slogan can stop analysis for fifty years.

Wendell Wilkie

There isn't going to be any final analysis.

John DeLorean

KEY TERMS

administrative systems (page 176)

corporate culture (page 180)

differentiation and integration (page 177)

holistic measures (page 180)

implementation (page 175)

information systems (page 177)

matrix organizations (page 176)

performance evaluation and compensation (page 179)

strategic business units (SBUs) (page 177)

unidimensional measures (page 180)

BIBLIOGRAPHY

Alexander, L. D., "Successfully Implementing Strategy Decisions," *Long Range Planning* 18 (June 1985), pp. 91–97.

Argyris, C., "The Executive Mind and Double-Loop Learning," *Organizational Dynamics* (Autumn 1982), pp. 5–22.

Bariff, M. L., and J. R. Galbraith, "Interorganizational Power Considerations for Designing Information Systems," *Accounting, Organizations and Society* 3 (February 1978), pp. 15–27.

Bettis, R., and C. K. Prahalad, "The Visible and the Invisible Hand: Resource Allocation in the Industrial Sector," *Strategic Management Journal* (January–March 1983).

Blackburn, R. S., "Dimensions of Structure: A Review and Reappraisal," *Academy of Management Review*, vol. 7, no. 1 (1982), pp. 59–66.

Bourgeois, L. J., "Performance and Consensus," *Strategic Management Journal*, vol. 1 (July–September 1980), pp. 227–248.

Bower, J. L., *Managing the Resource Allocation Process*, Harvard Business School Research Division, 1970.

Branch, B., and B. Gale, "Linking Corporate Stock Price Performance to Strategy Formulation," *Journal of Business Strategy*, vol. 4, no. 1 (Summer 1983).

Brunswik, E., *Perception and the Representative Design of Psychological Experiments* (Berkeley, CA: University of California Press, 1956).

Burns, T., and G. M. Stalker, *The Management of Innovation* (London: Tavistock Publications, 1961).

Cameron, K., and D. Whetten, "Perceptions of Organizational Effectiveness and Organizational Life Cycles," *Administrative Science Quarterly* 26 (1981), pp. 525–544.

Caves, R. E., "Industrial Organization, Corporate Strategy, and Structure," *Journal of Economic Literature* (March 1980), pp. 64–92.

Chakravorthy, B., "Strategic Self-Renewal: A Planning Framework for Today," *Academy of Management Review* (July 1984).

Chandler, A. D., Jr., *Strategy and Structure* (Cambridge, MA: M.I.T. Press, 1962).

Christensen, C. R., et al., *Business Policy: Text and Cases* (Homewood, IL: Richard D. Irwin, 1987).

Christopher, W., "Achievement Reporting — Controlling Performance Against Objectives," *Long Range Planning* 10 (October 1977), pp. 14–24.

Collier, D., "How to Implement Strategic Plans," *Journal of Business Strategy* 4 (Winter 1984), pp. 92–96.

Daniels, J., B. Pitts, and M. Tretter, "Strategy and Structure of U.S. Multinationals: An Exploratory Study," *Academy of Management Journal* (June 1984).

Davis, S. M., and P. R. Lawrence, "Problems of Matrix Organizations," *Harvard Business Review* 56 (May–June 1978), pp. 131–142.

Drucker, P., *Management: Tasks, Responsibilities, and Practices* (New York: Harper & Row, 1974).

Dutton, J. E., L. Fahey, and V. K. Narayanan, "Toward Understanding Strategic Issue Diagnosis," *Strategic Management Journal* 4 (October–December 1983), pp. 307–323.

Galbraith, J. R., "Matrix Organizational Designs," *Business Horizons* 15 (February 1971), pp. 29–40.

Galbraith, J. R., *Organization Design* (Reading, MA: Addison-Wesley, 1977).

Galbraith, J. R., and D. Nathanson, *Strategy Implementation: The Role of Structure and Process* (St. Paul, MN: West Publishing, 1978).

Hall, W. K., "SBUs: Hot New Topic in the Management of Diversification," *Business Horizons* 21 (February 1978), pp. 17–25.

Heany, D. F., and W. D. Vinson, "A Fresh Look at New Product Development," *Journal of Business Strategy* (Fall 1984), pp. 21–31.

Herbert, T., "Strategy and Multinational Structure: An Interorganizational Relationships Perspective," *Academy of Management Review* (April 1984).

Hirschleim, R. A., "Data Base — A Neglected Corporate Resource?" *Long Range Planning* 16 (October 1983), pp. 79–88.

Hobbs, J., and D. Heany, "Coupling Strategy to Operating Plans," *Harvard Business Review* 55 (May–June 1977), pp. 119–126.

Horovitz, J., "New Perspectives in Strategic Management," *Journal of Business Strategy* 4 (Winter 1984), pp. 19–33.

Hrebiniak, L. G., and W. F. Joyce, *Implementing Strategy* (New York: MacMillan, 1984).

Huber, G. P., and D. J. Power, "Retrospective Reports of Strategic-Level Managers," *Strategic Management Journal* 6 (April–June 1985), pp. 171–180.

Jaeger, A. M., and B. R. Baliga, "Control Systems and Strategic Adaptation: Lessons from the Japanese Experience," *Strategic Management Journal* 6 (April–June 1985), pp. 115–134.

Jelinek, M., and M. C. Burstein, "The Production Administrative Structure: A Paradigm for Strategic Fit," *Academy of Management Review*, vol. 7, no. 2 (1982), pp. 242–252.

Kantrow, A. W., "The Strategy-Technology Connection," *Harvard Business Review* 58 (July–August 1980), pp. 6–21.

Kast, F., and J. Rosenzweig, *Organization and Management Systems and Contingency Approach* (New York: McGraw-Hill, 1979).

King, W. R., "Using Strategic Issue Analysis," *Long Range Planning* 15 (August 1982), pp. 45–49.

Knight, K., "Matrix Organization: A Review," in R. M. Miles, ed., *Resourcebook in Macro Organizational Behavior* (Glenview, IL: Scott, Foresman, 1980).

Lawrence, P. R., and J. W. Lorsch, *Organization and Environment* (Homewood, IL: Richard D. Irwin, 1967).

Leontiades, M., "Choosing the Right Manager to Fit the Strategy," *Journal of Business Strategy* 3 (Fall 1981), pp. 58–69.

Lorange, P., *Implementations of Strategic Planning* (Englewood Cliffs, NJ: Prentice-Hall, 1978).

Lorange, P., "Strategic Control," in Lamb, ed., *Latest Advances in Strategic Management* (Englewood Cliffs, NJ: Prentice-Hall, 1983).

Lorsch, J. W., and P. R. Lawrence, *Organizational Planning* (Homewood, IL: Richard D. Irwin, 1972).

Lorsch, J. W., and J. J. Morse, *Organizations and Their Members: A Contingency Approach* (New York: Harper & Row, 1974).

MacMillan, I. C., and P. E. Jones, "Designing Organizations to Compete," *Journal of Business Strategy* 4 (Spring 1984), pp. 11–26.

Merchant, K. A., "The Control Function of Management," *Sloan Management Review* 23 (Winter 1982), pp. 43–55.

Miles, R., and C. Snow, *Organizational Strategy, Structure and Process* (New York: McGraw-Hill, 1978).

Mintzberg, H., "Organization Design: Fashion or Fit?" *Harvard Business Review* 59:1 (January–February 1981), pp. 103–116.

Mintzberg, H., "Power and Organization Life Cycles," *Academy of Management Review* (April 1984).

Mitroff, I., and R. Kilmann, "Stories Managers Tell," *Management Review* (July 1975), pp. 18–28.

Naylor, M. E., "Regaining Your Competitive Edge," *Long Range Planning* 18 (February 1985), pp. 30–35.

Nutt, P. C., "Hybrid Planning Methods," *Academy of Management Review* 7:3 (July 1982), pp. 442–454.

Ouchi, W., "A Conceptual Framework for the Design of Organizational Control Mechanisms," *Management Science* 25:9 (September 1979), pp. 833–848.

Pascale, R. T., and A. G. Athos, *The Art of Japanese Management* (New York: Simon & Schuster, 1981).

Pearce, J. A., III, "The Relationship of Internal Versus External Orientations to Financial Measures of Strategic Performance," *Strategic Management Journal* 4 (October–December 1983), pp. 297–306.

Peters, T. J., and R. H. Waterman, Jr., *In Search of Excellence: Lessons from America's Best-Run Companies* (New York: Harper & Row, 1982).

Rockart, J. F., "Chief Executives Define Their Own Data Needs," *Harvard Business Review* 57 (March–April 1979), pp. 85–94.

Rockart, J. F., and M. S. Scott Morton, "Implications of Changes in Information Technology for Corporate Strategy," *Interfaces* 14 (January–February 1984), pp. 84–95.

Rockart, J. F., and M. E. Treacy, "The CEO Goes On-line," *Harvard Business Review* 60 (January–February 1982), pp. 82–88.

Rothschild, W. E., "How to Ensure the Continued Growth of Strategic Planning," *The Journal of Business Strategy*, vol. 1, no. 1 (Summer 1980).

Schoderbek, C., D. Schoderbek, and A. Kefalas, *Management Systems* (Dallas: Business Publications, 1980).

Sihler, W. H., "Toward Better Management Control Systems," *California Management Review* 14 (Winter 1971), pp. 33–39.

Sloan, Alfred P., Jr., *My Years with General Motors* (Garden City, NY: Doubleday, 1963).

Snow, C. C., and L. G. Hrebiniak, "Strategy, Distinctive Competence, and Organizational Performance," *Administrative Science Quarterly*, vol. 25 (June 1980), pp. 317–336.

Stopford, J., and L. Wells, *Managing the Multinational Enterprise* (London: Longmans, 1972).

Tichy, N. M., "Managing Change Strategically: The Technical, Political and Cultural Keys," *Organizational Dynamics* (Autumn 1982), pp. 59–80.

Tichy, N. M., C. J. Fombrum, and M. A. Devanna, "Strategic Human Resource Management," *Sloan Management Review* 23 (Winter 1982), pp. 47–61.

Tilles, S., "How to Evaluate Corporate Strategy," *Harvard Business Review* 41 (July–August 1963).

Vancil, R. F., "What Kind of Management Control Do We Need?" *Harvard Business Review* 51 (March–April 1973), pp. 75–86.

Vancil, R. F., et al., *Formal Planning Systems*, Division of Case Distribution, Harvard Business School, 1968, 1969, 1970, 1971.

APPENDIX: PERSONAL STRATEGY

But education is the hope of the world only in the sense that there is something better than bribery, lies, and violence for righting the world's wrongs. If this better thing is education, then education is not merely schooling. It is a lifelong discipline of the individual by himself.

Jacques Barzun, *Teacher in America*

Thus far you have studied strategy in terms of organizations. In this appendix you will be the strategic manager formulating a strategy for your personal life. You will study the external environment for personal opportunities and analyze your own strengths and weaknesses. To put things into a time period, this appendix is based on a five-year planning period for your personal life.

THE PERSONAL EXTERNAL ENVIRONMENT

Significant factors in your external environment include (1) markets, (2) competition, (3) technology, (4) society, and (5) government.

Markets

The market of most immediate concern to students is the employment market. In analyzing the employment market, you as the "organization's" strategic manager, must consider the various market segments. The reactive student will wait for the employment market to reveal opportunities through student placement announcements, employment advertisements, and family contacts. The proactive student, on the other hand, will examine the various employment segments, using some of the following categories.

Geography (cities versus towns, seacoasts versus mountains, heartland versus borders)

Function (accounting, marketing, production, finance, research, human resources, administration)

Responsibility level (entry, executive trainee, line or staff management)

Industry (high-tech, retail, service including financial or advertising, distribution, manufacturing, governmental, nonprofit including education)

Using a strategic point of view means that you study not only the existing characteristics of these employment segments, but also trends in these characteristics. What expectations do you have for these segments three and five years from now?

Finally, the student asks what purchase (employment) decision criteria are being used by employers in these segments. These criteria might include cost, appearance, education, work experience, references, availability, motivation, and personal interests.

Competition

What are the present and potential alternative sources for you as an employee? Your competition is not limited to other students; it includes inter- and intra-organization transfers, promotions, and reassignments. Depending on the function and industry, your present or future competition could include automation. And some futurists expect an increase in the amount of services subcontracted to independent organizations. Evidence of the rise of third-party service organizations can be seen in the number of third-party personal and small business computer maintenance organizations such as Xerox, Arrow Electronics, TRW, and Honeywell.

Technology

The personal strategist asks the following three questions.

1. What present technology underlies the different employment segments?
2. What is the expected future technology for these same segments?
3. What is the rate of technological change?

Just as in the business world, you probably will get more valuable assistance in answering these questions from knowledgeable experts rather than from statistics about past trends.

Society

The cultural values and expectations surrounding you can be described in terms of the expected and presumed amount of influence. These sources of influence include close friends; family members; and role models from school, work, or other experiences. As personal strategist, you will analyze the relationship between yourself — the strategist — and these values and influences.

Government The student can be affected by governmental acts in many ways. You must analyze the present and future interactions between yourself and regional and federal governmental bodies, including

Military service
Source of financing
Employer
Regulator of employment
Influence in economy

For example, advanced study and graduate school may or may not be feasible for you, depending on the level of government support for higher education in terms of scholarships and loan guarantees. Administrative agencies of the government, including the Federal Trade Commission and the Agency for International Development (AID), employ graduates with business administration degrees. Most certainly, the level of employment demand concerns those responsible for influencing the economy through fiscal and monetary measures.

OPPORTUNITIES AND THREATS

After analyzing the external environment, the personal strategist next groups the identified positive and negative strategic signals into significant opportunities and threats. Opportunities might include such things as a major expansion by a local employer, a booming regional economy, or a national program of economic stimuli. Threats might encompass a population bulge in your age bracket, an increase in graduates with advanced degrees, or an increase in regional unemployment.

INTERNAL RESOURCES

Your resources include primarily intangible components, although you may have such tangible resources as investment capital or even production equipment. Your intangible resources include education, work experience, appearance, personality characteristics, and either personal or familial social and business contacts and relationships.

The personal strategist, recalling the earlier analysis of competition that comprised the assessment of the competitive factor in the external environment, prepares a strategic profile of personal strengths and weaknesses. Using this profile, the personal strategist next develops a distinctive competence.

What is it that distinguishes you from classmates and other competitors for employment positions? By answering this question you can determine your distinctive competence. Note that the concept of distinctive competence does not imply that you are the *only* one who has this or that strength or resource, just that it is an important strategic strength or resource. Keep in mind that your competitors also may share your strengths. Remember that strengths and resources include your planned future as well as existing present factors. Excellent communication skills might result in a future distinctive competence of high visibility and favorable attitudes with your employer and supervisors.

You also can use the life cycle model to suggest which strengths and weaknesses are especially critical. While desired strengths and competencies will vary from one employer to another, some strengths are particularly appropriate for various stages of your career. The ability to learn quickly can be presumed to be more important at earlier stages of your life than leadership capability, while the reverse may be true as your career progresses. Social relationships and verbal communication might be more important at intermediate stages of your career, while analytical skills might carry more importance early on in your business life.

PURPOSE

Just as the enterprise has a series of increasingly individualistic components of purpose, ranging from social goals to organizational priorities to personal values, the student also must review a spectrum of personal considerations. This spectrum includes physical, sensual, and material goals; mental and emotional values; and psychological and spiritual priorities.

The personal strategist must not only identify and define all the elements of personal purpose, but must recognize that

The spectrum is a mix of objectives and goals which may be competing or complementary.

Personal purpose is a guide to a general direction in life, but external environment factors and other circumstances can cause short-term courses of action that veer off from the desired target.

Changes do occur in either the relative weight assigned to various factors, or in the goals and priorities themselves.

Some priorities and goals are short term and others longer term. Some things, such as material rewards, may seem more important in one stage of life than in another. One relatively constant factor, responsibility to society, may be as difficult to define for an individual as it is to determine for the organization.

Clearly, determining and defining personal purpose is as subjective a task as is the definition of organizational purpose. Both tasks are limited and influenced by the internal and external environments. Put another way, some elements of purpose are adopted in response to other factors, and some elements are intrinsic.

STRATEGY FORMULATION

Personal strategy formulation, like its organizational counterpart, is easy to describe as a process yet difficult to perform. Simply put, the personal strategist uses personal purpose as the criterion for selecting opportunities for which he or she has a distinctive competence. In other words, what do you want to achieve? Which career opportunities, within the set of opportunities for which you have a present or a planned competence, will allow you to achieve your goals?

Many tools of the strategic manager, such as competitive response analysis, risk, synergy, and consistency assessment, also can help the personal strategist. Analyzing competitive response consists of considering people's future responses, which in turn depends on the nature of your competition. How competitive are (1) the current situation, (2) the power of suppliers and customers, (3) the threat of entry, and (4) the threat of substitutes? The personal strategist considers (1) the difficulty in obtaining a position, (2) the relative power of employee providers and of those offering employment, (3) the easiness of entry into a field, and (4) the employment alternatives and substitutes. This four-point review enables the strategist to determine the degree to which personal purpose must accommodate competitive realities. What compromises will your competition force you to make?

Risk assessment is an additional personal strategy tool. The spectrum ranges from high-security employment opportunities to high-risk positions. The decision about where to position yourself within that risk-security spectrum should be based upon your personal purpose.

Where does opportunity for synergy exist? What employment opportunity will provide you with a desired future competence, or will allow you to overcome a personal weakness while attaining other goals and objectives? How will your particular skills mesh with an employers' needs, products, or services so that the output of the whole is greater than the total output of the sum of each part?

The personal strategist asks if the formulated strategy is internally consistent — Is it free from internal contradictions and conflicts? — and if it is consistent with opportunities, personal purpose, and individual competence. Examples of possible conflicts and inconsistencies include

A job's travel requirement versus obligations to one's family

Learning objectives versus immediate income

Physical conditioning goals versus social entertaining job requirements

In formulating a strategy for the next five years, the personal strategist determines and then performs the specific steps required to carry out the formulated strategy. These specific steps and strategic objectives are the detailed plans to attain the formulated strategy. These plans should anticipate all major alternatives, provide decision criteria to use in making the choice between alternatives, and include schedules and timetables.

IMPLEMENTATION EXAMPLES

The personal strategist formulates a strategy of hard work in the investments field in order to become financially self-sufficient by age thirty-five, at which time the strategist might focus on such goals as raising a family and pursuing psychological growth. In implementing this plan, the strategist applies for a training program with most major securities brokers, and defines detailed contingency plans and criteria in the event (1) that no broker has a place in a training program; (2) that no broker offers a post-training position; and (3) that small regional brokers or banks must be sought out as employers.

In the final implementation phase of the strategic process, you must measure performance, asking (1) Am I progressing as planned? and (2) Are my original assumptions and conclusions still valid? Strategic evaluation is always subjective, so personal strategy evaluation is especially subjective. It is very difficult to measure subjective personal goals, such as the degree to which a job is challenging or whether or not you are happy. Nonetheless, the more advance planning you can do about how you will measure challenges or happiness, the more effective your evaluation will be.

Inherent resistance to change is a hindrance to accurate personal self-evaluation. Fear of the unknown and a lack of initiative may lull you into accepting lower and lower definitions and measures of such subjective things as challenges and happiness. Defining measures in advance provides one safeguard against lowering your standards.

You also need to step back and reassess the analysis of and conclusions about external opportunities, internal resources, and personal purpose. Have subsequent events supported or contradicted your judgments? Strategy is dynamic; periodically evaluating and updating your formulated strategy is an important aspect of the strategic process. You do know for certain that the external environment will change, and that your resources and personal objectives will grow and evolve.

OPTIONAL PERSONAL
STRATEGY ASSIGNMENT

Write a paper applying the strategic process to the next five years of your life. Since the grade will be given based solely on your ability to apply the strategic process, and not upon the actual content of the strategy you determine, you may choose to make your paper as impersonal or as personal as you like. You can describe a fictitious person in your paper and make it nonpersonal. On the other hand, the paper may be a more worthwhile learning experience for you if you consider personal objectives.

It also might be easier for you to structure your paper beginning with objectives, so that you can then review a much more narrow external environment. If you start with the external environment, you may spend time on alternatives (graduate school, ski bum) that you may be able to eliminate through your personal objectives.

EXECUTIVE COMMENTS

I do not believe that I am going too far when I say that modern man, in contrast to his nineteenth-century brother, turns his attention to the psyche with very great expectations. . . . To me, the cause of the spiritual problem of today is to be found in the fascination which psychic life exerts upon modern man. If we are pessimists, we shall call it a sign of decadence; if we are optimistically inclined, we shall see in it the promise of a far-reaching spiritual change in the Western world.

    Carl Jung, *Modern Man in Search of a Soul*

And the Quality, the arete *he has fought so hard for, has sacrificed for, has never betrayed, but in all that time has never once understood, now makes itself clear to him and his soul is at rest.*

    Robert M. Pirsig, *Zen and the Art of Motorcycle Maintenance*

This, then, is held to be the duty of the man of wealth: First, to set an example of modest, unostentatious living, shunning display or extravagance; to provide moderately for the legitimate wants of those dependent upon him; and, after doing so to consider all surplus revenues which come to him simply as trust funds which he is called upon to administer . . . the man of wealth thus becoming the mere agent and trustee for his poorer brethren.

    Andrew Carnegie

In our era, the road to holiness necessarily passes through the world of action.

    Dag Hammarskjöld

The human race has had long experiences and a fine tradition in surviving adversity. But now we face a task for which we have little experience, the task of surviving prosperity.

    Alan Gregg of the Rockefeller Foundation

For a long time they looked at the river beneath them, saying nothing, and the river said nothing, too, for it felt very quiet and peaceful on this summer afternoon.
"Tigger is alright really," said piglet lazily.
"Of course he is," said Christopher Robin.
"Everybody is really," said Pooh. "That's what I think," said Pooh. "But I don't suppose I'm right," he said.
"Of course you are," said Christopher Robin.

    A. A. Milne, *Winnie-the-Pooh*

If A = success, then the formula is A = X + Y + Z. X is work, Y is play, Z is keep your mouth shut.

Albert Einstein

BIBLIOGRAPHY

Baba Ram Dass, *Be Here Now* (San Cristobal, NM: Lama Foundation, 1971).

Berne, E., *Games People Play* (New York: Grove Press, 1967).

Bolen, J. S., *Goddesses in Everywoman* (New York: Harper & Row, 1984).

de Chardin, Teilhard, *The Future of Man* (New York: Harper & Row, 1964).

Tillich, P., *The Courage To Be* (New Haven, CT: Yale University Press, 1952).

Wilber, K., *The Atman Project* (Wheaton, IL: Theosophical Publishing House, 1980).

INDEX

Aaker, D. A., 89
Abbanat, R. F., 167, 170
Abell, D. F., 122, 170
Abernathy, W. J., 121, 122, 124
Ackoff, R., 170
Acquisition strategy,
   see situational strategies
Administrative systems, 176–177
Aguilar, F. J., 118–122
Aharoni, Y., 120–122
Alexander, L. D., 191, 194
Anderson, C., 89
Andrews, K. R., 14, 17, 67, 89, 170
Ansoff, H. I., 14, 17, 86, 89, 170
Argenti, J., 27, 29, 166, 170
Argyris, C., 191, 194
Astely, W. G., 170
Athos, A. G., 196
Austin, N., 172

Baliga, B. R., 192, 195
Bariff, M. L., 194
Barnett, J. H., 67
Barney, J., 124
Becker, L. C., 122
Bell, D., 67
Berg, N. A., 170
Bettis, R., 194
Bitondo, D., 171
Blackburn, R. S., 194
Bloom, P., 170
Boston Consulting Group
   and product portfolios, 142
Boulton, W., 122
Bourgeois, L. J., 194
Bower, J. L., 17, 170, 194
Branch, B., 194
Bright, J. R., 122
Brooks, H., 109, 122
Bruno, A. V., 90, 121, 123
Brunswik, E., 25–26, 29, 194
Brunswik, lens
   and managerial perceptions (working concept 7),
      25–26
Buchele, R. B., 89
Burgelman, R. A., 170
Burns, T., 191, 194
Burstein, M. C., 195
Business history, 14–16
Business policy, 8
Buzzell, R. D., 172

Cameron, K., 194
Carper, W. B., 67
Carroll, A. B., 65, 67
Capon, N., 67
Case method, 47
Case preparation, 47–52
Caves, R. E., 194
Chaffee, E. E., 28, 30, 167, 170
Chakravorthy, B., 194
Chamberlain, N. W., 17, 27, 30, 166, 170
Chandler, A. D., Jr., 4, 14, 17, 118, 122, 170,
      195
   see also stages of corporate development
Channon, D. F., 170
Chile and international copper, 126–133
Christensen, C. R., 17, 170, 195
Christopher, W., 170, 195
Clark, K., 122
Collier, D., 191, 195
Compensation and measurement systems, 179–185
Competence, distinctive,
   see distinctive competence
Competition,
   defined, 96
   Porter's model of (working concept 12), 106–
      108
   strategic signals of, 106
Competitive response analysis, 160–162
Congruence, 185–187
Consistency and evaluating strategy, 164
Contingency planning, 183
Cook, V. J., 90
Cooper, A. C., 120, 122, 170, 173
Coplin, W., 120, 123
Copper industry in Chile, 126–133
Corporate culture, 58–59, 180
Corporate development, stages of,
   see stages of corporate development
Customer needs analysis (working concept 11),
      103–106
Cyert, R. M., 17, 28, 30, 166, 170

Daniels, J., 195
David, F. R., 156–160, 170
David, S. H., 68
Davis, P. S., 120, 123
Davis, R. M., 68
Davis, S. M., 195
Day, G. S., 143, 170
Decentralization at General Electric, 12–13
   see also decentralized

Decentralized,
  stage three of corporate development, 4–7
DeMuzzio, E., 120, 122
Dess, G. G., 120, 123
Determining distinctive competence,
  see distinctive competence
DeVanna, M. A., 197
Development, stages of corporate,
  see stages of corporate development
Dhalla, N. K., 89
Dickel, K., 146, 172
Diffenbach, J., 120, 123
Differentiation strategy,
  see generic strategies
Directional policy matrix, 144–146
Distinctive competence, 83–86
  and comparative advantage, 83–84
  defined, 83
  in implementation selection, 185–187
  and levels of strategy, 85–86
  and market needs, 83
  and product life cycle, 83
Diversification,
  see growth matrix
  see situational strategies
Divesting,
  see exit strategies
Divisional management
  as decentralized stage two organization, 5
Donovan, N. B., 172
Doz, Y. L., 67
Drucker, P. F., 3, 17, 89, 92, 103, 123, 195
Dutton, V. E., 167, 170, 195

Edmunds, S., 123
Emery, F., 119, 123
Entrepreneur
  and stages of development, 4
Entrepreneurial,
  stage one of corporate development, 4–7
  see also stages of corporate development
Environment dependence spectrum, 116–117
Ethical values,
  see personal values,
  see also executive householder
Evaluating strategy, 160–164
Evered, R., 17, 20, 30
Executive comments, 16–17, 29, 66, 88, 122, 169,
  193–194
Executive householder, 22
Exit strategies, 154–155, 159–160
Experience curve,
  see product portfolios
External environment, 93
  changes in, 99–100

Fahey, L., 120, 123, 167, 170, 195
Farley, J., 67
Farmer, R. N., 133, 135

Ferguson, M., 123
Firstenberg, P. B., 67
Fitzpatrick, M., 67
Focus (or niche) strategy,
  see generic strategies
Fombrum, C. J., 197
Formulating strategy,
  defined, 136
  generic strategies, 151–152
  and levels of strategy (working concept 17), 139–
    140
  as part of strategic decision process (working
    concept 16), 137
  situational strategies, 152–160
Frederickson, J. W., 170
Freeman, R., 17
Frohman, A. L., 171
Functional,
  level of strategy,
    see levels of strategy,
  stage two of corporate development, 4–7
    see also stages of corporate development

Galbraith, J. K., 65, 67, 123
Galbraith, J. R., 7, 186–187, 194, 195
Gale, B., 194
Garland, J., 133, 135
General Electric
  and decentralization, 12–13
  and strategic business units, 12–14
Generic strategies, 151–152
Ginter, P. M., 28, 30, 171
Global markets, 135, 137
Glueck, W. F., 167, 171
Gold, B., 121, 123
Government, 97–98, 109–112
  defined, 97
  process of, 111–112
  strategic signals of, 109–111
Govindarajan, V., 171
Grant, J. H., 68
growth matrix (Ansoff's growth vector), 146–147
Gupta, A. K., 67, 171
Guth, W. D., 17
Gutmann, P. M., 168, 171

Hall, W. K., 171, 195
Halle, D., 97, 123
Hambrick, D., 89
Hanna, R. G. C., 30, 168, 171
Harrell, G. D., 155, 171
Harrigan, K. R., 21, 30, 154, 171
Haspleslagh, P., 143, 171
Hatten, K., 120, 122
Hatten, M. L., 67
Hayes, R. H., 90
Heany, D. F., 172, 195
Hedley, B., 171
Heibroner, R., 123

Henderson, B., 171
Henry, H. W., 89
Herbert, T., 195
Hicks, E. J., 120, 122
Hirschleim, R. A., 192, 195
Hise, R., 17
Hitchens, R. E., 172
Hobbs, J., 195
Hofer, C. W., 89, 144, 168, 171
Holistic executive householder, 22
Hopkins, T. J., 22, 30
Horovitz, J., 192, 195
Hout, T., 67
Hoy, F., 65, 67
Hrebiniak, L. G., 195, 197
Huber, G. P., 192, 195
Hussey, D. E., 89, 171
Hulbert, J., 67

Iacocca, L., 53–55, 67
Identifying opportunities and threats,
    see opportunities and threats
Implementation selection model (working concept
    23), 186–187
Implementing strategy,
    administrative systems, 176–177
    compensation and measurement systems, 179–
    185
    components of, 176–185
    defined, 175
    information systems, 177–179
    selection criteria, 185–187
Industry analysis (working concept 21), 148–150
Information systems, 177–179
Integration, vertical,
    see vertical integration
International business, 124–135
    complexities, 124–125
    host country power, 125–126
    life cycle, 133–135

Jaeger, A. M., 192, 195
Jelinek, M., 195
Jelinek, M., 195
Joint venture strategy, 159
Jones, P. E., 123, 196
Joyce, W. F., 195
Jung, C. G., 24, 30

Kantrow, A. W., 122, 123, 192, 195
Karger, D. W., 30
Kast, F., 195
Katz, R. L., 171
Kazanjian, R. K., 7
Kefalas, A., 196
Kennell, J. D., 172
Kiefer, R. O., 155, 171
Kierulff, H. W., 172
Kilmann, R., 192, 196

Kimberly, J. R., 67
King, W. R., 168, 172, 195
Kirton, M. J., 67
Kitching, J., 168, 172
Klein, H. E., 119, 123
Knight, K., 195
Kotler, P., 93, 123, 135, 170
Kotter, J. P., 18, 30
Kramer, R., 68
Krasler, O. J., 123

Lawrence, P. R., 191, 195, 196
Learned, E., 17
Lebell, D., 123
Lei, D., 89
Leibenstein, H., 67
Leidecker, J. K., 121, 123
Leontiades, M., 196
Levels of strategy,
    business, 9, 11
    corporate, 9
    defined, 9
    departmental (see functional)
    functional, 12
    purpose or mission, and, 62–65
    strategy formulation, and (working concept 17),
        139–140
    strategy implementation, and, 188
    working concept 2, 9, 11–12
Levitt, T., 89
Lindblom, C. E., 24, 28, 30, 166, 172
Linneman, R. E., 123, 172
Litschert, R. J., 67
Lorange, P., 18, 89, 196
Lorsch, J. W., 191, 196
low-cost producer strategy,
    see generic strategies
Lucas, H. C., Jr., 89

MacMillan, I. C., 123, 172, 192, 196
Makrodakis, S., 124
Malik, Z. A., 30
Managerial perceptions, 25–26
Managerial roles, 23–24
March, J. G., 17, 28, 30, 166, 170
Market competition matrix, 146
Markets, 93–96, 101–106
    borderless, 94
    customer needs analysis of, 103–106
    defined, 96
    global, 135, 137
    strategic signals of, 102
Mascarenhas, B., 89
Mason, R., 68, 146, 172
Matrix analysis,
    directional policy matrix, 144–146
    growth matrix, 146–147
    market-competition matrix, 146

product life cycle–competition matrix, 144–145
product portfolios, 142
space matrix, 146
Matrix organization, 176–177
McCormick, R. E., 123
McDaniel, S., 17
McGinnis, M. A., 28, 30
McGowan, R. P., 68
McIntyre, S. M., 90
McKie, J. W., 67
McNamee, P., 121, 123
Meadows, D. H., 123
Merchant, K. A., 196
Miles, R., 123, 196
Military strategic manager, 20–22
Mintzberg, H., 18, 23–24, 30, 56–58, 68, 172, 196
    and managerial roles, 23–24
    and organizational power, 56–58
Mission,
    see purpose
Mitchell, T. R., 170
Mitroff, I., 68, 192, 196
Moore, W. L., 123
Moran, T., 128–129, 135
Murphy, D. C., 89

Narayanan, V. K., 120, 123, 167, 170, 195
Naylor, M. E., 18, 28, 30, 196
New business strategy, 152
Newman, W. H., 68
Niche (or focus) strategy,
    see generic strategies
Nonprofit agencies, 68–70
Nutt, P. C., 68, 196

O'Connell, J. J., 18
O'Leary, M., 120, 123
Opportunities and threats,
    competition signals of, 106
    government signals of, 109–111
    market signals of, 102
    social signals of, 114–116
    strategic signals of, 101–102, 106, 109–111, 114–116
    technology signals of, 108
Organ, T. W., 30
Organizational power, 56–58
    configurations, 57–58
Organizational priorities, 56–59
    determination by power,
        configuration, 56–58
    working concept 8, 56
Ouchi, W. G., 68, 196

Pascale, R. T., 196
Patten, R., 168, 172
Paul, R. N., 172
Pearce, J. A., III, 172, 196

Penrose, E., 119, 124
Performance evaluation,
    see compensation and measurement systems
Performance measurement,
    see compensation and measurement systems
Personal values of managers, 54–56
Peters, T. J., 6, 16, 18, 89, 172, 196
PIMS (Profit Impact of Market Strategies), 86, 143
Pitts, B., 195
Planning and control systems,
    see information systems
Polli, E., 90
Porter, M. E., 67, 119, 124, 151–152, 171, 172
    model of competition determinants, 106–108
Power, D. J., 192, 195
Power, organizational,
    see organizational power
Prahalad, C. K., 67, 194
Precursor (working concept 15), 115–116
Product life cycle (working concept 10), 78–82
Product life cycle–competition matrix (working concept 19), 144–145
Product portfolio (working concept 18), 142–144
Profitability signals, 32–33
Profit Impact of Market Strategies,
    see PIMS
Purpose,
    defining, 61
    levels of strategy and, 62–65

Quinn, J. B., 172

Relative Earnings Multiple, 181–182
REM,
    see Relative Earnings Multiple
Resources, 71–73
Retrenchment, 159
    see also turnaround strategies
Riggs, J., 168, 172
Risk and evaluating strategy, 162–163
Robinson, R. B., Jr., 30, 172
Robinson, S. J. Q., 172
Rockart, J. F., 193, 196
Ronstadt, R., 68
Rosenzweig, J., 195
Rothschild, W. E., 90, 196
Rowe, H., 146, 172
Rucks, A. C., 28, 30, 171
Rudden, E., 67
Rumelt, R., 168, 172

Salter, M. S., 7, 90, 170
Sampson, A., 135
SBU,
    see strategic business unit
Schecter, S., 89
Schendel, D. E., 168, 172
Schenkel, S., 18, 30
Schoeffler, S., 90, 172

Schoderbek, C., 196
Schoderbek, D., 196
Schwartz, H., 68
Scott, B. R., 172
Scott-Morton, M. S., 193, 196
Seeger, J. A., 173
Shanks, D. C., 68
Shrivastava, P., 68
Sihler, W., 197
Simon, H., 30, 68, 166, 173
Single business strategy, 152
Situational strategies, 152–168
Sloan, A. P., Jr., 30, 197
Snow, C. C., 196, 197
Social goals,
  see societal goals
Societal goals, 59–61
Social responsibility, 60–64
  see also societal goals
Society,
  defined, 97
  precursor, 115–116
  strategic signals of, 113–116
Soleri, P., 108, 114, 124
South, S. E., 90
Space matrix, 146
Stages of corporate development,
  and evolution of strategic management, 8
  working concept 1, 4–7
Stakeholder analysis (working concept 14), 112–
  113
Stalker, G. M., 191, 194
Steele, L., 121, 124
Steiner, G., 30, 166–167, 173
Stevens, J. M., 68
Stevenson, R. H., 90
Stopford, J., 28, 197
Strategic analysis (working concept 9), 61
Strategic business unit (SBU),
  defined, 12
  illustrated at General Electric, 12–14
  implementation alternative, 177
  working concept 3, 12–14
Strategic financial analysis, 32–34
Strategic issue analysis (working concept 22),
  150
Strategic management,
  defined, 8
  evolution of, 8–9
Strategic manager,
  defined, 19
  holistic executive householder, 22
  military general, 20–22
  performance modes, 24–25
  roles, 23–24
  working concept 4, 19–20
Strategic mapping, 149–150
Strategic planning,
  defined, 8

Strategic process,
  defined, 10
  summarized, Figure 1.3, 10
Strategy evaluation,
  see evaluating strategy
Strategy, formulating,
  see formulating strategy
Strategy formulation,
  see formulating strategy
Strategy implementation,
  see implementing strategy
Strategy, implementing,
  see implementing strategy
Strategy, levels of,
  see levels of strategy
Strategy research, 14, 27–29, 65, 86–88, 118–121,
  166–169, 190–193
Strengths and weaknesses, 73–78
Strickland, A. J., III, 71, 90
Stubbart, C., 121, 124
Summer, C. E., 18
Susbauer, J. C., 92
Sutton, C. J., 18
SWOT,
  see opportunities and threats
  see strengths and weaknesses
Synergy, 73, 163–164

Taylor, B., 173
Taylor, J. W., 172
Technological innovation,
  phases of (working concept 13), 109
Technology, 96–97
  innovation phases, 109
  strategic signals of, 108
Thain, D. H., 7
Thompson, A. A., Jr., 71, 90
Thompson, J. D., 173
Threats,
  see opportunities and threats
Tichy, N. M., 197
Tilles, S., 197
Tock, D., 120, 122
Tollison, R. D., 123
Treacy, M. E., 193
Tretter, M., 195
Trist, E., 119, 123
Turnaround strategies, 153–154
Turner, J. A., 89
Tushman, M. L., 123
Tyebjee, T. T., 90

Ulrich, D., 124
Unterman, I., 68
Utterback, J. M., 121, 124

Values,
  see personal values
Vancil, R. F., 18, 197

Veblen, T., 124
Vertical integration, 152–153, 156–157
Vesper, K. H., 92
Viability signals, 32–34
Vinson, W. O., 192, 195

Wade, D. P., 172
Wallender, H. W., III, 68
Wasson, C. R., 90
Waterman, R. M., Jr., 6, 16, 18, 89, 196
Waters, J. A., 172
Weaknesses, strengths and,
    see strengths and weaknesses
Weber, C. E., 30, 168, 173
Wells, L., 28, 197
Wheelwright, S. C., 90, 124, 173
Whetten, D., 194
Williams, J. R., 90, 173
Woo, C. Y., 173
Wood, A., 65, 68
Workability and evaluating strategy, 164
Working concept, for numbers 1 through 23 see
    below:
    Brunswik lens and perception, (7), 25–26
    customer needs analysis, (11), 103
    defined, 3–4
    directional policy matrix, (20), 144–148

implementation selection model, (23), 186
industry analysis, (21), 148–150
levels of strategy, (2), 9, 11
levels of strategy and strategic decision process,
    (17), 140
military and holistic strategic managers, (5), 20–
    22
Mintzberg's organizational power, (8), 56–57
Mintzberg's roles and styles, (6), 23–24
Porter's determinants of competition, (12), 106
precursor, the (15), 115
product life cycle, (10), 78–80
product life cycle–competition matrix, (19), 144
product portfolios, (18), 142–144
stages of corporate development, (1), 4–7
stakeholder analysis, (14), 112–113
strategic analysis, (9), 61
strategic business units, (3), 11–14
strategic decision process, (16), 137–139
strategic issue analysis (22), 150
strategic manager, (4), 19–20
technological innovation, (13), 109

Yuspeh, S., 89

Zeithaml, C., 89
Zentner, R., 124